100 More Tales from All Our Yesterdays

100 More Tales from All Our Yesterdays

by Edgar Andrew Collard

Published by

The Gazette

MONTREAL

Other *Gazette* publications

The Gazette Style (1990)   *Joseph N. Gelmon*
Montreal Yesterdays (1989)   *Edgar Andrew Collard*
All Our Yesterdays (1988)   *Edgar Andrew Collard*
Montreal Then and Now/hier et aujourd'hui (1985)   *Bryan Demchinsky*

Published by

The Gazette

245 St. Jacques St.,
Montreal, Que., Canada H2Y 1M6

Watercolors and sketches — John Collins
Book design — Tom Carbray
Edited by Joseph N. Gelmon
Project co-ordinator — Reena Santini

Special thanks to the composing room staff of The Gazette

Canadian Cataloguing in Publication Data

Collard, Edgar Andrew, 1911-   ,   100 More Tales from All Our Yesterdays
ISBN 0-9692315-4-7

1. Montreal (Quebec) — History. 2. Montreal (Quebec) — Biography. I. Title.
II. Title: One Hundred More Tales from All Our Yesterdays.

FC2947.3.C65 1990 971.4'28 C90-090527-1 F1054.5.M84C65 1990

Printed in Canada

Illustrations by John Collins

CONTENTS

Lacrosse: the old manslaughtering style

"*Nothing has done more injury to Lacrosse than rough play in general.*" Dr. George Beers of Montreal wrote those words in 1869. He was the "father of lacrosse," the man who first drew up rules for the game and led it to become known as the national game of Canada.

Though Beers was the greatest advocate and promoter of lacrosse, he was well aware of its risks. Unless it could be played in a spirit of fairness, it could degenerate into a game of hack and hew. Beers recognized that accidents were always possible. In a game where stick was played against stick, anything could happen.

Accidents, however, couldn't explain all the injuries in lacrosse. He noticed "that certain individuals stand out so prominent for maiming their antagonists, as to suggest . . . more . . . than mere accident." Some players were maimed for life: "There are players carrying indelible reminiscences of rough play, who can testify to the injurious effects on the game, of the old manslaughtering style."

Such self-destructive violence in lacrosse was all the more deplorable because the game had otherwise so much to recommend it. Beers saw lacrosse as a nationalizing influence: "If the Republic of Greece was indebted to the Olympian games, if England has cause to bless cricket, so may Canada be proud of Lacrosse. It has raised a young manhood throughout the Dominion to active, healthy exercise and has, perhaps, done more than anything else to invoke the sentiment of patriotism among the young men of Canada."

It would have been hard to think of Montreal in those days without lacrosse. It had become part of the life of the people. What the game meant in the city was seen and described by a visiting Irish priest, Rev. M.B. Buckley from Cork. The Shamrocks were one of Montreal's greatest teams. Irish boys made superb players. Their parish priests entered into their enthusiasm and urged them on. Buckley described the Shamrocks as all parishioners of Father Hogan of Griffintown, and no doubt many of them were.

Hogan took Buckley to see his first lacrosse game, a match between the Shamrocks and a team of Indians from Caughnawaga. Hogan was "trembling all over with the excitement of fear and suspense for the success of his protégés." Buckley found "the whole scene . . . as bright and brisk as could be."

The game began. It was close and hard-fought all the way. Whenever the Shamrocks scored, "there was shouting and throwing up of hats, and the band played its most exultant strains." Then the Shamrocks won the final, decisive goal. What lacrosse meant to its spectators was seen by this visitor from Cork: "I cannot describe the wild joy of the spectators . . . . The air was filled with cheers. . . . It was a tremendous triumph, and Father Hogan was in ecstasies. He passed through the throng, and shook hands with all the 'boys'."

In all this excitement, the visitor from Cork still noticed that lacrosse must be a rough game. The players of the Shamrock team "stood puffed and perspiring and with hands all livid from the blows of their enemies."

Even Beers, as the "father of lacrosse," admitted that opportunities for violence were inherent in the game. But, while severely condemning deliberate violence, "the slashing and swinging and wounding by crosses," he didn't want the game to be condemned just because those playing it might be injured. After all, he pointed out, all sports are open to injuries. Collarbones are broken in football; men are drowned in yachting; a man might get maimed by the ball in cricket or get his hand or head blown off in duck or deer shooting. But this did not mean that all these sports should be abandoned or prohibited. Lacrosse was a manly sport. Players seldom complained. It was a "game for men, not dudes." In any case, he was hopeful. Roughness in lacrosse would wear itself out.

It didn't. The roughness grew worse and worse. On Aug. 31, 1912, Montreal's Irish Canadians were playing against the Tecumseh lacrosse team on the Maisonneuve grounds. Fines in that match grew so numerous that the referee refused to make the total public. In the early stage of the last period an Indian player named Yeaman was "struck over the head in a deliberate manner" by an opponent named Kane. He was carried off the field and replaced by a Tecumseh named Donald Smith. Then the real mixup began.

Smith and Kane started swinging at each other. All

SKETCHBOOK

John Collins

LACROSSE
GAME
IN THE
LAST
CENTURY

LACROSSE
STICK
OF THE OLD STYLE

players joined in. Reserve men on the line came onto the field and joined the fight. Police were called for fear of more serious trouble. They restored order. The match was resumed. When only 10 minutes of play was left, there was "another general mixup in which all hands took part."

The crowd, having come out to see a match, became sickened by this warlike spectacle. They were leaving the grounds, "many of the regulars expressing disgust at the sport they had been treated to."

The crowd that left the field on that Saturday afternoon symbolized a far wider desertion of lacrosse by its spectators. The national game of Canada was losing its national audience. There were other and deeper causes for the decline in lacrosse's popularity. Fashion in sport was bringing changes. In the same way that the ski was gradually displacing the snowshoe, baseball and football were gradually displacing lacrosse.

There is no doubt, however, that the lacrosse players who had been deliberately injuring one another had also been injuring the game. Beers, for all his enthusiasm and hope, had rightly warned that lacrosse itself was being maimed by "the old manslaughtering style."

The men who built the Victoria Bridge

The construction of the Victoria Bridge in the 1850s not only connected Montreal with the mainland of the South Shore. It also stimulated the growth of a cluster of communities along the Montreal waterfront in the neighborhood of Bridge St., the street leading to the bridge's entrance.

In any Victorian industry the workers had to live near their jobs. They had to walk to the workplace, and be there early in the morning. Building the Victoria Bridge brought thousands of workers to that area of the waterfront. And the work of construction went on for more than five years. Sufficient housing for the sudden arrival of so many workers didn't exist; the employer had to provide it.

Though the Victoria Bridge was built for the Grand Trunk Railway, the contractors were the British firm Peto, Brassey and Betts. They had the obligation. James Hodges, chief engineer of the project, said the workers were "provided with a comfortable range of dwellings close to their work." The contractors also provided a building as a sort of community centre. On Sundays it could be used as a chapel, on weekdays as a schoolhouse for the workers' 80 children and as a library of 1,000 books.

Despite these accommodations, life for the workers was hard and hazardous. During the years of construction, 26 lives were lost. Most died by drowning. Nearly every man working on the bridge was a good swimmer. But the river at that stretch was merciless. Though boats and lifebuoys were always ready, anyone who fell in had little chance of rescue.

Workmen building the piers (and there were 24 piers to be built) did their work on patches of man-made dry ground on the riverbed. These dry areas were artificially created by square cofferdams, sunk below the water until they touched bottom. Water was then pumped out of them. Those working at the bottom of these enclosures had the eerie awareness that the level of the river was far above them. Any accident might send the river plunging in, drowning everyone below.

Nor did the danger lie only in a breakdown of the enclosure. Water might rise up from the bottom. This happened on June 26, 1858. A blow from a pick among the boulders at the bottom tapped a spring. Black, thick water spurted up. At first it was like a thin fountain, no thicker than a man's finger. Workmen gathered round to watch. They called it "a spring of ink." The thin spurt swelled into a torrent. Workmen ran for their lives. In half an hour the cofferdam was filled to river level.

Risks of drowning continued even in the winter. As construction progressed, winter work became possible on the bridge's superstructure. In 1859 winter construction of the central span of the Victoria Bridge was being carried on. Workmen reached the site by walking over the ice for about a mile. Even in March, when the ice was becoming soft, construction was pressed ahead. The contractors were working to a deadline. They were eager to get as much work done as possible before the ice broke and drifted away. They knew all work would then have to be suspended until the river was clear.

On March 24, 1859, the ice was getting "very rotten, with a great deal of water upon it." Weather had turned mild. The temperature was 40 degrees Fahrenheit. Heavy rain fell. Work on the central span was hurried. About 5,600 more rivets needed to be driven in before the span could be completed. Next day, about 2 in the afternoon, several faintly dark lines, like ridges, appeared in the ice about half a mile above the bridge. Some questioned whether they really were new: perhaps they had been there before, though unnoticed. Ridges grew larger. Tremors were felt on the ice covering the entire Laprairie Basin. Twenty miles of the river's surface began to move.

Hodges, the engineer, said: "A panic immediately seized all hands and most of the men were for running for the shore." But the shore was nearly a mile off. They soon thought they had better remain on the bridge. The ice movement proved brief. Stillness returned. Men went back to their work, "with a quaint remark or two." On March 26, a sharp frost made safer ice. Work was progressing well. By that afternoon the central span was in place, supported by the piers at both ends. The work had been completed just in time. On March 27 the ice was unsafe. No workmen could reach the bridge. Next day the ice split apart, and began shoving its

SKETCHBOOK

John Collins

The FIRST VERSION OF THE VICTORIA BRIDGE WAS A COVERED ONE —A LONG TUBE-LIKE AFFAIR

SCENE AT ITS OPENING AS THE VICTORIA JUBILEE BRIDGE the open type Montrealers recognize

way downstream.

Hazards of winter work on the St. Lawrence came not only from the treacherous ice but from the cold itself. The contractors' problem was how to keep their workers from freezing. Men went to work with thick gloves, heavy coats, fur caps and heavy handkerchiefs over most of their faces, "so that only a very small portion was visible." Just below the bridge St. Mary's current never froze. Vapor rose from open water. Workmen at the bridge might be covered with icicles. Many were frostbitten, some seriously.

Work had other hazards, no matter what the season might be. Lumber companies in springtime sent their timber downstream in rafts, with the heavy logs lashed together by ropes. Crews aboard had trouble managing the unwieldy mass. Coming on in the swift current, rafts sometimes crashed into barges where the bridge-builders were at work.

Then there was cholera. In 1854 James Hodges wrote: "Early in July, the cholera made its appearance, making sad havoc amongst our men. In one case, out of a gang of 200 men, 60 were sick at one time." The contractors, having provided their workers with housing, provided them with medical services also. At a cost of 1,000 pounds annually they retained the services of five of Montreal's most prominent physicians. One of them, Palmer Howard, served as oculist for snow blindness, a common affliction among the men who worked in the glare of the sun on the snow-covered ice of the river.

When the long years of work on the bridge were over, many of the workmen departed. Some returned to the British Isles; some settled in other parts of Canada; some went to the U.S. Others, living in the dwellings provided by the bridge contractors, had grown attached to the district down by the river. They stayed there.

Montreal and the 'Rebecca' of Ivanhoe

"You are now looking at the Rebecca who was the real heroine in Sir Walter Scott's famous novel *Ivanhoe.*" Henry Joseph used to say this to visitors as he pointed to the portrait of Rebecca Gratz by the American artist Thomas Sully. It hung on the north wall of his Montreal drawing room.

Rebecca Gratz was the unmarried daughter in a rich Jewish family in Philadelpha. When Henry Joseph's mother, Sara Moses, was left an orphan while still an infant, Rebecca Gratz, her aunt, had taken her into her own home and brought her up. In 1848 Henry Joseph's father, Jacob Henry Joseph, married Sara and brought her from Philadelphia to Montreal.

The claim that Sir Walter Scott modelled his Rebecca on Rebecca Gratz may seem strange, since he never saw her in his life. Scott had heard about her, however, from the American author Washington Irving, perhaps best remembered today for his *Sketch Book* with its tale of Rip Van Winkle. Irving was one of the literary circle — the coterie of celebrities — that met in Rebecca Gratz's Philadelphia home.

While travelling in the British Isles in 1817, Irving visited Sir Walter Scott at his house, Abbotsford, on the Tweed. At that time Scott was at work on *Ivanhoe,* which was to be the best selling of his many novels. He mentioned to Irving that he was thinking of introducing "a female Jewish character" into the new book. Irving at once told him that he knew a woman in Philadelphia who had just the qualities Scott might need for such a character. He described Rebecca Gratz — her many talents, her suavity of manner, her liveliness, her kindness, her uprightness and her unyielding faith in the God of Israel.

Scott listened attentively. As soon as Irving had finished speaking, Scott exclaimed, "You have given me my Rebecca!" When Ivanhoe was published in 1820, Scott sent a copy (the very first copy, it is said) to Irving. He asked: "How do you like your Rebecca? Does the Rebecca I have pictured compare with the pattern given?"

Much information on Rebecca Gratz is in the collection of her letters published in Philadelphia in 1929 by the Jewish Publication Society of America and edited by Rabbi David Philipson. These letters describe the marriage of Rebecca's niece, Sara Moses, to Jacob Henry Joseph in 1848. Joseph went to Philadelphia for the wedding. It was private. At once they left for Montreal. Letters from Sara in Montreal to her aunt in Philadelphia spoke of "her content so absolute."

The Joseph family had been very agreeable to her. Her mother-in-law had been "affectionate and cordial in her reception, and his sisters pleasant companions." Sara was much interested in her drives about the countryside. Very fond of music, she was enjoying the fine bands of the Montreal garrison.

Sara and her husband lived at first in a Montreal hotel. There they had apartments with "private entrance and table." Eventually they moved to a house in the Près de Ville Terrace (sometimes called Près de Ville Place). *Mackay's Montreal Directory* defined the terrace as being on la Gauchetière at the head of Côté. Later they lived in Dorchester House, near where the Queen Elizabeth Hotel now stands.

Rebecca Gratz admitted that the child she had "reared and cherished so dearly" could "hardly be transferred to other protectors without reluctance and misgivings." Before the marriage she had established through inquiries that "the gentleman Mr. Joseph of Canada" was "a young man of irreproachable character — a merchant in good business and respectable connections." In the late summer and early autumn of 1851, Rebecca Gratz spent about a month with her niece in Montreal. She was astonished by the difference between Montreal and the cities she had known in the U.S. Here was a city almost medieval in some of its narrow streets, with imperfect pavements and low stone houses. She heard as much French as English spoken by the inhabitants. At every turn she seemed to be in a foreign country.

The loveliness of Montreal soon impressed her — the city "on the bosom of the noble St. Lawrence," the fine quay, the great dome of Bonsecours Market, the many steeples. The mountain, rich in foliage, made a magnificent background. At the waterfront on a clear day "fantastic white clouds . . . reflected in the water . . . added greatly to the prospect, and gave

JOHN COLLINS SKETCHBOOK

**REBECCA GRATZ —
As painted by the American
Artist THOMAS SULLY**

a fine impression."

She found that her niece in the Près de Ville Terrace was "very pleasantly situated in a retired part of the city," with "good neighbors on the street." Looking from her bedroom window in the terrace, she saw "a large garden opposite belonging to the Friars, where fruit and vegetables are abundant and the black-robed inhabitants are seen daily from my chamber window — book in hand strolling for hours together." What she saw was the grounds of Les Frères des Ecoles Chrétiennes. Their large property occupied the entire block from Côté to Cheneville and from la Gauchetière to Vitré.

By 1851 Jacob Henry Joseph was on his way to becoming one of Montreal's principal citizens — an enterprising financier active in railways, banks, telegraphs, construction, real estate and many other projects. He held public offices, such as vice-president of the Montreal Board of Trade, and was one of the prominent members of the Spanish and Portuguese Synagogue.

Rebecca Gratz lived to the age of 88. She was honored and respected to the end and for many reasons. In addition she was always of unique interest as the original of Sir Walter Scott's Rebecca. The English novelist William Makepeace Thackeray described Scott's Rebecca as "the sweetest character in the whole range of fiction." From time to time Rebecca Gratz was asked whether it was really true that she was the model of this heroine in *Ivanhoe*. Her reply was a nice mixture of pride and modesty: "They say so, my dear."

Royal magic that opened faraway doors

In October 1909 something took place in Montreal that was called a miracle of modern science. On that day King Edward VII opened the doors of the new Royal Edward Institute in Montreal. This was the institute's first building. It stood in the area between St. Monique and St. Geneviève Sts., expropriated in 1930 to make way for the Canadian National Railways terminal. The king not only opened the doors, but in the same instant he turned on all the lights and ran the royal standard to the top of the flagmast. And yet, all the while, King Edward was 3,000 miles away, just outside the dining room of West Dean Park in Sussex.

To see something so amazing — something that had never happened before in the history of the world — invited guests assembled under the canvas of a huge marquee which had been erected in front of the new hospital. It was a day of heavy autumn rain. The coachmen on the carriages were dressed in their rubber raincoats, with rubber sheets covering the blankets over their legs. As each carriage reached the wooden steps that led to the marquee, a police constable with an umbrella covered the guests as they stepped out.

The chairman of the gathering, Sir George A. Drummond, made the opening speech. It was an important day for Montreal, he said, that at last it had a hospital for treating tubercular patients. A dramatic change had come about, because the bacillus of tuberculosis had been discovered. No longer was tuberculosis to be considered as "consumption," a mysterious wasting away, of unknown origin, and with no known cure. "The discovery of the bacillus of tuberculosis," said Sir George, "has changed utterly the treatment of the sufferers."

Other speakers followed. Among them was Lt.-Col. Jeffrey H. Burland. He and his sisters had built the hospital as a memorial to their father. He described how the magical ceremony had come to be planned. Through the governor-general, Earl Grey, the king had consented to bestow his name upon the hospital. Encouraged by the royal consent, Burland said he had then sought to have the king become the hospital's patron. Again the king consented.

Encouraged to be even bolder, he made the request that the king would open the doors of the hospital. Again came royal consent.

The king had not been in Canada since 1860 when, as the 18-year-old Prince of Wales, he came to open the Victoria Bridge. He was never to come to Canada again. The ceremony of opening the new hospital was to be accomplished by pressing down a key in West Dean Park where he was staying as the guest of Mr. and Mrs. William James. Electric current would be sent to Montreal. There the audience under the marquee would see the doors opening, the lights coming on and the standard running up the flagstaff.

Such an event, without precedent, needed weeks of planning. The arrangement was that as soon as the king pressed the key at West Dean Park, the electric current would flow along a wire to the Chichester post office, five miles away. From Chichester it would flow for 55 miles over a reserved wire to the central post office in London. Then it would pass on to the Commercial Cable Co. in London's Royal Exchange. By submarine cable it would be carried 400 miles to Waterville in Ireland. From Ireland it would set out across the ocean by another submarine cable. Reaching Canso, 2,100 miles distant, it would move the 400 miles over the CPR's wires to Montreal. It would all be a scientific marvel, demonstrating how small science was making the world of the 20th century.

In Montreal, the time was being watched closely. Dr. R.W. Philip, a medical visitor from Edinburgh, was speaking — at considerable length. His speech was interrupted, with apologies, by Burland. It was now 4 p.m., he said, and it would be 9 p.m. in Sussex. At that moment King Edward would be leaving the dining room of West Dean Park. He asked Sir George Drummond to close the silver switch on the table before him; this would establish the connection between the hospital and West Dean Park. It was said that "a wave of patriotic emotion appeared to pass over the entire assembly. The great gathering leaned forward, tense and breathless; every eye was fixed on the brass lever to the left of the door of the Institute, which, it had been explained, would set the power in motion."

ROYAL EDWARD INSTITUTE

KING
EDWARD
VII

John
Collins SKETCHBOOK

The minutes passed. Nothing broke the silence but the heavy rain beating on the roof of the marquee. The guard of honor of the Prince of Wales Fusiliers stood motionless, waiting for the command to give the salute. Meanwhile, in West Dean Park, the king had left the dining table. Accompanied by his host and hostess and a few guests, he went into the hall outside the dining room door. Officials of the general post office stood waiting by a table, where the apparatus had been set up. The king pressed the key.

In Montreal a soft whirring sound announced that the motor had been set in motion. Instantly the royal standard was seen running up the staff. From roof to cellar the new institute burst into light. The doors swung open. The guard of honor presented arms and the band struck up God Save the King. At West Dean Park the king stood beside the apparatus to wait for a signal from Montreal. Five minutes after he had sent the current on to the hospital a sharp clicking came in the little machine on the table. It was the signal that all had gone well. The king went back to the dining table, stopping for a moment to order that a congratulatory message be sent over the wire.

What had happened at the opening of the Royal Edward Institute captured the imagination of the world. The newspapers marvelled. "The march of science has seldom been more strikingly exemplified than it was last night," declared the Dundee Courier. And the London Westminster Gazette's comment was: "The progressive knowledge of the only partially explored world of natural forces has opened many doors, and will, thanks to our scientific explorers, open many more."

The Hélène of Ile Ste. Hélène

In Canada, the name of Hélène de Champlain has endured for centuries in the island in the St. Lawrence opposite Montreal. Her husband had first seen the island on a voyage of exploration in 1603, but gave it no name at that time. On another voyage to Montreal in 1611 he was newly married — his wedding with Hélène Broullé had taken place only five months before. "In the middle of the river," he wrote, "there is an island about three-quarters of a league in circumference . . . and I named it Ile Ste. Hélène."

(It was customary in the 17th century to honor people by naming places after the saint whose name they bore. Many of Montreal's oldest streets were named in this way.)

When Champlain married Hélène Boullé in 1610, he was about 40 years of age; she was not quite 12. Though the marriage took place, a marriage contract was drawn up and signed and a dowry paid, Champlain was not allowed to live with his bride for another two years. Hélène was considered old enough to marry, but not yet old enough to be a wife.

Hélène is reputed to have been beautiful, lively and spirited. For Champlain, she had other attractions. He was rather poor. Her father, one of the secretaries in the king of France's household, was rich and influential. Hélène brought her husband a dowry of 6,000 livres, a substantial sum.

The disparity of age was only one of the oddities of their marriage. They lived together only a few years of their long married life. Champlain was too preoccupied with his work far away in Canada to spend much time with his wife in France. In 1624, after 14 years of seeing little of each other, Champlain decided to bring his wife to join him in Quebec. It did not prove a happy experiment. The sea voyage was her first; the passage was unusually rough. The few buildings Champlain had erected at Quebec had fallen into disrepair during his absence. The main one, the Habitation, had rain seeping through its roof.

Hélène spent four hard, cheerless years in this tiny, uncomfortable outpost at Quebec. She was without the amenities of her accustomed lifestyle. There were only four or five women in the settlement. Her sense of her social status, and her husband's position as head of the settlement, seemed to oblige her to stand aloof from some of them. Her time was largely spent as a benefactor among the Indians. She picked up a working knowledge of the Algonquin language. She taught Indian girls the Catholic catechism and appears to have aided them when they were ill.

Among the Indians she became a sort of cult, almost an object of worship. Her appearance, manner and clothes were all new to them. Most of all, they were awed by a little mirror she carried, suspended from her belt. Indians gazing into the mirror were astonished to see themselves. They believed everything was somehow contained in that miraculous piece of reflecting glass.

Even in Quebec Hélène did not have much of her husband's company. He was away most of the time on voyages of exploration or on trading expeditions among the Indians. She found life lonely, bleak, boring, harsh. Menace from the Iroquois made it dangerous as well. Four years was enough. Champlain took her back to France. From that time on, they lived together only during the brief intervals while he was in France. She never returned to Quebec. He left France for Quebec on his last voyage in 1633. They never saw each other again.

In France Hélène lived in her mother's house. Through most of her life she lived the strange widowhood of a woman whose husband was away so long and so far that he was almost dead to her.

Over the years she turned more and more to religion. She wished to enter a convent. Vows of celibacy would make little difference to her: she was already leading a celibate life. Her absentee husband, however, refused to give his permission. The strange, empty marriage continued till Christmas Day in 1635. On that day Samuel de Champlain died in Quebec. Even his will added another oddity to their marriage. He had ignored the marriage contract of 1610. Instead of leaving all his possessions to his wife, he left everything to the Virgin Mary. His estate was to be used for the benefit of a chapel he had founded in Quebec — dedicated to the Virgin, as Notre Dame de Recouvrance. Hélène, with her religious feelings, did nothing to contest the will. It was contested, nevertheless, by her first cousin,

SKETCHBOOK

John Collins

Restaurant
HELENE de
CHAMPLAIN

Marie Camaret, wife of Jacques Hersault, comptroller of customs at La Rochelle. The will was annulled. The marriage contract prevailed.

The matter of her husband's will, and other concerns, preoccupied Hélène de Champlain for the 10 years following his death. In 1645 she felt free to carry out her wish to become a nun. She entered an Ursuline convent in Paris as a novice. She could not adapt her ways easily. She was too old for the role, too independent by nature and custom. In 1648 she chose a different role. She would found a new convent and be its benefactor. With permission from Msgr. Dominique Séguier, bishop of Meaux, she founded the new convent at Meaux with a gift of 20,000 livres, together with furniture and other equipment. She wished to humble her proud spirit by some conspicuous act of humiliation. With the bishop's permission, she wrote down all her faults.

At a gathering of the religious community she read them out. This solemn ceremony she performed on her knees. Her feet were bare. A rope hung about her neck. A lighted taper was in her hand.

Those who founded new convents were accorded special privileges. Bishop Séguier granted them to Hélène, who had become Sister Hélène de Saint-Augustin. She would not have to rise for mass at 4 a.m; she would have a somewhat better diet than the other nuns; she would be allowed to have a fire in her cell; she would have a lay sister to wait on her as a servant.

Hélène lived in the convent at Meaux for six years. She died five days before Christmas in 1654. Hers was a good death. She expired "in the odor of sanctity," meaning that she had attained an eminent degree of "charity, from a pure heart and a good conscience, and an unfeigned faith."

When a clerk's job was anything but dull

Anyone today who thinks of the office worker of the 19th century is likely to picture a Bob Cratchit type, spending a life of dull drudgery on a high stool, writing with a scratchy quill pen. No doubt the picture is, in general, accurate. But the 19th century had so much adventure that at times even office workers were drawn into it. Some were sent out of their offices on missions of excitement and danger. For them, on such occasions, life was anything but dull.

In 1819, George Davies was sent on just such a mission. He was a clerk in the office of Bridge and Penn — Samuel Bridge and Turnton Penn. These prominent auctioneers had their office on St. Paul St. When the office was opened one winter morning, the great iron chest was gone. At that time Montrealers were beng robbed left and right by a gang from the Eastern Townships. This same gang had been flooding the country with counterfeit coins. It was not broken up until 1824.

The police, after the robbery of the Bridge and Penn office in 1819, had traced the path of the robbers in the snow down to the waterfront. There the chest was found. It had been forced open. The firm had kept its business papers in it. All were gone. Without these papers Bridge and Penn could scarcely hope to carry on.

The best they could do was to advertise the loss and offer a reward of 50 half-eagles — a coinage amounting in value to $250. About a month passed. No reply came. Then Bridge and Penn received a letter postmarked Sherbrooke. It informed them that all their papers were safe. They might get them back if they handed over the reward, in gold. The reward, however, would have to be paid according to the robbers' strict instructions.

The firm was to send a messenger. He must be "a self-possessed man." He must come entirely alone. He must carry no firearms. He must give no hint to anybody as to why he had come to the Townships. He was "not to be too inquisitive" about the source of the instructions given him.

Samuel Bridge and Turnton Penn looked over their clerks for one with enough self-possession, discretion and courage to carry out this mission. Their choice was George Davies. Davies was given the 50 golden half-eagles — no inconsiderable weight. He went to the hotel in Sherbrooke. There he was handed a letter. He asked no questions about its source. The letter instructed him to remain at Sherbrooke for two days. He was then to go to a certain inn at Hatley and ask for another letter. The letter handed him at Hatley only directed him to return to Sherbrooke for two days. He was then to go to Compton and inquire for another letter. The letter at Compton only told him to go back to Hatley. Davies travelled back and forth for nearly two weeks.

At last he was given a letter with definite instructions. He was to put the money in his pocket. He was to ride about three miles on the road to Compton, until he came to a very noticeable tree (which was described) on the right hand. There he was to dismount. He was to lead his horse 100 yards or so into the woods. There he was to tie it up. From this spot he was to go on foot along a sufficiently well-marked footpath for about half a mile. He would come into a small clearing. In the centre of the clearing was a stump of a tree newly felled. Upon this stump he was to place the money, and there he would find the bundle of stolen business papers.

Davies set out toward Compton. He came to the distinctive tree on the right side. He followed all his instructions. On the stump in the clearing he picked up the documents. He left the money.

Davies made his way back along the wooded path, relieved that his mission seemed to be accomplished. When he was about halfway to the road, two men jumped out from the undergrowth. Each held a musket, aimed at him. They ordered him to stand still

Time passed — it seemed a long time to him, though perhaps it was only a few minutes. Then the sound of a shot came from some distance away, somewhere near the clearing he had left.

At once the two men lowered their muskets. They disappeared into the woods. Then Davies understood what had happened. The whole procedure had been prearranged. The two men with the muskets had held him up until a shot fired by a confederate at the stump gave the signal that the

SKETCHBOOK

John Collins

BANK
OF
MONTREAL
ST. JAMES STREET

money had been left there. If he had taken the business papers but not left the money, he never would have got back to the road.

Other employees in other offices were sent on dangerous missions, on which they had to be equally discreet, equally self-possessed. Among them was Henry Dupuy, one of the first employees of the Bank of Montreal after its foundation in 1817. Dupuy, in old age, wrote an account of his adventures. It was published in full by the Montreal Board of Trade in 1893.

Dupuy's adventure took place when the Bank of Montreal stood just west of its present location on Place d'Armes. The site is now covered by the bank's westward extension. In those days no express companies took charge of shipping money or other valuables on behalf of the banks. The banks had to make arrangements of their own. Bank employees were often selected to travel with large sums.

Dupuy was ordered to bring a large sum in coins to Montreal from the Bank of Montreal's branch in Kingston. The journey was made in February.

Dupuy packed the coins in boxes and kegs. He hired a stagecoach. They set out before daybreak. Snow was falling steadily. Roads became scarcely visible. Between Brockville and Cornwall they came to a steep hill. The harness snapped. There was nothing they could do but carry the boxes and kegs from the bottom of the hill to the top.

Dupuy and the stagecoach driver couldn't handle the job. Dupuy went looking for assistance. He waded through snow nearly up to his hips. He came to a hut and tried to persuade the man there to come to his help. The man was attending a sick person and didn't want to leave, but in the end he agreed. The three of them got the coins to the top of the hill.

The situation, from the point of view of security, could hardly be worse. Dupuy was stuck in the snow with boxes and kegs of coins on a lonely stretch of road, with a stagecoach driver who was swearing "at a great rate" and a total stranger he had persuaded to come out of his hut. But eventually he made it. "I felt very much relieved," said Dupuy, "at our safe arrival in Montreal."

The murders on the Chemin du Roi

A murderer's house once stood on the north side of René Lévesque Blvd. (formerly Dorchester). It was about halfway between Guy and St. Mathieu, on the spot where the iron gates are today — the entrance gates to the avenue leading to the convent chapel.

The murderer was Jean-Baptiste Goyer, known as Bélisle. His house was small. Being indolent, and spending too much time at a tavern in town, he did not make much from his farm. His neighbors were Jean Favre and his wife. They were hard-working and prosperous, with a good house and well-run farm. Their house was at the crossroads, where the road from Côte des Neiges village (the road of which the present Guy St. forms a part) met Dorchester, then called by a grand name: "le Chemin du Roi" — the King's Highway.

The Favres may have been well aware of their superior position. Jean Favre is said to have boasted to Bélisle about how much money he had been able to lay aside. Envy, resentment and avarice could all have been at work in Bélisle.

He was not a murderer on impulse. His plans were carefully prepared. Early in May 1752, he made a point of telling the Favres, and as many of his other acquaintances as he could, that he was making a journey to Quebec — a long trip in those days. He closed his house on the Chemin du Roi. He disappeared from his usual haunts in town.

While he was believed to be away in Quebec, Montreal was appalled by news of a double murder. Jean Favre and his wife were found dead in their house. Both had been murdered savagely. The motive was obvious. Nothing had been broken into except the chest or cupboard where Favre kept his money. Other chests and cupboards had not been touched. The murderer had known exactly where to go to get what he was after.

Bélisle did not reappear in town until two weeks after the murders. He went to a tavern. He was told what had happened to his neighbors. He appeared amazed, horrified, indignant. No suspicion might have been attached to him if he had kept his expenditures down to the usual small amounts. But he began spending money as he had never been able to spend it before. His visits to the tavern became more frequent, his outlays more conspicuous. He displayed a new and lordly generosity, buying drinks all round.

More than this, Bélisle's horror at the murder of the Favres was overdone. He seemed obsessed with the crime on the Chemin du Roi. He had a theory that began to sound too much like an alibi. He said he was convinced that one of the devil-may-care type of fur-traders, a "coureur de bois," must have killed the Favres. Such a person could easily have come out of the woods, committed his crime, then disappeared back into the woods with the money. No one could ever expect to trace such an elusive murderer. Therefore the crime could never be solved.

This insistence that the crime was unsolvable, combined with Bélisle's sudden and inexplicable affluence, made him appear a prime suspect. He was arrested, but denied having anything to do with the death of his neighbors. Law officers at that time regularly employed torture to force an unco-operative suspect to tell all he knew. Bélisle broke down under the pain. He made a full confession.

He admitted that he had never gone to Quebec. He had put the story out only to conceal his tracks. He had kept himself hidden in his house, waiting for a dark night. According to his story, he had never planned to kill the Favres. All he meant to do was to creep into their house while they were asleep. He knew where their money was kept. He had, however, prepared himself for armed burglary: he had come with a pistol and a knife.

Bélisle had broken silently into the house after the Favres had gone to bed. As he was in the act of taking the money, he was alarmed by a sound and a sudden light. He turned. Jean Favre stood in the doorway of the room, a candle in his hand. Bélisle fired his pistol. Jean Favre, wounded, called for his wife and flung himself at Bélisle. They struggled and swayed. Bélisle reached for his knife. He kept plunging it into Favre until Favre's body went limp.

Mme. Favre appeared just as her husband fell. She rushed at Bélisle. He turned his knife on her, striking her again and again in the breast. When she slumped to the floor, he looked around the room. His eye fell on a spade. He smashed her skull with it. With the

SKETCHBOOK

John Collins

The CROSS OF THE GREY NUNS

two dead bodies lying beside him, he went for the money. He gathered it up. In the dark of the night he made his way to a cove in the river. There he had a canoe, hidden and ready. He paddled all night. When dawn came over the Chemin du Roi, he was already far out of sight, his alibi established.

Bélisle suffered an atrocious penalty for his atrocious crime. He was "broken on the wheel." This execution was carried out on a scaffold in what today is Place Royale. A wheel was laid flat on the scaffold. Bélisle was bound to it. His bones were beaten and broken and he was left to die, with "his face turned to the sky." A custom of the time was to bury murderers at a crossroads. Bélisle's broken body was taken to the crossroads where the Chemin du Roi and the road down the west side of Mount Royal met. There a big Latin cross, painted the color of blood, was raised over his grave — a lasting warning of the terrible end of those who took the

blood of others in a crime.

About 100 years later the Gentlemen of St. Sulpice, at one time seigneurs of the entire island of Montreal, decided to release some of their vast land holdings. They intended to keep the portion of the immense Priests' Farm above Sherbrooke St., but they would sell land to the south. The Grey Nuns, wishing to move from their old location on Place d'Youville, chose the area between St. Catherine and Dorchester and between Guy and St. Mathieu. This block was known as the "terrain de la croix rouge." Here stood the "murderer's cross." The widening of the streets had already made it necessary to relocate the cross some distance back from its original site. The sisters replaced it, about 1870, with the cross to be seen near the corner of Guy and René Lévesque today. It stands on a little mound. But the color is no longer murderer's red. It has been subdued to a dark brown.

The exemplary life of a Christian Indian

Only a few feet from Sherbrooke St., a Huron Indian, François Thoronhiongo, lies buried. His grave is in one of the round stone towers that stand just beyond the wall of the Grand Séminaire on Sherbrooke St., near the head of Fort St. He was, by his piety and by his uprightness, an example to the Christians and the admiration of the unbelievers; he died at about 100 years of age on April 21, 1690.

The conviction began to grow among the missionaries that the only way to nurture faith among the converted Indians was to separate them from the pagans and establish them in Christian communities. In Montreal this was being done by the Sulpician missionaries. They had established a community of Christian Indians on the southwestern slope of the mountain, in the area now occupied by the Grand Séminaire and part of the Priests' Farm.

François Thoronhiongo came to join the settlement of Christian Indians on the slope of Mount Royal in 1677. He had been converted and baptized in the wilderness by the Jesuit missionary Jean Brébeuf. As a Christian, he very probably had suffered persecution among the unconverted Indians of his own tribe. Worse had followed. The Iroquois, as the enemies of the Hurons, had attacked his village and carried him off as a slave to their village of Tsonnonthouan. Through all these tribulations he kept his Christian faith.

It was the Indian custom that a slave taken in battle was set free when his master died. The time for Thoronhiongo's liberty came. He set out from Tsonnonthouan to join the Christian settlement at Montreal. He brought with him a son, his son's wife, and a granddaughter, aged 6. The granddaughter's name was Gannensagouas.

In the Indian village he proved to be a rare asset. He was noted for his respect for the priests, his frequent prayers in the church. He was patient and kind to the old: he built or repaired their cabins.

Thoronhiongo had every reason to be satisfied with his granddaughter. She became one of the Indian children taught by the nuns at the mission under the direction of Marguerite Bourgeoys and was baptized as Marie-Thérèse on June 28, 1681, at the age of 14. The experience of the nuns of New France in trying to educate the Indian girls under a convent system had not often been satisfactory. But Marguerite Bourgeoys and her assistants were having more promising results with some of the Indian girls in their mountainside mission near Montreal.

The faith of a few of the Indian girls seemed so real and dependable that they were admitted as nuns of the Congregation of Notre Dame. The second to be admitted was Thoronhiongo's granddaughter, Gannensagouas. She had learned how to speak, read and write French. She had the qualifications to become a teacher of other Indian girls at the mission. She had also been judged to have the true spirit of a nun. Special praise was given to her modesty. Abbé Belmont of the Sulpicians said that she was never known to have looked any man in the face, but kept her eyes averted.

While Thoronhiongo's granddaughter honored him, his son disgraced him. He was a libertine. He laughed at the missionaries. He refused to be baptized. Then, to crown his sins, he quit the community, leaving his wife pregnant. He went back to live among the Iroquois in Tsonnonthouan.

In the midst of this humiliation, old François Thoronhiongo became blind. Yet nothing shook his faith. The grandson, born after his father had left the mission, was growing up. Every day after dinner he would lead his blind grandfather to the church and leave him there till evening. His prayers, the old account says, were for his son.

François Thoronhiongo was growing old — so old that when he died in the spring of 1690, they said he was 100. Probably no record of his birth existed; they only guessed at his years.

His little grandson at the mission had grown to be a young man. In the same year the grandfather died, the grandson was old enough to be a "brave" and to go to war. He took part in an expedition against the Iroquois — an expedition half French and half Indian, commanded by de Beaucourt. At the foot of the St. François rapids, on a river named the Kentsage, they encountered a band of Iroquois from Tsonnonthouan. They fought viciously. The Iroquois were defeated. Thoronhiongo's grandson took a prisoner and led him back as a slave.

The traditional story, like many such old accounts,

TOWERS
FORT DES MESSIEURS

is centred on an extraordinary coincidence. When he came home, wild rumors flew through the mountain mission. Indians came running. The slave he had brought back with him was his own father. Neither had recognized the other; they had never seen each other before they met in the battle on the Kentsage River.

The missionaries hoped that Thoronhiongo's son would see something miraculous in his return to the settlement as a captive, led by his own son. Perhaps, they said, he would now consent to be baptized. But he seemed as insolent and unyielding as ever. Within a few days he had a change of heart. Slaves were often roughly treated. He was ill with fatigue after his long forced march through the winter woods. He grew worse and seemed sinking into death.

In his last hours he remembered the Christian prayers that Thoronhiongo had taught him and recited them aloud. The missionaries were called to give him baptism. He is said to have received it with humble contrition, and died while the missionaries exhorted and prayed.

Five years later Marie-Thérese Gannensagouas, Thoronhiongo's granddaughter, died. Her life as a nun in the Congregation of Notre Dame had been exemplary. She was buried in the chapel at the mission, as her grandfather had been buried before her. In the 1790s the chapel was demolished. The bones of grandfather and granddaughter were then removed to the eastern tower. The towers were part of the stone fort built about 100 years before to protect the Christian Indians from attacks by the Iroquois.

Women's liberation: 1903 style

Mrs. John Lovell believed in women's liberation. And the year was 1903.

She had been asked to give a "little talk" to the High School for Girls. She was clear and forthright. She told the girls what their role ought to be in the years ahead of them. Mrs. Lovell knew all about girls. She had brought up a family of her own. And she had taught her own school for young ladies.

In fact, she opened that school in September 1877. The classes were held in the Lovell house, on the site now occupied by the Bay. This school was something between a school and a college. Mrs. Lovell maintained it for seven years. By that time McGill was beginning to admit women to its classes.

Mrs. Lovell taught her own version of women's liberation. She was not thinking how women could liberate themselves by aggressive self-assertion in a man's world, or what had been regarded as a man's world. For her, liberation and self-fulfillment had other meanings. She thought of women as liberating the world from worry by their cheerfulness; liberating it from weariness by their cozy, well-ordered housekeeping; liberating the world from its evils by their own uprightness of character; liberating it from harshness by their politeness and tact; liberating it from stress by their composure and calm.

And, she was convinced, only by liberating the world from so many evils and distresses could woman fulfil herself. Only in this way could she set herself free — free from selfishness, free from meanness, free from vulgarity, free from contention.

Mrs. Lovell rejected the argument that routine household chores, within the confines of the home, imprisoned a woman, frustrated her potential, made her a slave of others instead of a free person in her own right. Anyone who would regard the home as a female prison would, in Mrs. Lovell's opinion, have lost touch with the realities of life, with human and social needs. "It is the place," she said of the home, "where love learns its lessons, where life is schooled into discipline and strength. Where character is moulded. Out of the homes of the community comes the life of the community."

Of course, there was work to be done in the home — routine work at that. But it would be drudgery — soul-destroying drudgery — only to those who had lost sight of its purpose. No work is tedious and menial if it leads to the comfort and happiness of others. And housework, well done, produces more practical happiness than any other work in the world.

In Mrs. Lovell's "little talk," that word "service" keeps recurring. Woman, she believed, is liberated by service. She is imprisoned when she thinks of herself alone. There is the cooking. It is more than the preparation of food. It makes a happy family table, where the cares and perplexities of the day may be forgotten and the world made to look brighter again. And cooking is an act of gracious hospitality. A guest feels his welcome in what has been thoughtfully prepared for him.

A woman's role in the home, however, is not merely to do the housework and to do it well. She has, in her own attitude and manner, to set the household tone. A home must be at peace, if it is to be a home at all. One discordant life in a household mars the harmony, even as one instrument out of tune mars the music of an orchestra. If that discordant life is the mother's, then the whole home is on edge, and tense, and miserable. "What one does," Mrs. Lovell warned, "the others are apt to do, and thus the habit grows until little but sharp speech and unseemly wrangling is heard in the home where the conversation might have so much in it of sweetness and profit."

If women are to be the spreaders of peace, they must have peaceful voices. They ought to heed Shakespeare's words: "Her voice was ever soft, gentle and low, an excellent thing in woman." A soft, low voice would smooth for others the jar and clamor of life. "How often," she recalled, "the spell of beauty is rudely broken by coarse, loud talking. How often you are irresistibly drawn to a plain unassuming woman whose soft, silvery tones render her positively attractive. In the social circle, how pleasant it is to hear a woman talk in the low key that always characterizes the true lady. In the sanctuary of the home how such a voice soothes the fretful child and cheers the weary heart."

Woman would not find her liberation in adding to

SKETCHBOOK
Union and St. Catherine
John Collins

the struggle, controversy, competition of the world — or in proving that she can hold her own in the arena. Her role is to be tactful, to avoid pain and annoyance. The definition of a lady is like the definition of a gentleman: one who never gives pain. Her role is to foresee pain, to save others from it by her skilful management: "When a woman is possessed of tact, she sees as if by second sight any little emergency as likely to occur. The woman of tact not only perceives the variations which are constantly taking place in the atmosphere of social life but she adapts herself to them with a facility which the law of love enables her to carry out so as to spare her friends the pain and annoyance which so frequently arise from the mismanagement of familiar and apparently unimportant affairs."

Mrs. Lovell by no means suggested that a lady should devote herself so much to housework as to neglect literature and art. She should keep up with her reading. It was quite compatible with some kinds of housework. "The darning of stockings need not be irksome," she suggested. "One can have a book of poetry near by and read a few lines at a time without retarding her work." She should visit as many art exhibitions as she can. She should keep a scrapbook to "preserve notable speeches and events." If she has the opportunity, she should travel abroad to study great architecture. All such studies would enrich her mind, improve her conversation, enlarge her influence. Mrs. Lovell had a word of warning: "But while the mind and character of women ought to be cultivated with a view to their own being, they ought not the less to be educated with a view to the happiness of others."

Mrs. Lovell's "little talk" in 1903 to the High School for Girls had expanded into a full discourse on the role of women. She did not believe that true values could ever change. The mission of women would always be "to live for others."

If they ever set out to live for themselves, they would find out (perhaps too late) how much they had missed in life.

Montreal's 'social assembly'

In Old Montreal, at the end of the 18th century and in the early 19th, the sort of amusements enjoyed in the long, idle, pleasure-loving winters depended on one's position in Montreal's social structure. A Montrealer said that the town's social classes were "as distinct and impenetrable as the castes of India." And in winter the lines between the classes were clearly defined by the Montreal Social Assembly.

The Assembly was really a wintertime club, meeting for dancing and supper. Each year in December the "managers" met to plan the winter's program. These managers were all-powerful; they decided who should be invited to join the Assembly and who should be passed over. Those who had social ambitions in Montreal at that time longed or hoped to be included. If no invitation was received, they were "out" — not just out of the Assembly, but out entirely.

About 1784, Simon McTavish was one of the managers of the Assembly. He was prominent in the North West Co., the Montreal-based partnership of fur traders whose aggressive energy was rivalling the Hudson's Bay Co. He was reputed to be the richest man in Montreal, perhaps Montreal's first millionaire. From his exalted social position McTavish had a great part, possibly the most influential part, in selecting the 70 members of that winter's Assembly. He admitted, even boasted, that he had been ruthless in "drawing the line." He pronounced the Assembly to be "the cream of the town."

Two Montrealers who thought highly of their social status found themselves outside the line McTavish had drawn. One of them was Robert Jones, a prominent physician. The other was a Mr. King — a man now obscure in history but who must have had some claims to social recognition in his day. The doctor and King were furious with Simon McTavish. They felt McTavish, by excluding them from a group he openly called "the cream of the town," clearly implied they were of an inferior social status. They met McTavish at the Exchange Coffee House. King demanded an explanation. He used harsh words. McTavish grew angry. What then took place was described as "a boxing match."

Simon McTavish was a proud man, often called "the Marquis" or "the Emperor." He was not accustomed to being spoken to rudely in public, or to being boxed about. Next morning he sent a challenge to King to fight a duel. He may have sent a challenge to Jones also, or the doctor may have challenged him. In any case, duels were arranged between McTavish and both his outraged critics.

By the time McTavish and King met on the duelling ground, their anger had had time to cool. McTavish explained he had had no intention of excluding King from the Assembly. King then said he was sorry matters had gone so far. They shook hands and parted amicably enough. Jones, however, was not to be so easily reconciled to his exclusion from "the cream of the town." He and McTavish met for their duel at the Windmill, on Windmill Point, near the waterfront. Apparently any explanation McTavish might have offered was not accepted. The duel went ahead. Jones's shot took effect. It entered McTavish "a little above the groin and lodged near the skin in the back." Luckily for McTavish, no bone was touched. The bullet was easily extracted.

McTavish soon recovered. He went on to enjoy the social pleasures of the Assembly. The excluded Dr. Jones had to console himself with the thought that he had at least caused this manager of the Assembly some pain and inconvenience.

A glimpse of a gathering of the Assembly in 1805 is given in the memoirs of William Henderson. It took place in the Exchange Coffee House on St. Paul St., near the northeast corner of St. Pierre. "After some six or eight country dances," wrote Henderson, "the company had descended to the supper room. . . . The good things had been disposed of, toasts and songs succeeded."

The Exchange Coffee House, fashionable enough in its day, was completely eclipsed about 12 years later when John Molson opened the Mansion House on the site now covered by the eastern end of Bonsecours Market. The Montreal Social Assembly moved at once into quarters suitably elegant. The ballroom, where the Assembly met, glittered with splendors. From its ceiling hung chandeliers imported from London at a cost of about 1,000

Jøhn Collins SKETCHBOOK

Rue Bonsecours at St. Paul

pounds. The ballroom's curtains cost more than 140 pounds, its ornamental plastering more than 490 pounds.

The Montreal Social Assembly met in the Mansion House to celebrate the queen's birthday in January 1817 (the birthday of Queen Charlotte, consort of King George III). The "cream of the town," numbering 230, was there. The Assembly was "unusually brilliant and crowded." At this January gathering in the ballroom of the Mansion House, dancing commenced about 8 p.m. It was "kept up with great spirit" until midnight. The ladies and gentlemen then "paired off" and withdrew to the supper room.

The ceiling was hung with green boughs, the walls were covered with the colors of all nations. While the members of the Assembly were at supper, the band played at intervals. There was singing. No fewer than 14 toasts were proposed. It was 3 a.m. (seven hours after the meeting had begun) when the Assembly broke up and "the cream of the town" streamed out of the Mansion House door into the cold January night.

Montrealers not invited to join the Assembly had humbler pleasures of their own. Those who had no claim to social distinction of any sort could attend a type of assembly known as the "free and easy." These "free and easy" gatherings were generally sponsored by hotel-owners. But their hotels were all very different from the stately Mansion House of John Molson.

Advertisements for "free and easy" assemblies all combine the same two features: a warm invitation to all, coupled with a stern warning that the rude and rowdy would not be tolerated. Such was the advertisement for George Gibson's British Hotel in 1837. The advertisement begins:

"COME AND SEE A FREE AND EASY, HELD every MONDAY EVENING . . . conducted under the same principle as was so highly approved of last winter. None admitted but the friends of good order, friendship and harmony."

Harry Norris's Gilbert and Sullivan

For more than two decades Montreal had Gilbert and Sullivan all its own. And it was the real thing. The repertoire of operettas was presented in Montreal by the man who had been the director of the Savoy Opera Company (the D'Oyly Carte company) — the historic company that had originally produced the operettas in the days of Gilbert and Sullivan, and continued to produce them in the same style after Gilbert and Sullivan were dead.

Those who took part in the Gilbert and Sullivan operettas at London's Savoy Theatre were known as Savoyards. Montreal, too, had its Savoyard, one of the most celebrated of them. This director was Harry Norris, who died in the 1970s in Hampshire, England, in his 93rd year.

He first knew Montreal in the 1920s, when he brought the performers of the Savoy Opera Company on tour to His Majesty's Theatre. In 1929 Norris, after 10 years as director of the Savoy Opera Company, decided to leave London to settle in Montreal. He came as a newlywed, with his wife, Doris. She, too, was a Savoyard: she had joined the company as a singer in 1923. They both taught music in Montreal. Doris taught piano and singing. Harry taught singing (notably at the McGill Conservatorium) and the violin as well. Harry also served as organist and choir director of Montreal West United Church.

Harry Norris showed his audacity. He would turn the amateurs of the St. Lambert Operatic Society, and later those of the Montreal West Operatic Society, into groups of Savoyards — Montreal's Savoyards. He was not to be content with the ordinary level of amateur performance. He would select the performers carefully. Then he would raise them up to a level not far short of the professional standards he had known. His wife would help not only with instruction in singing; she could manage the staging of the plays — the scenery, the costumes, the whole movement of the players. Together they set to work.

Early every autumn the search for talent began. By the end of October the cast would have been chosen. In weekly rehearsals Harry worked with the choruses, Doris with the principals. After the first few months, rehearsals were increased to twice a week. In the last four or five weeks the whole cast would be brought onto the stage for rehearsals together.

Nothing succeeded like their success. Their Gilbert and Sullivan productions gained so high a reputation that amateurs with talent competed to take part. The choice for the Norrises became wider: they could afford to be increasingly exacting, increasingly selective. Some of the same players reappeared through a number of years, gaining immensely in experience and training. Yet it remained an amateur cast — businessmen, artists, salesmen, housewives. "They come because they love it," said Doris. "They love to sing and it's relaxing for them."

And they were coming from a wider and wider territory. One of the performers came in from Huntingdon. He stayed with the Norrises on rehearsal nights. Harry and Doris had the cheerfulness, the bubbling good humor of the operettas. Harry, in particular, a bald, bespectacled Englishman, had about him a buoyancy, a chuckling quality, touches of wit and satire.

Though he was very demanding of his performers, he was not mean or bitter. He gave the performers the Gilbert and Sullivan spirit, the lightness and gaiety, the sense of highly accomplished fun. They got the spirit. Many were transformed by it into real Gilbert and Sullivan interpreters. By first-night time the cast had been disciplined into precision. Doris worked hard with the backgrounds and the scenery. The operettas must not only be well performed: she saw to it they were well staged. For *The Pirates of Penzance* she devised an attractive Cornish coast, for *The Yeomen of the Guard* the imposing gloom of the Tower of London.

She and her husband, as professionals, were aware of one of the worst traps amateur performers might fall into — the danger of allowing the comic situations in Gilbert and Sullivan to sink into burlesque. The lightness, the cleverness of the operettas must be upheld; they must not become merely coarse and blunt. They were light operas, not vaudeville.

The Norris productions of Gilbert and Sullivan were not only popular. They won critical praise. Thomas Archer, *The Gazette's* music critic, was an

Englishman who had seen the Savoyards in London; he could make comparisons. He wrote: "Top honors . . . invariably go to Mr. Norris. . . . He conducts the music with uncommon refinement and precision and can bring out the felicities better than anyone I know of. He imparts his wisdom and enthusiasm to everyone participating so that a show . . . is given a unity of style which makes it an authentic work of art. We can ask for no more."

In 1963 the Norrises decided to retire to England; they wished to be near their son, Peter, and his wife. They were given a true Gilbert and Sullivan farewell. It was a singing farewell by many of the amateurs he had trained. They came aboard the Franconia at the port of Montreal. A piano was brought out on deck. In brilliant sun, under a blue sky, interrupted only by occasional blasts from ships' sirens, they gathered round the piano to sing songs from *HMS Pinafore.*

The Norrises came back to Montreal on a long visit. Even as visitors, they could not stay away from Gilbert and Sullivan. In 1968 they produced *Pinafore* for the St. Paul's Operatic Society, in the Lachine High School. Harry Norris was then over 80. But he was described as "conducting with his customary vigor and meticulous attention to detail," while his wife had everything under control backstage.

It was a remarkable record of devotion to the Gilbert and Sullivan tradition.

Harry Norris used to say: "The extraordinarily clever humor and satire in Gilbert's librettos have an ageless appeal to both the ordinary man and the intellectual."

And Doris Norris would say: "Sullivan believed that each operetta should have at least one tune which the public would go away whistling."

They were both right.

Age of Wonders: demons and talking heads

The first half-century of Montreal's history might well be called the Age of Wonders. In those early years, the dividing line between the natural and the supernatural was extraordinarily thin. To Montrealers in that 17th-century era, the supernatural, though stranger than the natural, seemed just as real. It was almost part of everyday experience.

The explanation of such weird beliefs is obscure. Perhaps people in Montreal then gave supernatural explanations for natural phenomena. Perhaps their imaginations made the unreal seem real. Whatever the explanation, the old narratives of the time, again and again, give literal accounts of the most fantastic occurrences.

Demons were said to be not merely "forces" or "influences." They were persons. Even as God sent his angels to guide and help mankind, the devil sent his demons to terrorize and torment. According to the narrative, a particular demon was sent by the devil in the 1690s to spread fear in the new Hôtel Dieu. The previous hospital had been destroyed by fire. A new building was under construction on St. Paul St. at the corner of what is now St. Sulpice. The nuns did not wait for it to be finished. They moved in as soon as the first storey was ready for occupancy.

According to the beliefs of the time, the special mission of demons was to harass and thwart any good project. A new hospital, as a work of charity and compassion, would be a natural place for a demon's antics.

It was said that the sisters had no sooner moved into the new hospital than a demon arrived to terrify them. He ran about in the night, a big candle in his hand. He dashed from window to window. Passers-by caught sight of him. They came to the sisters to report what they had seen.

In the hospital the demon raised a horrible racket. Piles of building materials still lay about. It sounded as if he was turning them over and tumbling them down into the cellar. At other times the demon went to the top of the building. There he could be heard working all night long with axe and saw, as if he was a carpenter. Other nights he would spend running about on the roof, like a frisky young horse. Three times, the nuns said, they heard him walking the length of the dormitory. He clattered by, as if in wooden shoes. The demon was later heard leaping up and down the main staircase, as if pursued. Then he rolled an empty barrel down the stairs, top to bottom. With this last defiant gesture, the demon left.

This story is not unusual. Montrealers in the 17th century shared this belief. They regarded the devil as the awesome lord of evil, whose agents were always lurking everywhere.

This was believed to be true on the very day when Montreal was founded in 1642. Maisonneuve, acting for the pious Society of Notre Dame, had come to the island with a few followers to set up a "Ville Marie." It was to be a missionary settlement in the dangerous Iroquois country.

After coming ashore, they gathered at the waterfront. It was a serene May morning, with sunshine and birdsong. But they felt certain that demons must be all about them, trying to defeat this undertaking, which they had consecrated to the Virgin Mary. In celebration of their arrival, they fired cannon. Father Vimont, a Jesuit priest, was there. He wrote: "The thunder of the cannon reverberated over the whole island. The demons, though accustomed to thunder, were no doubt dismayed at a sound that testified to the love we have for our great Lady."

This sense of the horrible presence of demons was only one of the supernatural beliefs of the time. Freakish miracles were frequently reported. Particularly grotesque was the tale about the head of Jean St. Père. This Jean St. Père was one of the original Montrealers, who came ashore with Maisonneuve in 1642. On an October day in 1647 he was at work roofing houses. Iroquois suddenly appeared. He was "savagely shot at and killed." The Iroquois cut off his head. They carried it off with them.

John Collins SKETCHBOOK

ST. PAUL
and
ST. SULPICE

place, then in another. They tried to cover it, so the voice could not be heard. Still, St. Père spoke to them.

So outlandish a tale presented something of a problem for Dollier de Casson. After all, he was a historian, setting down what he believed to be the facts. The story seemed to have excellent authority. Yet it strained his credulity. The tale, he felt, ought to be included in his history. Yet he felt reluctant to assume full responsibility for its truth. He hedged and he did it discreetly: "If anyone doubts this, I give the thing for what it is worth just as I receive it from people of good repute. . . . That being the case, I felt obliged to relate the matter in all simplicity."

Grotesque as belief in the supernatural might be, it could, at times, assume a wild and frenzied poetry. This kind of supernatural vision was most evident during a long series of appalling earthquakes. These earthquakes of 1663 shook Montreal, as they did the whole St. Lawrence Valley. It was said that the approach of the earthquakes was announced when serpents appeared in the sky — serpents "which entwined themselves with one another and flew through the air with wings of fire."

This fabulously poetic account reached its height in the vision of the battle in the heavens. "For 40 days," wrote one narrator, "we saw . . . men on horseback who rushed through the air richly robed and armed with lances, like troops of cavalry; steeds ranged in squadrons which dashed forth against each other; combatants who joined battle hand to hand; shields shaken; a multitude with helmets and naked swords."

In Montreal's Age of Wonders in the 17th century there was this inclination, even this readiness, to believe in the wonders of the supernatural. Yet the note of detached skepticism is heard from time to time.

In relating one of many miraculous happenings, Dollier de Casson could say: "Whatever may be the case in this wonder, I have given you the facts so that you may believe as much as you wish."

The bizarre story of what happened was recorded in the 1670s by Montreal's first historian, Dollier de Casson, superior of the Sulpicians. St. Père's head hurled reproaches at the Indians as they went off with it. Though St. Père had never known the Iroquois language, he now spoke it. According to the story, the Iroquois heard the voice from time to time both night and day. It scared them; it would not leave them alone. They tried putting the head in one

Wit and compassion at the bar of justice

She refused to give her age. It was during a court case, with Justice Thomas J.J. Loranger on the bench. The lawyers questioning her did all they could to have her state how old she was. Still she refused. The judge raised his eyes to the ceiling. "Surely you can see, gentlemen," he remarked, "that she is refusing to incriminate herself."

Loranger was a justice of the Superior Court of Quebec from 1863 to 1883. Often in the course of a trial he would interpose a touch of irony. One of the cases he heard in Montreal's courthouse on Notre Dame St. (known today as the old courthouse) concerned a money-lender who was suing a customer for repayment of $50. The lawyer for the defendant (the customer) was cross-examining the money-lender (the plaintiff). He was trying to make him admit that he had lent the money at the shocking rate of 50 per cent. The plaintiff was doing his best to avoid answering. He kept saying that he was a big businessman, accustomed to large transactions. "Don't bother trying to get him to reply," said Justice Loranger to the lawyer for the defendant. "I understand. The plaintiff wishes to say that he never steals except in a big way."

In the 19th century the law was the profession, next to the church, to which educated French Canadians most aspired. The result was an extraordinary number of talented and remarkable judges. One of the most notable among them was Joseph Rémi Vallières de Saint-Réal. His judgments were masterly in reasoning and in language. He was also known as a wit, rapid in repartee. Vallières, a strikingly good-looking man, had his portrait painted. Another judge, Jean Roch Rolland, viewed it. "It's certainly a handsome portrait," he commented rather spitefully, "but it doesn't look much like him." A little later, Rolland had his own portrait painted. Vallières viewed it. "Ah!" he remarked. "It's certainly not a handsome portrait, but it looks just like him."

Vallières was appointed chief justice for the district of Montreal in 1842. While brilliant intellectually, he was sensitive emotionally. He was seen to weep in court during some heart-rending cases. One day a poor Irishman was brought to court. This immigrant, unable to find work, found himself destitute in a strange land. He had to feed his children. Necessity and despair had driven him to steal two loaves of bread. A witness explained the circumstances. Vallières refused to hear any more. He stood up. "So help me God!" he exclaimed. "Poor man. I think I would have done the same thing, if I had been in his place." The charge was dismissed. One commentator remarked: "Not quite judicial, perhaps. But how admirable!"

The 19th century at times produced men of extraordinary politeness. These lawyers, after education in church schools and colleges, had been taught good manners. One of the most remarkable examples of this *politesse* was the Montreal lawyer Côme Séraphin Cherrier, after whom Cherrier St. in Montreal is named. He practiced law in the city for more than half a century. Three times he declined appointments to the bench, the last time an offer of appointment as chief justice. To see Cherrier walking along a street was to see politeness in perpetual motion: "His hat was always in his hand, as he bowed left and right, often without knowing the people to whom he was being so polite." In the evening he never left his law office without saying goodnight to everyone, even the clerks. One evening, after he had left and gone some distance, he began wondering whether he had said goodnight to his law partner, Antoine Dorion. He could not go on, but retraced his steps to the office. "I beg your pardon, M. Dorion," he said, "but did I say goodnight to you before I left?" "Certainly," Dorion reassured him. "Ah! That makes me feel a lot better. Let me say goodnight to you again, M. Dorion." He left with a free mind.

Such scrupulous *politesse,* carried almost to excess, was seen in Augustin Norbert Morin, who was appointed a judge in the Superior Court in 1855. In the years while he was a practicing lawyer, a beggar called every day at his office. Morin's courtesy had made him vulnerable to the unscrupulous. Sometimes this beggar would go so far as to call several times in the same day. He could always count on a polite reception and something out of Morin's pocket. One day Morin was overwhelmed with work. The return of the beggar irritated him. He told him

John Collins SKETCHBOOK The Old Courthouse

to get out. "Look here, my friend," he said, "you're really getting unreasonable. You're no gentleman." Startled and saddened, the beggar turned and went out. Scarcely had the door closed when Morin, terribly upset by what he had said, dashed hatless into the street. He overtook the beggar. At once he apologized: "My good friend, I certainly beg your pardon. I shouldn't have spoken to you that way. I didn't have any intention of suggesting you're not a gentleman. No, no, I assure you."

Not all Montreal lawyers were by any means as polite as Cherrier and Morin. A lawyer who could be very abrupt was George Etienne Cartier, a man who grew great in politics and became one of the most important Fathers of Confederation. In politics, he could be rough with those seeking free advice. To one such advice-seeker he retorted: "Why don't you get to work? If you studied hard enough, you could learn for yourself what you want me to tell you. How do you think I found out? By sleeping?"

The bench and bar of Montreal saw in those years a great variety of character and characteristics among its French-Canadian members. A lawyer of another type was Joseph Alfred Mousseau. He was the perpetual optimist. Such optimism was all the more remarkable in that he lived a life of disappointments, of good beginnings and poor endings. His political career was first in Ottawa, then in Quebec. He was a member of Sir John A. Macdonald's cabinet, and later the Conservative premier of Quebec. Though Mousseau achieved prominence, he failed to retain the confidence of others. Eventually he was led to understand it would be best for him and for the party if he retired from politics. He was appointed a puisne judge of the Superior Court. He died after only two years on the bench. Yet through all his disappointments, he remained good-humored, cheerful, hopeful. Always his future was brightened with imaginary rainbows. A friend asked him: "If you were sentenced to be hanged, would you still be the happy optimist?" Mousseau replied: "Certainly, I would expect the rope to break."

The nuns' cheerful, unrelenting discipline

"At the stroke of 12, the Sisters entered two by two, followed by the lady-superior with a prayer-book in her hand. She clapped the leaves of this together in signal for them to kneel, to rise, to kneel again and rise, while they repeated . . . their prayers. . . . The ungraceful gowns of coarse gray, the blue checked aprons, the black crepe caps, were the same; they came and went with the same quick tread, touching their brows with holy water and kneeling and rising now as then with the same constrained and ordered movements."*

In these words the American writer William Dean Howells described his visit to the chapel of the Grey Nuns in Montreal in the mid-Victorian era. What he pictured was the regimental precision of the nuns, the unison of their movements, the way they were ordered and disciplined. The resemblance to regimental drill was real. As one nun herself remarked, the discipline of the convent was accepted by those who entered the religious life as soldiers "do that of their military calling, without question."

An example of the severity of convent life in Victorian Montreal was seen in the case of Eulalie Durocher. She was to become known in religion as Mother Mary Rose, founder and first superior general of the Sisters of the Holy Names of Jesus and Mary, at Longueuil. In the 1840s she was a postulant, on probation in the first stage of her training as a nun. She was assigned to the most menial and uninviting tasks: "she would fetch and bring, she would sweep and scrub." When she moved on to the next stage, as a novice, she was rigorously trained in self-denial and in the humble spirit.

The novice-master was an Oblate from France, Rev. J.F. Allard, later a missionary bishop in Africa. He aimed to cure the novices of any egotism they might possess. They were made to have a low opinion of themselves, to forsake self-esteem and any complaisant views they might have of their own spiritual excellence. Such hard training was considered indispensable.

When Eulalie eventually, as Mother Mary Rose, became the founder and first superior of an order of nuns, she taught the postulants and novices the same discipline she had herself endured, though she mingled her strictness with kindness.

Mother Mary Rose was particularly strict about the period of silence — the silence to be observed from "evening prayer until after the morning meditation." One day, in her room, she overheard two sisters violating the silent period by talking in the corridor. She at once left her room and ordered them to kneel down where they were, in instant penance for their delinquency.

She was not a superior who imposed austerities on others while avoiding them herself. Though the superior, she practiced the same self-abasement. Her principle was: "It is the lowliest and most servile work that should be most eagerly sought; we need it; it helps to keep us humble." During the hours of teaching, while the nuns and their pupils were in their classrooms, she went about cleaning baths and toilets. If one of the servants happened to see her, and asked to do the work instead, she would reply: "No, my dear, I must practice humility."

The results of this sort of self-discipline, rigorously and habitually taught and practiced, were seen in moments of crisis. As with regimental training, persistent attention to discipline in little things was preparation for the greater moments of self-sacrifice. It was seen in the typhus epidemic of 1847. Irish immigrants were landing sick or dying on the Montreal waterfront. Nuns were called to care for them, at the risk of their own lives, in the hospital sheds erected by the government at Point St. Charles. In the Grey Nunnery, the sisters were addressed by Mother McMullen:"In sending you there I am signing your death warrant, but you are free to accept or refuse." Years of convent training were put to the test. The nuns all stood up. They said together, in a sort of chorus, "I am ready."

The same response came from other religious orders, both in the typhus of the 1840s and in epidemics of cholera. In 1854, in the middle of the night, a man came knocking at the door of the Sisters of Charity of Providence, in Montreal. His wife and two children were dying of cholera. Would the sisters come to help them? The superior, Mother Gamelin, went into the dormitory. She rang a bell to awaken the sisters. "My dear daughters," she said, "sisters are wanted for cholera patients; who will be the first to go?" At once she had her volunteers.

John Collins SKETCHBOOK
Chapel of the Grey Nuns—

The same discipline was seen in other emergencies. A number of instances are given in the autobiography of a Victorian fireman, Capt. William Orme McRobie. Several times he was called when fires broke out in convents. Always he was astonished by the absence of any panic among the nuns. One of these fires was in the convent of the Congregation of Notre Dame, then on St. Jean Baptiste St. in Old Montreal. In the chapel, while the sisters were at a service, the gauze and drapery around the altar caught fire. Firemen rushed in with axes and an extinguisher. They began cutting away the burning wood round the altar. "All this time," said McRobie, "the nuns never budged, but remained reverently on their knees, with their eyes turned heavenward. . . . The heat and smoke were . . . considerable, but they never flinched or moved."

The most remarkable feature of a life of such unrelenting and unwavering discipline was the mood of cheerfulness that went with it. Part of the rule was that self-discipline and humility should be accepted joyfully. Of Mother Mary Rose it was said that "she discountenanced sadness, and caught and recommended the joy which is of God." Such cheerfulness in convents was seen by an English traveller, James S. Buckingham, who came to Montreal while on a North American tour in 1839. He was first taken to see the convent of the Hôtel Dieu. Though the duties of the nuns were "severe," and their diet "scanty and simple," he remarked: "They appear to be very happy." Buckingham then visited the Grey Nuns, in the convent then on St. Ann's Market, now Place Youville. After he had seen the building, the mother superior introduced him to some of the nuns. Buckingham wrote: "These were all engaged in needlework of various kinds; but all entered cheerfully into conversation. . . . There was nothing gloomy in their appearance or deportment; on the contrary, they were not merely serene, but cheerful."

Mount Royal Park as its architect saw it

From the time Mount Royal was acquired by the city of Montreal as a public park, disputes raged about what should be done with it.

Those who wished as far as possible to preserve it in its natural state came into conflict with those who wanted to"put it to use" — to develop it and erect buildings on it for some form of public entertainment. The controversy, once begun, has never ended.

How old all the modern disputes are may be seen by going back to Frederick Law Olmsted. He was the landscape architect who designed the park for the city of Montreal in the 1870s. Olmsted was the foremost landscape architect on the American continent. He remains one of the greatest of all time. He designed Central, Riverside and Mount Morris parks in New York, the Back Bay Fens at Boston, the grounds of the Capitol in Washington, the park at Niagara. He was the first commissioner for the national park at Yosemite.

In many ways Olmsted had taken on an unusually interesting project. He had been engaged to make a park out of a mountain. He saw at once that a mountain should not be treated as if it were just another civic park. It required very different treatment. Precedents set by other parks should be set aside as unsuitable. The mountain, by nature, had "dignity, serenity and strength." These were the qualities to be conserved. The very fact that it rose above the city would make it ideal as an area where the city dweller could get away from the noise, the pollution, the tensions of the streets into the quietness and solitude of unspoiled nature.

All suggestions to "citify" the mountain should be resisted, Olmsted urged. Once such suggestions began to be carried out, where would they end? The mountain would become just another part of the city. Its real value would lie not in making it more and more like the rest of the city but in maintaining the contrast that it offered.

Though Mount Royal was neither high nor large, as mountains go, Olmsted saw "in its different parts no little variety of mountain form and feature." At some points it commanded magnificent views of the city below. From its interior, which sloped into a valley, the city could no longer be seen or heard. Its

very existence seemed to disappear. The visitor found himself in secluded peace. Nothing should be done, Olmsted insisted, to "prettify" Mount Royal. It was no place, for instance, for flower beds. Flowers should flourish. But they should be wildflowers, in keeping with the scene.

It would be well to remember, Olmsted said, that the "original Gardener of Eden" knew his work better than any human gardener since. "And remember," he added, "that it is the lilies of the field, not the lilies of the garden, that we are bid to consider." Nor should the superb mountain scenery be marred by the introduction of buildings that could just as well be erected somewhere else. He warned against the introduction of "prospect-towers, club-houses, and fanciful houses of entertainment." All such intrusions would be bringing the city into the park. Mount Royal should serve Montrealers in the same way as national parks serve whole nations. It should preserve the experience of unmarred nature. But only a few people could visit national parks, and fewer still could go frequently. Mount Royal was nearby, and Montrealers could go there as often as they wanted.

Olmsted soon became aware that the future of Mount Royal would not depend upon his principles. It would rest on no steady principles of any kind. The future of the mountain would be in the hands of municipal politicians. They had no knowledge or understanding of landscape architecture. They did not even have any continuity. They came and went, carried in and out on the ebb and flow of political fortunes. Incoming politicans, he found, tended to look with disfavor on whatever had been done by their predecessors in office. They felt they had to do something different to justify their election. Their new ideas might be hasty and superficial.

What was worse, many of the new ideas of politicians were not even their own. They came from outside influences — from "selfish, partisan, and speculative objects, and puerile, shallow, temporizing, spendthrift interests." It was these interests that would have "undue weight" and would "overrule." Whenever Olmsted heard a new idea from a municipal politician, he suspected it was "a yielding to demands which it would be impolitic to

further resist."

Olmsted had no faith that his principles for the future of Mount Royal would be protected by such politicians. His hope that the "dignity, serenity and strength" of the mountain would be respected was based on one thing, and one thing only: the informed, consistent, resisting power of public opinion. Again and again, in the generations after his death, Olmsted's principles have found understanding and support.

A remarkable example of his surviving influence came in 1959. The Montreal Parks and Playgrounds Association sent a letter to the executive committee at city hall, concerning a proposal to make parking lots within the park itself: "Mount Royal Park [is] a refuge of tranquility and beauty in the heart of the great metropolis. As city life becomes progressively more noisy, hectic and uncomfortable, such a refuge, within relatively easy reach for the citizens, becomes

more and more valuable, especially as the free open countryside is pushed further and further away from the city limits."

Olmsted in his day had always to counter the repeated charge that his ideas were too artistic, too lofty, not down to earth and practical enough. He was called a dreamer, an unworldly idealist. To such charges he replied that what he urged was as important in the practical sense as any other municipal responsibilities. He would say to his critics: "The possession of charming natural scenery is a form of wealth as practical as that of wholesome air, pure water, of sunlight unobstructed by smoke and fog; as practical, then, as that of sewers, aqueducts and pavements. Insofar as the management fails to constantly serve that end; insofar, especially, as it runs counter to it, you must judge those responsible for it as you would judge those responsible for leaky sewers."

The sham battle of Notre Dame de Grâce

On Thanksgiving Day, Oct. 18, 1906, an army was advancing to capture Montreal, moving from Lachine eastward. It entered the Benny Farm. Then the battle began: it had encountered the defenders of Montreal. The battle line formed along the line of Madison Ave.

This was only a sham battle, taking place to give officers and men of Montreal's militia some practice in field manoeuvres, under conditions simulating war — the real war that seemed a grim possibility in the clouded future. Military umpires were observing the manoeuvres. At the end, they would pass judgment on how well the Montreal militia had done.

In 1906 convenient open country was available for a sham battle on a large scale. The land from western Notre Dame de Grâce to Lachine was little more than farms, except for Montreal West, then little more than a village. Farms also stretched north and south, up to Côte St. Luc Rd. and beyond, and down to the CPR tracks. The defending "Blue" forces took up a good line when they chose Madison Ave. In front of them lay the open fields, offering no cover for an advancing enemy. At the left flank, a little below Sherbrooke St. (then known as Sherbrooke Extension), the land fell away from a bluff. A little in front of Madison Ave., the Benny Farm came to an end. The land at Madison offered good cover: it was orchards, woodlots or thickets.

The manoeuvres of 1906 were planned seriously. The "Red" force was to be the invader, the "Blue" force the defender. About 2,200 militiamen were to take part. As would be assumed in real warfare, the attacking forces would be the stronger; they were assigned about 1,400 men. The defenders numbered about 800. The opposing forces were more or less complete. Each had infantry, cavalry, batteries, engineers, service corps, medical units and field ambulances. The Red force gave a realistic effect of field artillery in action with the thunder of blank shells from their new rapid-firing 4.7 guns. The Blue force had been left without the blank shells they had been expecting from Halifax. They had to make do with lighting firecrackers in their guns' barrels.

The Red invaders were commanded by Lt.-Col. E.B. Ibbotson, the Blue defenders by Lt.-Col. F. Minden Cole. The Red force advanced to attack the line the Blue force had taken up — the line centred on Madison Ave. In the attack the Highlanders, under Lt.-Col. George S. Cantlie, were on the right (the south); the Victoria Rifles were at the centre; the Prince of Wales Fusiliers (the 65th) were on the left (the north). The Red forces came on with spirit. The Blue defenders, fighting in front of their main line, kept falling back "in spurts." But soon the chief fault in the advance showed up. Ibbotson's different units lost contact with one another. The line was now advancing in pieces, not as a connected whole.

At one point, near the centre, the results became ludicrous. When a gap opened up, the advancing 65th and the defending 53rd became mixed together, a milling, bewildered mob. They did not even realize they were foes. They were eagerly asking each other where the enemy was. Only gradually did they realize what the situation really was and draw apart to continue the battle. On the south of the advancing force another wide gap opened. Cantlie's Highlanders pressed forward with such impetuous zeal as to lose all touch with the Victoria Rifles. They went so far as to move beyond Madison Ave. and were actually behind the defending line. There they came upon a gun, with no one to protect it but its crew. At once they captured it. Unquestionably, it had been a gallant, determined onrush, in the old Highland spirit. Cantlie seemed in a position to force the defenders to retreat on their south flank. But the umpires doubted that the Highlanders, having become isolated from the rest of the attacking forces, were strong enough to create real disaster for the defence. They might, in fact, have placed themselves in danger of being surrounded.

The battle developed mainly at the centre, along the line of Madison Ave. The infantrymen of both sides had been supplied with blank cartridges for their rifles. Concealing themselves as best they could, they kept up a lively fire at each other.

Immense crowds of Montrealers had turned out to witness the battle of Notre Dame de Grâce. For more fun they moved forward to the front line. They sat about, picnicking in the fields, among the "Lots for Sale" signs. Though the fighting line was

six miles long, sightseers crowded it all the way.

In the afternoon the umpires declared the battle was over. They did not believe that the battle line was likely to change much more. In any case, the crowds were so dense and near that further manoeuvres were almost impossible. Though a number of the soldiers on both sides had been required to play dead or wounded, the real military casualties were limited to scratches on thorny bushes or barbed-wire fences.

The officers gathered for a dinner at the Windsor Hotel. After dinner, the umpires gave their opinions. The chief umpires were General Lake and Colonel Buchan. They said the Blue defence forces had won. Though suffering losses and difficulties, Colonel Cole had established and held an effective defensive line. But the umpires went on to say that both sides in the battle of Notre Dame de Grâce had much to learn.

One battery on the defence side had committed a breach of military etiquette: it had fired on its own men for three-quarters of an hour. "It is generally wise," remarked Lake, "first to make sure you are not firing on your own men."

Both sides had left their cavalry with vague orders. As a result the cavalry had moved about vaguely and had no effective role.

Though much remained to be learned, the umpires had nothing but praise for the fine turnout and for the keenness shown by all these citizen soldiers. It was this esprit de corps that had brought out 2,200 men on a Thanksgiving Day, into the fields and orchards, to fight the battle of Notre Dame de Grâce. It was serious preparation. Nine years later most of the same officers and men who fought the battle of Notre Dame de Grâce would be fighting on the battlefields of the Great War.

The shrine on St. Catherine St.

The chapel of Notre Dame de Lourdes stands at 430 St. Catherine St. E., near the corner of St. Denis. It serves no specific or limited area, but every year it draws about 200,000 visitors. They come from anywhere, from everywhere.

This chapel was built under the inspiration of two events in the life of the Roman Catholic Church in the 19th century. The first, in 1854, was the declaration by Pope Pius IX of the dogma of the immaculate conception of the Virgin Mary. It was "a doctrine revealed by God." Therefore it "must be believed firmly and constantly by all the Faithful." According to this dogma, the stain of original sin (received by all mankind from the sin of Adam in the Garden of Eden) was not merely removed but excluded from Mary's soul. Her soul, from the moment of its creation and infusion into her body, was clothed in sanctifying grace.

The second, in 1858, was the report by a peasant girl, Bernadette Soubirous, that the Virgin Mary had appeared to her 18 times between Feb. 11 and July 16, near the town of Lourdes in the French Pyrenees. Bernadette was gathering firewood on the bank of a river near Lourdes. It was then that she saw, as she later testified, the first in the series of manifestations of the Virgin Mary in a riverside grotto. On one of these appearances the Virgin Mary had spoken: "I am the Immaculate Conception." At first Bernadette was censured. She was even arrested twice. In the end she convinced the authorities of the reality of her visions.

In Montreal, a member of the Sulpicians, Abbé Hugues Lenoir, became determined to commemorate the pope's declaration and Bernadette's visions, and together, in a shrine. His plan received the approval of the bishop of Montreal, Msgr. Ignace Bourget. The land on St. Catherine St. was donated by a lawyer, Côme Cherrier, a pious layman of St. Jacques Parish. The Sulpicians subscribed generously. Other help came from far and wide.

Napoléon Bourassa, the man charged with artistic responsibility for carrying Abbé Lenoir's idea into reality, was said to possess all the talents. His versatility was amazing. Apart from being an architect and a painter, he was a sculptor, a musician, a gifted public speaker, an art teacher, an extensive writer on the needs and principles of art, as well as the author of romantic novels. He even had a considerable grasp of law, having been a law student before he turned to art as a career. His youngest child, Henri Bourassa, became a prominent nationalist, and founded Le Devoir in 1910.

When Napoléon Bourassa gave up the law for art, he first studied for several years under the French-Canadian portrait painter Théophile Hamel. In 1852 he set out for Italy. It was the turning point in his life. In Italy he came under the influence of a group of painters who had set themselves up in a deserted monastery at Sant' Isidoro. Led by Johann Friedrich Overbeck, they were convinced that the highest art is religious art and that mural or fresco painting is the most effective form of religious art.

Derisively known as the "Nazareners," they believed the need was to turn away from all modern tendencies. The true models were to be found in the art of the 15th century. They sought to imitate its devout severity, its emphasis on design and purity of line. The effect of the Nazareners on the art of the world spread far. It was felt in Germany and France. In England it affected the celebrated pre-Raphaelite painters. When Napoléon Bourassa returned from Italy to Montreal he brought the aims and theories of the Nazareners with him. He had the supreme opportunity to put such aims and theories into practice when he was commissioned to create the chapel of Notre Dame de Lourdes.

He approached his task with dedication. To him art had become an apostolate. It was one of the most meritorious ways of serving God.

A remarkable feature of the chapel is that it was the artistic creation of one man. In the role of architect, he drew up the plans. In the role of painter, he covered its extraordinarily high walls with murals. In the role of decorator, he directed the gilding, woodcarving and other ornamentation. Bourassa drew up the architectural plans for the chapel in the Romanesque-Byzantine style of the Renaissance period. He gave the chapel three domes. The central dome measures 120 feet from the ground to the top of its cross. In fact, one of the features of the chapel is its height in relation to its ground

SKETCHBOOK
Notre Dame de Lourdes

— John Collins

space. The nave, for instance, is as high as it is long. It measures 50 feet in both directions. Such unusual height in a small building achieved two effects. It imparted a feeling of upward aspiration and it provided vast wall space for the mural paintings.

In the building are actually two chapels, one above the other. A basement chapel is devoted to the theme of Lourdes and Bernadette's visions. The Lourdes grotto, in which the Virgin Mary was said to have made her miraculous appearances, is reproduced at the altar. In the upper chapel, the dogma of the immaculate conception is dramatized in Bourassa's series of murals. One series depicts the foreshadowing of the dogma in Biblical history. It begins with a painting, on the roof of the nave, of the promise of redemption made to the sinful Adam and Eve. It includes, on the right side of the nave, the prophets who foretold the Virgin, such as Isaiah, who declared: "Behold a virgin shall conceive." The statue over the main altar represents the Virgin standing on clouds. White mystical light, from a source unseen, streams upon her, as in the description in the last book of the Bible: "a woman clothed with the sun."

This vast project was Bourassa's principal achievement, though he planned and decorated other churches with his murals. There are not many descriptions of Napoléon Bourassa's personal appearance. Photographs show him as a courtly looking figure, with a beard in the fashionable style of Napoléon III. John Watts, the first curator of the National Gallery of Canada, spoke of him as kind and hospitable and as "one of the old-school Frenchmen with fine manners."

Opinions differ as to the quality of Bourassa's painting. But the chapel of Notre Dame de Lourdes is of enduring historical interest. It reflects, with extraordinary intensity, two of the most ardent religious developments of Roman Catholicism in the 19th century.

Winston Churchill in Montreal: 1929

On Monday, Aug. 12, 1929, Winston Churchill arrived in Montreal with what he called "the Churchill troupe" — his brother, Major John Churchill, DSO, his son, Randolph, and his brother's son, John G. Churchill.

There was an interruption on his arrival that did not annoy him at all, but gave him so much amusement that he mentioned it later in a press interview. Harry Stafford of Montreal crashed through the small official group that was welcoming Churchill at Windsor Station. He was a former captain of the Manchester United Football Team, and had worked for Churchill in Manchester in the election of 1906. This abrupt interruption Churchill later described as "a pleasing informal touch."

The next day Churchill was to address the Canadian Club of Montreal. At no time in his life did he take the making of speeches lightly. He had been at the Château Frontenac at Quebec, keeping himself much of the time in seclusion while he worked at his text. He also did some sightseeing; he saw the usual places a tourist to Quebec visits. He had lunch with Lieutenant-Governor Henry George Carroll at Spencer Wood and was guest at a small dinner party in the Garrison Club. All the while the speech was on his mind: he was working out its structure, satisfying himself with its phrases.

Yet this speechmaking was all a voluntary effort on his part, for he was in Canada on a holiday. That year Britain's Conservative government had been defeated. Labor was in power. Churchill was no longer the chancellor of the exchequer: he was only a private member, with time to travel, to write, and to talk. It was an agreeable interlude in his life, not one he would wish too long prolonged, but a recreation while it lasted. It was not his first visit to Canada. He had come in 1900 as a young veteran of the South Africa War. At that time he had given lectures on his South African experiences.

On this Monday morning in 1929, at 1:30, Churchill left Quebec for Montreal in a private car placed at his disposal by the CPR. And that Monday evening president Edward Beatty (not yet Sir Edward) gave a dinner in his honor at the Mount Royal Club. While in Montreal Churchill spoke about his interest in his visit to Quebec. The city had

reminded him of Scotland: it was a castle on a cliff, like Edinburgh, while the Quebec Bridge reminded him of the bridge over the Firth of Forth. He could not then foresee that he would one day, as prime minister, return to Quebec's castle on the cliff, to decide, at a Quebec conference, the fate of the world.

Interviews were given, too, by Churchill's brother, the major. He had served with the Australians through much of the Great War. They had won his admiration, as had the Canadians. "The Canadians and the Australians were terrific," said Major Churchill. "The Germans felt that the British people could be understood, but they couldn't quite fathom the fellows from the Dominions."

On Tuesday, Aug. 13, at the Canadian Club, it was said that "probably no previous speaker had an audience of such proportions" as Winston Churchill. Ballroom, Rose Room, galleries, corridors and platforms were filled wherever chairs could be placed. Loudspeakers carried the speech in the corridors. Yet thousands, it was said, had to be turned away. It recalls the era of the 1920s to read the list of the guests who were at the head table. The singular magnetism of Winston Churchill, even in 1929, had given the opportunity of seeing, hearing and meeting him an irresistible attraction. The club's guest list included a roll call of "principal citizens."

Churchill was received with prolonged applause; everyone stood. He began speaking slowly, but he gave himself time to work his speech up to its climax and finish within the time allotted speakers at the Canadian Club. Loudspeakers were primitive in those days; Churchill was faced with a large disk. It was noticed that he curtailed the vigor of his presentation a little so that his gestures and the disk would not collide.

"You have made great progress," he remarked. "I come back after 29 years to Montreal, 29 eventful years, and I find that the city of Montreal is five times as large and probably 20 times as wealthy as when I left it last, only a little more than a quarter of a century ago." Old Britain could not be expected to make that kind of progress; it was not a new country. But he came to give assurances to anyone who might doubt the future of that venerable island in the sea. The Churchill touch was beginning to appear in the

SKETCHBOOK

John Collins

The WINDSOR

THE WINDSOR HOTEL

words: "Nevertheless, I feel, when I come here, that I have a right to tell you I come as the representative of one progressive, developing, expanding community, to land on the shores of another."

Churchill dwelt at some length on questions of trade. He hoped that the whole Empire might find its way to become one vast trading community, a sort of common market. But it was not in this part of his speech that his heart lay. His real concern was with defence, with the security of the peace of the world.

The year 1929 was one when disarmament was in the air. Armies were being reduced, and air forces — even navies. Churchill sounded his sombre caution. Disarmament could go too far, too soon. This was not the way to the peace of the world. The first thing was to do away with the causes of anxiety and suspicion that make nations feel they must arm for their protection.

The shadow of things to come was in his doubts about the wisdom of extracting heavy reparations from defeated Germany. He was saying in Montreal in 1929 much what he was to say as prime minister in 1945: that Germany, once defeated, must be welcomed back, not ground down. "We see great dangers — there are undoubtedly great dangers," he told the Canadian Club, "in nations drawing generation after generation immense tribute from Germany . . . as a penal consequence of defeat in war." The hope of mankind — the hope of preventing another terrible war — lay in trying "to heal the wounds of war."

Churchill made speeches from Montreal westward across Canada. He worked at them all carefully, in hotels and trains. He let it be known that no two of his speeches would be the same. And with him on that Canadian tour of 1929 he brought his painting kit. He might have painted in Montreal; he was here several days. Certainly he painted from the roof of his hotel in Vancouver and in other parts of Canada. He was a statesman out of office, but, while following his recreations, he was brooding always over the hopes and dangers of a very unsettled world.

Evergreen Hughes on snowshoes

The night was Christmas Eve, the year 1870. Members of Montreal's snowshoe clubs had gathered for the Mountain Steeple Chase. They were to race on snowshoes from the gates of McGill College (wooden gates in those days), across the campus, up McTavish St., by the path just west of the high stone wall of Sir Hugh Allan's house, Ravenscrag, and then right over Mount Royal to the Bellevue Hotel in Côte des Neiges.

Eight racers had turned out that Christmas Eve for the contest. Away they went at the signal. The night was dark. When they were on the mountain, far away from the reflected lights of the city, they could hardly see to keep the track. But the race was concluded. The winner (a man named Gilroy from the Alexandra Club) had covered the whole course in 27 minutes.

Among the contestants was Nicholas Hughes. He did not win. He did not even come second or third. By 1870 he was aging and past his prime. Old Hughes had turned out nevertheless, ready to contend with the best, even though it meant running on snowshoes right over the mountain, on a dark Christmas Eve. Though Hughes could no longer come first in open contests, he remained first in another sense. He was the symbolic snowshoer, the very embodiment of the sport in Canada. Back in 1840 he had been one of the little band of enthusiasts who formed the first organized showshoe club in Montreal — the first, they claimed, in the country.

Until that time snowshoeing had not been a sport. It was simply the means of travelling over the snow — the means used by Indians, trappers, fur traders, explorers. Nicholas Hughes had been one of the few to turn snowshoeing into a recreation. By the year 1870 few of the original band of 1840 remained. But Nicholas Hughes was still active in the sport he had helped to create.

Hughes on snowshoes, making light weight of his years, was something special. Nicholas Hughes became for snowshoeing what Herman Johannsen was later to become for skiing. They called Johannsen "Jackrabbit." They called Hughes "Evergreen." "Evergreen" Hughes, and the other sporting snowshoers, took the name of the Montreal Snow Shoe Club. In 1869 they adopted the blue tuque with the red tassel. From then on they were popularly known as the "Tuques Bleues."

Through most of the Montreal Snow Shoe Club's first 30 years Hughes was president. When he relinquished the office in 1871, the club would not let him go. It gave Hughes the unique title of "honorary permanent president." He was to be part of the club till the day he died. Tributes and honors were showered upon him. He was "Hughes of Ours" — "Hughes the Soul of Snow Shoeing." Always he was "the life and soul of parties." At the club's dinners he might be accorded Highland honors — the members standing to toast him, with one foot on their chairs. On March 25, 1876, Evergreen was given a dinner by the members and presented with "a handsome cup as a tribute of the club's respect and esteem."

Old Evergreen proved that he deserved his name. Only a few days previously the island had been smothered by a blizzard. He had important business that day at Pointe Claire. Nothing was moving. The railway "was hopelessly blocked up and the roads impassable." Evergreen simply took down his snowshoes (those "companions of many a tramp"). Through a "tearing gale," he reached his destination.

The story the Tuques Bleues liked to hear best from Evergreen Hughes was the one about the race with the British garrison officers in the 1860s. At that time Montreal was one of the garrison cities of the British Empire. Invasion from the U.S. was feared. Garrison officers and their men had to take training on snowshoes. Two officers of the 47th Regiment, Lt. DeBalinhard and Lt. Prevost, had been entertaining Nicholas Hughes at their regimental mess. Conversation turned to snowshoeing. The officers ridiculed the idea that the civilians of the Montreal Snow Shoe Club had the training or stamina to stand a long tramp. Nicholas Hughes would not put up with overseas snobbery. He challenged the officers to a race.

It would be a long one — nine miles, from Montreal to Laflamme's Hotel in Lachine. Hills, woods, valleys would make it a rough course. As they made ready to start, the racers faced an additional test: a boisterous head wind. They set out. President

John Collins SKETCHBOOK

McTAVISH
The ROUTE OF THE
SNOWSHOERS

Hughes took the lead at once. He had younger club members with him. They did not wish to pass him, but feared the wild pace would do him in. The lieutenants tried to take the lead. Every time they tried, Hughes outpaced them. The lieutenants began to trail. The distance lengthened. At Lachine the three men of the Montreal Snow Shoe Club reached Laflamme's first. When the lieutenants arrived, all sat down, as good fellows, to an amiable dinner.

Evergreen Hughes knew how to grow old gracefully. Toward the end he withdrew from competitions. Now he had a new role: the helper and counsellor of young men just joining the club and learning how to manage snowshoes. Evergreen in this role as mentor to the young is pictured by Dr. George W. Beers, also an outstanding snowshoer and the "father of Canadian lacrosse."

Beers describes a typical new member: "He has enrolled his name, and stands in the full glory of his new rig. . . . 'Evergreen' Hughes takes him under the shadow of his wing; ties on his shoes, shows him how to make them glide one over the other in walking, so as not to keep his legs unnaturally apart and tire his loins." If a new young snowshoer fell flat on his face, Hughes would soon be at his side, setting him upright again.

This role of helping up the young gave a certain mellow charm to Evergreen's last years. He also had the satisfaction of seeing the foundation in the 1880s of the Montreal Amateur Athletic Association. He had done all he could to encourage this coming together of the city's athletic clubs. Old Evergreen Hughes seemed likely to go on forever. When he died, after living to see the MAAA's first year of existence, the Tuques Bleues would not let his memory die with him.

He was not forgotten when the club made its tramps by night over Mount Royal. The members would make a detour through Côte des Neiges Cemetery. They would tramp in Indian file to Evergreen Hughes's grave. There they would form a circle in the moonlight, casting their long shadows over the snow. Joining hands around the grave, they sang Auld Lang Syne.

Duelling: the code of honor vs. the law

For about 100 years the tendency of the law in Montreal was to regard duelling as outside its jurisdiction. The prevailing legal view was that duellists were not criminals or miscreants. They were gentlemen, settling private disputes. They were settling them in a gentlemanly way, according to the honorable and civilized procedures "affairs of honor" required.

Even when a duellist was killed, the law did not consider his death as murder. After a fatal duel in Montreal in 1838, a coroner's jury had to reach a verdict. The names of all taking part in the duel, principals and seconds, were public knowledge. They were published in the newspapers. Yet the jury declared itself of the opinion that the deceased "came to his death, in consequence of a gunshot wound inflicted by some person unknown."

So little was duelling regarded as a violation of the law that many Montreal lawyers fought duels. Some of them later became judges. In at least two cases they became chief justices. Occasionally, however, the law interfered to prevent a duel from taking place. But it usually acted only if the person challenged was so afraid to fight, or at least so reluctant, that he called on the police for protection.

A case of this kind occurred in 1838. A Montrealer, Robert Weir, felt he had been maligned by an item in the Quebec Mercury. He went at once to Quebec, taking with him Montreal lawyer Aaron Philip Hart to act as his second. Hart was familiar with duels. He had fought at least two of them, both with other lawyers. Weir and Hart put up at Payne's Hotel. Hart called on William Kemble, proprietor and editor of the Mercury. Kemble gave an explanation. Hart deemed it "altogether unsatisfactory." He asked Kemble to name someone to act as his second. A duel would have to take place.

Hart returned to Payne's. He told Weir what had happened. That evening, while dining at Payne's, Hart was called from the table. The inspector of police was there, with a constable and a warrant. Weir and Hart were charged with "an intention to commit bodily harm." They were taken before a magistrate, who required them to give bail to keep the peace. No duel took place. But Kemble became the victim of public ridicule. Another newspaper,

L'Ami du Peuple, remarked with astonishment on "the energetic manner in which one of our contemporaries has backed out of a quarrel."

Another instance of a duel stopped by the police occurred in 1848. The contestants were George Etienne Cartier (later the statesman who played a decisive role in bringing about Canadian confederation) and Joseph Doutre, a Montreal lawyer and journalist. An item in the Montreal newspaper L'Avenir had accused Cartier of deserting the battlefield of St. Denis during the Rebellion of 1837. Cartier burst into the office of L'Avenir. He demanded to know who was responsible for that item. Doutre accepted responsibility.

The duel was about to take place on a secluded ground in the countryside behind Mount Royal. The seconds had just finished measuring the paces the contestants would have to cover before they would turn and fire. With dramatic timing the police appeared. They were guided to the spot by Cartier's brother Damien. The police told the contestants to leave the ground at once. They were to go directly home. Next day they would have to appear before a magistrate.

The magistrate let the two off with a warning. That might have been the end of the matter. But L'Avenir would not leave Cartier alone. It published another item. This time it reported a rumor that was going about town that Cartier, afraid to fight the duel, had connived with his brother to have the police intervene. Cartier, of course, had to issue a second challenge. This time the law had to be evaded. Cartier and Doutre went beyond the island of Montreal. They met near Chambly. Fire was exchanged. Neither duellist was wounded. The matter ended.

Gradually the public attitude toward duelling changed. Some said the change was due to the increasing commercialization of society. People were becoming more interested in making money than in upholding a spirit of chivalry inherited from the Middle Ages. Practical common sense was making the duel ridiculous. One of the last duels initiated in Montreal was as late as 1879. By that time duelling in town was almost unknown. It had become only a quaint memory, a tale told by very old men.

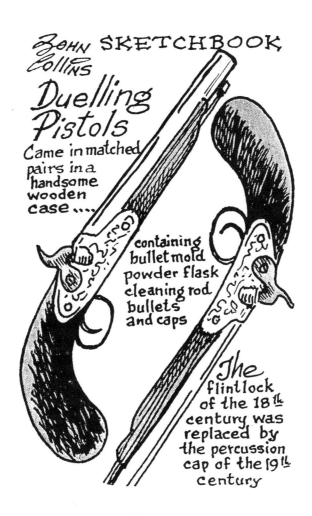

John Collins SKETCHBOOK

Duelling Pistols

Came in matched pairs in a handsome wooden case ....

containing bullet mold powder flask cleaning rod bullets and caps

The flintlock of the 18ᵗʰ century was replaced by the percussion cap of the 19ᵗʰ century

Details of this late duel are intriguing, though rather sparse. It was to be fought by two young men, a Mr. Savage and a Capt. Kirwan. Savage was secretary of a society or club that held dances, called Winter Dances, "attended by the best families in the city." The captain applied for admission. In fact, he applied twice. The first time he was told by the secretary that he could not be admitted because he was a stranger, unknown in Montreal. The second time, though he offered to furnish letters of introduction, he was rejected because there was "no room."

Kirwan was enraged. He called those who had rejected him liars and cowards. Savage took offence at Kirwan's words. He challenged him to a duel. Savage and Kirwan, together with their seconds, met for the combat at Professor Richardson's gymnasium on St. James St. Paces for the duel were measured on the gymnasium floor. The seconds, as was customary, considered whether a last-minute reconciliation was possible. Kirwan conceded he had nothing against Savage personally. He even realized

Savage was "well known to be a liberal man." In rejecting Kirwan's applications Savage had not been expressing any personal spite. He had, in his capacity as secretary, only been carrying out instructions from others.

The seconds agreed that the principals in the duel really had no grievance against each other. In the circumstances "no retraction of any kind was necessary." Principals and seconds left Professor Richardson's gymnasium together. They adjourned to a downtown hotel. There they celebrated the happy ending in convivial friendship.

Actually this duel could never have come off. Two magistrates, with two constables, had been waiting at the entrance of the gymnasium. If "an understanding had not been arrived at between the principals, the minions of the law would have intervened to prevent bloodshed."

By 1879 the law, from once being passive about duelling, had become active. It reflected the changing attitude of society. In Montreal the age of duelling was definitely over.

Graves in the vast, dark crypt

Montreal's most dramatic burials took place in the darkness of the day. When the funeral mass was over at Notre Dame Church in Place d'Armes, often the procession did not move outdoors to the Roman Catholic cemetery. It moved down into the immense crypt under the church. In that deep darkness it had to make its way by the light of tapers to where the earth of the floor had been turned up for the new grave. Beyond the light of the tapers the darkness swerved and fluttered.

The awesomeness of the crypt nearly overwhelmed sensitive visitors. Many years later (apparently in the 1920s) an Ottawa lawyer, J.K. Foran, described his visit: "A lighted taper is required, and the visitor is led into a damp corridor with vaulted roof and iron doors. . . . The clang of the feet upon the stone pavement, the grating of the iron hinges, the hollow reverberations, the tablets lost in the funereal gloom . . . in a word, all the surroundings bespeak the presence of the departed. . . . Our tapers burn dimly and the subterranean dampness becomes oppressive. We take a farewell glance along the sombre corridors and beneath the arched vaults and then turn toward the iron door, through which no ray of light from the outer world can ever penetrate. With a grating noise the heavy barrier opens and we step out once more into the light, life, noise and din of our vast city."

Burials were being made in the crypt of the previous Notre Dame Church, which had been built in the French regime. This church stood partly in front of today's church, covering Notre Dame St. and extending some way into the south side of Place d'Armes. When the present church was built in the 1820s, the bones of those buried in the old were reinterred in the new. They lie in long trenches (the "fosses"). The crypt of the new church was apportioned for various burials. Under the sanctuary were three vaults. In one were buried the Christian Brothers (the teachers of boys), in the second, the sisters of the Congregation of Notre Dame (the teachers of girls), in the third, the Sulpician clergy — the Gentlemen of St. Sulpice. Near the western wall of the crypt were the graves of the principal Roman Catholic families of Montreal — families with such prominent names as Berthelet, Desrivières, Perrault,

Roy, Parthenais, Rocheblave, Beaudry, Mondelet, Pelletier, Dufresne, Chaboillez.

By the middle of the 19th century these indoor burials at Notre Dame had become out of accord with more modern attitudes. Ramsay's guidebook of 1856, in describing Notre Dame, says: "At present, however, these interments are discouraged, as the new cemetery lately opened [at Côte des Neiges] . . . is justly considered a more appropriate and more beautiful resting place." Such indoor burials have long ago ceased. Burials along the west wall took place for only nine years — from 1831 till 1840. The last of the Sulpicians to be buried under the sanctuary was in 1874.

Today the crypt of Notre Dame has little of the mood of mystery. It has electric lights. With the flick of a switch the vast gloom vanishes. All but one of the ancient graves are now hidden. Action had to be taken to safeguard the church as far as possible from the hazards of fire. Concrete covers the whole floor. Fire-resistant materials line the walls, the ceiling, the old wooden beams. So far from being a cave of hoary mystery, the crypt now is featureless, rather reminiscent of the smooth monotony of a hospital corridor.

The modern transformation of the crypt has left only one grave visible. It is marked by a cross on the floor and a tablet on a pillar. This one grave singled out for perpetual honor holds the bones of the architect of Notre Dame Church, James O'Donnell. This Irish Protestant, who had distinguished himself as an architect in New York, was brought to Montreal to design the great church and to act also as the engineer supervising its construction.

O'Donnell wore himself out in the project. He worked at top speed. The huge building took only 35 working months to erect (no work could then be done in winter), and he had to depend on the primitive equipment and relatively unskilled workmen available to him at the time. "I have been a slave to the building since its commencement," he wrote. In his letters are dark references to his race with death.

A little while before he died, in 1830, O'Donnell was converted to Roman Catholicism. Notre Dame Church became his tomb. "When he embraced the

Bohn Collins SKETCHBOOK

GRAVE OF
JAMES O'DONNELL
—NOTRE DAME CHURCH

Catholic faith," says the tablet above his grave, "he wished that his ashes might rest in this place."

The practice of indoor burial in Montreal is continued in only one place — the Cathedral-Basilica of Mary Queen of the World and St. James the Major. On the Mansfield St. side, midway between the altar and the doors, is a chapel of Italian marble mosaics. It is separated from the aisle by bronze gates of open filigree work. There, in the centre of the chapel, is a sarcophagus containing the remains of Bishop Ignace Bourget. His effigy in bronze lies across it.

When Bourget died in 1885, the cathedral had not been completed. He had been living in retirement at Sault au Récollet and wished to be buried in the cemetery there. Though he was persuaded to consent to burial in the unfinished cathedral, he set conditions. He did not wish his cathedral burial to be a unique or special honor. He agreed only if tombs would also be provided for his predecessor,

Bishop Lartigue (who had been the first Roman Catholic bishop of Montreal), and for all the bishops and auxiliary bishops of the future.) His wishes were carried out. On the same day Bourget was buried in the cathedral — June 18, 1885 — the remains of his predecessor were buried there also: they had been transferred from his original grave in the chapel of Notre Dame de Piété (since demolished).

The graves of Bishop Bourget and Bishop Lartigue were made in the crypt of the cathedral in 1885. Nearly 50 years later their remains were brought up into the new marble chapel, built between 1931 and 1933. In this chapel all the bishops of Montreal now lie: Bourget in the central sarcophagus, the other bishops in tombs in one wall, the auxiliary bishops in tombs in the wall opposite.

There are many empty tombs in the walls of that marble chapel, tombs reserved for the bishops and auxiliary bishops of generations, even centuries, to come.

The archdeacon had no doubts

On an evening in 1928 a *Gazette* reporter had one of the surprises of his life. He had been sent on one of the dullest of all possible assignments — a church annual meeting. It turned out to be dramatic, even sensational. It was the annual meeting of St. George's Anglican Church on Dominion Square (on the part now called Place du Canada).

St. George's had a new rector; this was his first annual meeting in Montreal. Rev. A.P. Gower-Rees, formerly rector of a large parish in Bradford, Yorkshire, was a sturdy, broad-shouldered man with rosy English cheeks. When the time came for him to speak at the meeting, he followed no text. He told the parishioners their church had been allowed to sink into a deplorable condition. The parish was disorganized, the building was in disrepair. Immediately he listed, one item after another, all that had to be done to get things in order.

When he had finished, he looked at his startled parishioners. Then he added: "If you don't like what I'm saying, and if you won't do what I am asking, just let me know. I have here in my pocket a return ticket to England. I'm only asking you to do what must be done. If you won't do it, I'll go where I can be of more use."

Gower-Rees was a strong man, undoubtedly. In the Great War he had been an army chaplain, twice mentioned in dispatches and awarded the Military Cross. He was a muscular Christian who refereed English football matches. His parish in Bradford was huge and parts of it were rough. He knew what it was to enter pubs on Saturday night, to battle for some of his parishioners and bring them home.

Gower-Rees had come to St. George's at a critical time in its history. Churches had once clustered in and around Dominion Square. One by one they were being abandoned, sold, demolished. At St. George's the same tendency toward moving away was evident. The sale of the church had been under negotiation before the outbreak of the war. It was to be replaced by a hotel — marvellously situated, right opposite the main entrance to Windsor Station. The outbreak of war caused the negotiations to collapse. But with the idea of moving constantly in mind, little was being done to maintain the church. Why repair or decorate a building that might soon be torn down?

The new rector would have none of these counsels of removal. In a big city like Montreal churches were needed to witness to the reality of religion, right at the heart of things. As an army man he did not like the idea of retreat. No church could be more strategically placed than St. George's. Its parishioners ought to be thanking God and taking courage.

The reporter hurried back to *The Gazette* with his story of the most dramatic annual meeting he had ever attended.

As the bishop of Bradford had said, Gower-Rees had a "remarkable power of putting things through." He got his way at that first annual meeting, he had his way at every other annual meeting — and in between meetings. Eventually he became archdeacon (and he openly thought he ought to have been bishop). "The archdeacon," as he was commonly known, was the most practical of men. To get improvements started, he was seen down on his knees. This time he was not in prayer, but varnishing the church floors. Later linoleum was laid. He and the sexton did the work between them.

The archdeacon looked into everything himself; he would take nobody's word for anything. St. George's roof began to leak. Roofing estimates were high. The archdeacon climbed ladders. He poked in the drainpipes with his stick. "The pipes are plugged," he declared, "that's all."

Gradually he began to form an endowment fund. At one vestry meeting he asked permission to invest some available money in Hydro bonds. One of the vestrymen, Jackson Dodds, general manager of the Bank of Montreal, interposed. "Rector," he said, "you know very well you've already invested that money in those bonds. You're not asking for permission; you're asking for ratification."

Opportunity came when the Laurentien Hotel was planned. The hotel would need land just north of the church — land then occupied by the old rectory of St. George's and the old parish hall. The archdeacon, though having some of Montreal's most prominent businessmen in the vestry, took negotiations into his own hands. The hotel acquired rectory and parish hall, but at a price — the

SKETCHBOOK

John Collins

ST. GEORGE'S CHURCH

archdeacon's price. "Whenever I go into the lobby of the Laurentien Hotel," he would say, "orders are sent to the cashiers to lock up their drawers."

One day Archdeacon Gower-Rees came to *The Gazette* with a proposition. He offered to write a religious article every week for the editorial page. More than that, he would write the religious editorials as well at Easter and Christmas. And he insisted on doing it all for nothing. He just wanted to broaden his city ministry. His offer was accepted, very readily.

Even in summertime he refused "to take a holiday from the Lord." From his country house at Cap à l'Aigle, in the Lower St. Lawrence, his articles would still arrive, as prompt as ever. Altogether he must have written 600 articles and editorials for *The Gazette.*

He would reach out to help anyone, anywhere. At his study at St. George's was a lineup of people in trouble, waiting for his counselling. "I'm a practical psychiatrist," he would remark. "I listen to what they say, then I tell them, 'This is your problem'." As he spoke, he swerved his hand through the air, then came to a sudden stop.

No doubt the archbishop's very confidence, his own certitude, strengthened many who consulted him.

He helped the doubting because he had no doubts.

A bachelor's bequest to his city: music

Back in the 1920s a rich bachelor lawyer drew up an unusually imaginative will. He provided that a substantial portion of his estate, nearly $250,000, should finance band concerts in perpetuity to entertain the people of Montreal in summertime. Ever since his will came into effect, bands have been paid to play in Montreal's parks. The concerts have varied with the different bands and with the type of music selected, but all have shared the unique atmosphere of music played outdoors on a summer evening.

Such evening band concerts have taken place because of provisions in the will of this man, who died in 1923. The rich bachelor lawyer was Charles Sandwith Campbell, KC. Campbell was not a Montrealer by origin. He was born in Kingston, the son of Sir Alexander Campbell, one of the Fathers of Confederation, a law partner of Sir John A. Macdonald, a member of several of Macdonald's cabinets and, finally, lieutenant-governor of Ontario.

His son, the founder of the band concerts, decided to settle in Montreal. He had good reason. He wished to specialize in corporation law and Montreal, in those years, was the centre in Canada for that type of practice.

Here firms of corporation lawyers had clustered, all actively engaged (at times almost feverishly) in setting up companies, adjusting and revising their charters, and arranging the legal complexities of vast mergers. With this kind of practice, an able and successful corporation lawyer had much to do and was highly paid for doing it.

Charles Campbell was well educated for his career. He was sent to Bishop's College School in Lennoxville, on to Cambridge for arts and law, then back to graduate in law from Laval. Eventually Campbell headed the firm Campbell, Meredith, Allan & Co. (later known as Heward, Holden & Co.). His list of clients was dazzling: the Allan steamship line, the Canadian Pacific Railway, the Montreal Harbor Commission, the Hudson's Bay Co., the Montreal Light, Heat & Power, and three banks — Molsons Bank, the old Ontario Bank and the Merchants' Bank.

For many years he was conspicuous in court. He came prominently into the news as chief counsel in the famous litigation between the Dominion Coal and Dominion Steel companies. This case he fought through the Canadian courts and on to the privy council. But, like many corporation lawyers, he gradually withdrew from court practice. After all, court practice was "contentious law" — arguing in legal disputes. Important as it was, he felt his time could be better spent in advising and guiding clients in his office on how to set up their corporations, or to modify their corporate structures. In that era, the next best thing to being a capitalist was to be an adviser to capitalists.

Charles Campbell soon had the means to indulge his tastes. Most rich men acquired a country estate. He did also. His estate at Dorval gave him the opportunity to indulge his chief sporting interest, the breeding of horses for the racetracks. He was convinced that no amount of breeding among Canadian horses would ever assure a supply of really competitive racers. The breed would have to be improved by importing fine horses from foreign stables.

As a breeder of horses Campbell had notable success. In a single season his horses might be coming first in three to seven races each. But suddenly, in the autumn of 1913, Charles Campbell made a startling announcement. He was giving up horse-breeding in Canada; he would have nothing more to do with it. He gave his reasons. The Canadian government's regulations seemed senseless and frustrating. They had taken all the pleasure out of his hobby. They would compel him to be a loser in horse racing. He did not care to endure enforced inferiority. Campbell felt he should be free to import fine horses for breeding. He should, in fact, be encouraged.

Campbell had appealed to the customs department to make clear where he stood. Customs had passed him along to the agriculture department. It passed him along to the National Record Committee. This record committee was not a government department but a private group, a non-elected body of breeders and dealers.

The committee refused to recognize as reliable the stud books kept in England, France and the U.S. It would consent to the free importation of breeding

SKETCHBOOK *Bandstand in the Park*
John Collins

horses only if such imports were recorded in its stud book. And the committee members laid down their own conditions.

Campbell had had enough: "Over . . . one animal . . . I have had eight months of correspondence and experienced enough to deter anyone from importing." He sold his racing farm at Dorval. He bought a big estate near Bedford. Here he carried on scientific farming; the farm became one of the most admired in the Eastern Townships.

After nearly 40 years of practice, he almost gave up corporation law. He remained a consultant at his old law firm, but was seldom seen in town. One June day in 1923 he left his law office in the Merchants' Bank building and returned to Bedford. On Monday he was "attacked with a violent heart seizure." Dr. Henri Lafleur of the Montreal General Hospital hurried out to Bedford. He found Campbell so ill that he spent the night there. Nothing could be done. Campbell died in the morning. He was 65.

Charles Campbell, described as being of "a quiet, retiring disposition," expressed himself most freely in his will. It was enterprising and novel, sensitive to needs ignored by other testators.

The will began with the usual gifts to relations, friends and employees. He was generous to various hospitals. Then the more unusual legacies began to appear. He remembered his old horse Kodak: it was to be cared for by a small trust fund. Then two-fifths of his estate (amounting in total to nearly $500,000) was given to the people of Montreal. He left one part to purchase vacant lots in the congested parts of the city of Montreal to make playgrounds for young children — playgrounds that must not be too far from "their parents' abodes."

The remaining fifth was to "be retained by the trustees and the income applied to encourage the playing on summer evenings of bands of music in public places handy to the congested parts of said city."

When Scots curled on the St. Lawrence

The Scots were so strongly present in Montreal by the early years of the 19th century that they decided to make use of the St. Lawrence ice as a rink for curling. In Scotland they had curled on frozen ponds. Now, in Canada's deep frosts, they had a river stretching out for their amusement.

In January 1807 a group of Scots in Montreal (described at the time as "some natives of North Britain") formed the Montreal Curling Club (later the Royal Montreal Curling Club). It was the first curling club in Canada, and older than any in the U.S. Its rink was the ice on the river. Over the years it moved about the river, wherever a good sheet of smooth ice was to be found. Sometimes it played on the ice just below Bonsecours Church. Frequently it curled "on the canal basin, near Wellington bridge." One unusual match was played behind Molson's Brewery, on the ice of St. Mary's current. Ice seldom formed over the current; when it did, the surface might be rough. But this time — on the last day of March 1820 — the ice was "smooth and keen, and the rink about the usual length."

When the river ice formed well, it was beautiful for play. But the St. Lawrence had its own whims, and some unaccommodating habits. It was not really fit for play until at least the middle of January. Any winter thaw made its surface dull and sticky. When March came, the warmer suns of midday would soften a surface that had been firm at dawn. This meant that enthusiastic curlers, eager to prolong the season, had to get up early in the morning and be on the river while the ice was still favorable for play. That match on the last day of March in 1820 was certainly unusual — all the more so in that the play went on past noon. Most March games had to be played as soon as possible after daybreak. In 1807, the year the club was formed, a game was "played on the river, a little below the port, at 5 a.m."

Curling was not then a game known or played outside Scotland. Few knew what these Montreal Scots were doing when they went out on the river with their "irons." These irons were, in any case, peculiar; they were the best they could get in Canada. They were not stones at all, but iron balls of different sizes. The lightest weighed 45 pounds, the heaviest 65. They did not run as well as the Scottish whinstones in mild weather, or when the sun shone bright and warm. But in most kinds of Canadian weather they served the purpose as well. They had one great advantage: they could not be cracked or broken.

Those who happened to be on the river and saw a group of citizens (all of them prominent) solemnly sending these iron balls over the ice could not make out what it was all about.

Gradually curling on the river ice in front of Montreal became more familiar. A second club was formed in 1843. It was another gathering of Scots, as its name indicated: the Thistle Curling Club. In 1845 arrangements were made between the two clubs "to play a bonspiel on the first good ice, three rinks, four players on each side." It was the first of the long series of matches between Montreal and Thistle. Transporting the heavy irons and other equipment onto the ice of the river was a serious problem. Neither club had a house of its own, where the equipment could be kept close to the rink. The problem was solved by keeping the equipment in a storage shed in town. A sleigh, bearing all that was needed, could quickly be driven from the city to the ice, whenever and wherever called for.

Montreal artist James Duncan drew a sketch in the 1850s depicting a curling match in progress. The game was being held on the ice just below Nelson's monument, which appears clearly in the background. A flagpole has been set up. Round its base are set a number of wicker-covered vessels, or demijohns, providing warm stimulation to the players, as might be required. The teams contesting the game are not specified.

Despite the demijohns beside the flagpole, these games on the ice chilled the players to the bone, for there was no protection from the river winds. But arrangements were made for warmth and refreshment as soon as the games were over. The players would retreat to one of Montreal's hotels or chophouses. They would have only a little way to go, as all hotels and chophouses were near the river. The first rules and regulations drawn up by the Montreal Curling Club provided that the members should meet every Wednesday to play on the ice till 3 p.m.

Three early 19th-Century stones used on the St. Lawrence River

The "IRON"

and The "GRANITE"

SKETCHBOOK
"CURLING ON THE RIVER"
from an engraving of the 1850's

John Collins

In wintertime that was judged to be the latest hour possible, as the days were short and the fading sunlight obscured the game. At 4 p.m. the members would dine at Gillis's Inn.

Toward the middle of the 19th century the curling clubs had begun to play some of their matches indoors. They made rinks in sheds — sometimes the same sheds that were used in summertime for the business of the port. These sheds at least sheltered them from the wind. But indoor ice could not compare to river ice at its best. The match between Montreal and Thistle was played indoors in March 1845, only because "from the unfavorable state of the weather it was found impracticable to procure rinks on the river as originally intended." By about 1870 curling on the river had practically ceased. The city was growing uptown; the river had lost its old closeness and convenience. But the clubs continued to concede that the ice of indoor rinks could not be compared to the best river rinks of other days.

In 1876 this deficiency was mentioned when the Thistle Curling Club was trying to get its indoor ice in shape for the competition for the Governor-General's Medals. The club had devised a method of "shaving" the ice. It had set a special blade about three feet long, in a strong wooden frame. The frame was weighted with one or more curling stones. It was dragged by ropes across the rink, from end to end.

"Our object," said a spokesman for the club, "being to make the sheet of ice true and level; in fact, like a billiard table." This ingenious procedure was necessary because flooding an indoor rink would never be enough in itself. "The possibility of a perfectly level sheet of ice might be found on lake or river," the club went on to say, "but our experience leads to the conclusion that in the . . . rink . . . is almost impossible to obtain it by simply flooding."

The coming of artificial ice in the 1920s eased or solved most of the problems of indoor rinks. But for many of the earlier years after curling had moved off the river, the older members retained a fondness in memory for the naturalness of play on nature's own rinks.

Immigrants at Lachine: on the way west

"The wharf, alongside of which was the boat, presented a heterogeneous mixture of bedding, baggage, trunks, men, women and children, all laid in one heterogeneous heap. The crew and male passengers were busily employed in tumbling this promiscuous group into the boat."

Such is the description, written about 1820, of the immigrants setting out from Lachine by bateau on the long inland journey to Upper Canada. Montreal was the head of ocean navigation on the St. Lawrence. The immigrants had to walk or travel by coach or wagon the nine miles from Montreal to Lachine. There they set out (before steamboats or canals) by the slow progress of the bateau, propelled against the current and even up the rapids by nothing more than oars, sails, ropes or poles.

Bateaux were about 30 feet long, heavily built to stand the knocks and strains of the river. They could carry great weights; passengers and baggage were crowded into them. There was no protection from the weather, except perhaps an awning.

Very few descriptions of the immigrants embarking at Lachine have survived. The description of the "heterogeneous mixture" being tossed into the bateau is perhaps the best; for though its writer was anonymous (calling himself only "The Itinerant") he had an eye for what was taking place, and a detached amusement in what he observed. He had a mind freer from preoccupation than the immigrants, as he was a traveller, taking the route for the sake of what he might see — "for I like to 'keep moving'," he said.

The "packet boat," he found, was only a bateau with an awning. The awning, it seemed, was the added luxury that had given the bateau its "packet" status. He stood at the wharf amid baggage, beds and squalling brats. He admired the captain, a man well used to handling immigrants. The crew was a "set of ugly, shabby looking fellows," a mixture of races — French Canadians, Yankees, Dutchmen and Irishmen. They were far from the disciplined crew of an Atlantic schooner, and joined "the general clamor, by ranting, roaring, singing and swearing in chorus."

The Itinerant watched the confusion. A husband, wife and four small children, all dirty, bustling and bewildered, were trying to get their baggage aboard. They found they had left behind the box with the children's "duds." The wife asked the captain to wait while her husband went ashore to get it. "Where is it?" the captain wanted to know. "He must be quick, I'll be off in 10 minutes." Then it was found that the children's "duds" had been left in Montreal. The poor mother sat down and wept. The father, standing mute and overwhelmed with the misfortune, was hustled on board by the crowd.

"Tak' up the bairn," said a Scots wife to her husband, "he'll tumble o'er the bank." "Come here, Tammie," said the father, "come to me, my wee callant, ye manna gang there." He reached toward the boy, but the boy dodged into the crowd. The father went after him and carried him screaming and struggling to the bateau. In the bustle the boy's hat went into the river. The loss of the hat seemed to excite the crowd as much as if the boy had gone into the water with it. A boatman fished it out and put it on the boy's curly head. But the boy was surly and stubborn; no threat of punishment would make him say thanks. A shoe fell from the foot of another child, just as its father was handing it to the mother in the bateau. It sank in the river, and they had to face their journey with a one-shoed child.

The captain stood looking toward the inn nearby, pulling out and putting up his watch. The Itinerant wondered who was expected. Out of the inn came "a genteel-looking middle-aged gentleman . . . with a female of an elegant figure leaning on his arm. The rear was brought up by two men carrying a large trunk between them, and their other hands occupied, the one with a travelling bag, the other with a birds' cage containing a pair of canaries." Here was something that was needed to complete the picture: the army officer, put on half-pay when the army was reduced in size, and come out to make his way in a world quite unsuited to his tastes or habits.

All were now aboard. The boatmen had to make their way to the oars, but the boat was so crowded that it was a struggle.

An immigrants' bateau was a strange jumble: "In the forepart of the boat was a motly [sic] mass of male and female, old and young heads — peeping over the gunwhale; which in their ill-adorned and

JOHN COLLINS SKETCHBOOK *Lachine waterfront* —

uncombed state, combined with the tattered dirty dresses, formed a picture which would defy the ever varying pencil of a Hogarth to portray. The bundles of baggage piled in heaps, seen at a distance, intersected the line of the horizon like a haystack; but on a nearer view seemed like a rocky mountain in miniature. Seated among this chaos of ruins the rowers were seen pursuing their see-saw vocation with steady regularity. The rest of the group seated under the awning in the stern, differed in the appearance of their dresses, and had an aspect approaching what might be termed cabin passengers."

It was late afternoon of a serene summer day. As the bateau moved slowly along the shore of Lac St. Louis toward Pointe Claire, the sun began to set. The clamor on board had been so raucous that The Itinerant could scarcely hear what the army officer seated next to him was saying.

But with the calm that came at the end of the day, silence fell over the bateau: "The tranquility of the scene produced a corresponding quietness in the beholders, as is always the case. The squealing and caterwaling of the children in the bow of the boat became more and more faint as the sun descended. It had been incessant during the afternoon . . . but at last the drowsy god accomplished what had defied the scoldings, threats, promises and beatings from the mothers, and laid the little imps in calm repose under his oblivious veil, and left those so inclined to enjoy the full pleasure of a contemplative mood."

Ships that never came in

Many a ship sailed out of Montreal and disappeared, and many a ship expected in Montreal never arrived. So far from these disappearances being regarded as unusual, they were expected, as part of the natural hazards of shipping.

Before radio communication, a ship might have no way of signalling distress, except by rockets or the firing of a gun. Such signals might be seen or heard from the coasts. But a ship far at sea might signal in vain, alone with disaster.

An item in *The Gazette* on June 5, 1834, reported that nearly 20 vessels had gone down at sea since the opening of the navigation season. In addition to its own list of "melancholy disasters," *The Gazette* reprinted items from the Halifax Royal Gazette and the Miramichi Gleaner. They reported further heavy losses.

Lists of losses included not only ships known to have gone down, but many others that had sailed into silence. Such lists were headed: "Vessels Not Heard Of." Whatever their ports of destination might have been, they had been steered by fate into the unknown, engulfed in the mystery of the sea.

When Montreal merchants ordered stock from overseas, they looked forward to its arrival "by the first fair wind" of spring. Often they began advertising their wares in advance, hoping to stir anticipation among their custmers. But such stocks might never come.

In 1844 Edward and George Wright, china merchants on St. Paul St., were advertising in *The Gazette* that they were expecting tablewares "of the very best manufacture and style." These wares were "daily awaited." They had been shipped from Liverpool aboard the Parana — a fine new brig, making its third voyage, and known to be capable of a fast crossing. But at the time these advertisements were appearing in *The Gazette,* this ship and its cargo were already at the bottom of the sea.

When a ship given up as lost arrived after all, the passengers described the terror of sailing close to death. One of these passengers was an 18-year-old Scot, Sanford Fleming (later Sir Sanford). He sailed for Montreal on the ship Brilliant in 1845. The ship ran into furious storms. "Slept little or none all night," he wrote in his diary, "and we thought sometimes we were like to be pitched out of our berths."

One night the sea seemed about to close over them. A cargo of iron bars had broken loose. It was rolling about in the hold, pounding one side of the ship and then the other. "It did not seem possible that the ship could withstand such pounding much longer," wrote Fleming. The Brilliant seemed about to go down, and simply be listed among "Vessels Not Heard Of." Fleming wrote a farewell note to his father. "I sealed the letter in a bottle and threw it into the sea," his diary says, "thinking it might be the last letter I should write, and that it might perhaps reach my father."

Terror in the age of sail almost became frenzy when all hatches were shut to keep waves from plunging into the ship. Passengers then felt imprisoned, trapped like rats. Another emigrant, Hector McLean, described the sensation of being held below deck after lights were prohibited for fear of fire. In the dark, waves could be heard pounding the ship's sides like cannonballs.

McLean's widowed mother, with the eight children, had set out from Belfast for Canada in 1843. They sailed in the ship Catherine. On May 17 "a terrific storm arose and soon the sea was running mountains high." McLean later wrote in his memories of the night below the closed hatches: "Passengers were gathered in groups here and there weeping, wailing and praying. Children were cleaving to their mothers, and wives to their husbands, expecting every moment to be swallowed up. It was a night never to be forgotten. . . . My mother drew us around her that at the last we might all be together, but morning broke and found us alive."

Hatches were thrown open. Passengers were released. When they came on deck, they saw what the storm had done. Nearly everything had been swept away. Even some of the bulwarks were gone. The ship was leaking. The captain ordered the crew to the pumps. Exhausted by the night of storm, they refused. Passengers were then compelled to take their turns. The pumps were kept working day and night.

The sinking of a sailing ship generally meant the loss of everyone aboard. Only rarely were survivors

SKETCHBOOK

The DERELICT SHIP

found by another passing ship. Even then, survivors were likely to be very few.

The Gazette reported such a rescue in June 1825: "The Alexander picked up Capt. Smith of the brig Cumberland, of and from Liverpool [together with] two passengers and three men, the survivors of the crew of that vessel, which they were obliged to abandon at sea in Long. 35."

Occasionally the drifting hulk of an abandoned ship was encountered on the sea lanes. It would be heavily waterlogged, awash in the sea, waves streaming over it. Lt. Francis Duncan, who was stationed with the Montreal garrison on Ile Ste. Hélène in the 1860s, had seen such a drifting wreck on his journey over the Atlantic. It left a haunting memory: "As we approached, all doubt was cleared

away — a wreck it was, with the topmasts broken short off, bowsprit gone, no boats left, and the sea breaking over it as it reeled heavily to every wave. We passed within a very few yards of her, and shouted, but there was no answer — not even a dog seemed to be on board. No boat could have got alongside in the sea that was running; so, reluctantly, we had to bear away . . . but often since then one thinks with sadness of that tossing hull, with the wind howling through the damaged rigging, and the waves beating on her deserted deck."

The sea, in such an age, was called "the gray old widow-maker." Frequent losses were accepted with resignation at the port of Montreal as the unavoidable hazards "against which human skill is unable at times to guard."

The man who built a church of his own

Among Montreal's many churches, one has a unique history. St. Thomas Anglican Church, now on Somerled Ave. between Rosedale and Mariette, but originally down on Notre Dame St., was a church built and owned by one man. He was Thomas Molson, second son of John Molson, founder of the brewing family and its fortune in Montreal.

Thomas Molson owned St. Thomas Church entirely. It was his private property. Though it was an Anglican church in its form of worship and its clergy, the bishop of Montreal had little authority over it. St. Thomas, in fact, was so much private property that the city of Montreal would not accord it the usual exemption from taxes granted to church-owned land and buildings. As private property it was assessed. Molson had to pay personal taxes on it every year.

The church stood close to the brewery on Notre Dame St. E. (the part of Notre Dame St. then called St. Mary's). Extensions to the brewery buildings now cover the site. Building the church in 1841 cost Thomas Molson 2,330 pounds, an impressive sum in the money value of that time.

The Anglican bishops of Montreal (Rt. Rev. George Jehoshaphat Mountain, titular bishop, and, later, Rt. Rev. Francis Fulford) were disturbed by St. Thomas's peculiar position. They tried their best, severely at times, to induce Thomas Molson to bring his church into more regular relations with the diocese. Molson would not give in. He would not even allow his church to be consecrated. If this was done, he was afraid, the bishop might have stronger claims upon it.

In 1852 he lost his church — not by an invasion of episcopal authority but in a devouring fire. On a July day fire broke out in a house on the east side of St. Lawrence Main. The weather had long been dry and intensely warm. Strong winds from the west drove the flames eastward, "like water pouring down a rapid." The fire reached Molson's Brewery. On the Molson property a number of buildings were ruined. Among them was St. Thomas Church.

After the fire, Thomas Molson seemed to be making no immediate move to have his church rebuilt. Bishop Fulford encouraged the erection of a new church, St. Luke's, in the area — a church that would be independent of Thomas Molson and under the bishop's full authority. St. Luke's Anglican Church, built nearby on Dorchester St., soon attracted the Anglicans living in the neighborhood, including those who had formerly gone to St. Thomas. This move by Bishop Fulford discouraged Thomas Molson from re-erecting his church. But on a visit to England, his idea of having a church of his own was revived.

On this trip Molson became acquainted with a new religious denomination. It seemed to suit his own outlook. This denomination was known as the Countess of Huntingdon's Connexion. It had been founded in 1748 by a widow of high rank, wealth and influence — Selina, countess of Huntingdon, a daughter of Earl Ferrers. She had been attracted by the evangelical spirit of the Methodists. The sect she founded was a blend of Methodism and Anglicanism. Her sect was legally established in 1783 as a distinct religious body. It attracted Thomas Molson because each church belonging to the Connexion remained autonomous.

Molson joined the Countess of Huntingdon's Connexion. Before leaving England, he bought 250 copies of the Connexion's hymnbooks. Obviously his desire to have another privately owned church had been rekindled. Before long, a new St. Thomas Church rose on the site of the old. With towers at either end, it was a far larger and more imposing church than its predecessor.

The extent of Molson's revived enthusiasm was seen in his decision to give his new church a set of chimes that was, he believed, far beyond anything else to be found in Canada. These chimes were the same as those in the Royal Exchange in London. They cost him as much as he had paid to build the entire first church. The quarter-hours were chimed on two bells, the hours on the deep-sounding 15-hundredweight bells. Every three hours all eight bells played one of three tunes twice over — the Vesper Hymn, the Blue Bells of Scotland, or Home Sweet Home.

In addition to his church, he built a college. This Molson's College, an impressive building, was erected between the church and the river. His plan

JOHN COLLINS SKETCHBOOK

ST. THOMAS
ANGLICAN
CHURCH
N.D.G.

was that it would serve, among other aims, to train young men for the ministry of the Countess of Huntingdon's Connexion and provide ministers for other churches across the country.

Nothing, however, turned out the way he had hoped. No large congregation came to his church. Teaching at Molson's College was begun but soon dwindled to a close. By the early 1860s Molson gave up his efforts. He rented Molson's College to the British government as a military barracks and his church as a garrison chapel.

These, in the nature of things, would be only temporary arrangements. In a new will he provided for the future of St. Thomas Church. A very different future it would be. The church was to be fully united with the diocese, as "an evangelical church appertaining to the Church of England." He left rentals from houses in Molson's Terrace, a row of houses south of the church, as an endowment. Only one stipulation recalled his old independent attitude. He wanted the nomination of the rector of St. Thomas to remain with his descendants in a direct

line. Thomas Molson did not live long after drawing up his will. He died in January 1863. Arranging the final settlement took time. But on Sunday, July 28, 1867, St. Thomas Church was at last consecrated.

Much, however, had changed over the years. The area around Molson's Brewery had become highly industrialized. Few people were now living nearby. In 1906 the congregation moved northward. It built a new St. Thomas Church on Sherbrooke St., at the corner of de Lorimier Ave. Members of the Molson family remained interested in the church and made large voluntary contributions toward meeting its needs.

The shift of population continued. By the 1940s most of its people had moved to the suburbs in the west end of the city. The church at Sherbrooke and de Lorimier was sold. The present St. Thomas Church on Somerled Ave. in Notre Dame de Grâce was built in the early 1950s. Among the links with the past are the clock and chimes — the same clock and chimes that Thomas Molson brought from England for his church in 1857.

The old street characters of Victorian days

Henri Julien, the French-Canadian artist, drew a sketch in 1876 of an old blind fiddler and his little dog. They were to be seen any day at the foot of Nelson's monument on Notre Dame St. or down among the farm wagons of the Bonsecours Market. A pathetic pair they were, but the man made a lively sound with his fiddle. He was part of the street scene in Montreal in the 1870s. He was respected in his day, missed when he had gone.

Today such characters are hustled in the crowds, ignored by people who have no time to notice them. But in the small Montreal of more leisurely days the street characters had their place in the scheme of things. Their picturesqueness was welcomed.

The old blind fiddler at the foot of Nelson's monument was only one of many street musicians. And street musicians meant more when recorded music was still unknown and no music came over the airwaves. A voice, or an instrument, drew attention. Passers-by lingered to listen. During this period — 1875 to 1878 — two French singers appeared in Montreal. They were wandering musicians — "chanteurs ambulants." One was without an arm, the other without a leg. They claimed to be wounded veterans of the War of 1870 between France and Prussia. They sang, with spirit, patriotic songs about the day when the captured French provinces of Alsace and Lorraine would be free again.

Another singer of that time used to take up his place on the northeast corner of Notre Dame and St. Pierre Sts. His name was Forget. They used to say that Forget was no Adonis. His big head, covered with bushy hair, was pierced by two eyes that looked in opposite directions. In a hoarse voice, he sang an everlasting lament for the girl who had broken his heart. Forget became one of the sights of the town. The cabmen would show him to tourists. The street singers were followed by another order of musicians — the organ-grinders. Heard too closely, the street-organ's puffs and wheezes might be distracting. But heard a block away, through an open window, on an evening in early spring, the music of the organ-grinder might echo with the very spirit of remote romance.

By the year 1900 Montreal still had about 50 organ-grinders. One of the last of them to survive was Arthur Lachapelle. He was small and old, with long white hair over his shoulders, and a worn brown hat with a wide, turned-down brim, and a solemn, dignified way of bowing his thanks whenever a coin was given him. He used to turn the handle of his old organ on St. Catherine St. in front of one or other of the big department stores. Times grew hard for him toward the end. In 1954 he said: "Today everyone has music in their homes. There is no need to go far to hear what they would like."

While Forget had been grotesque, Lachapelle, in his wistful way, was handsome. He had never lost his pleasure in his work in the street. "I enjoy my work," he said, when nearly 75, "not only because I like music and believe others do, but I like being my own boss."

Other picturesque figures on the streets of Montreal were the apple women. They would sit at points of vantage, often at the street corners. From makeshift stands, they offered their stock to the passers-by, or they would go from office to office, selling apples from a basket. Rumor had it that they used to spit on the apples to polish them, but it was not believed by everyone, and heeded by few.

Most of the old apple women were real characters, who knew how to pass a few genial words with their customers. But they were very poor, often widows with no other income. Enduring rain, wind and cold, they were pathetic figures. The Montreal poet George Martin wrote a poem in the 1880s on "The Apple Woman."

Montreal's Victorian street scene also had the candy-sellers. From 1880 to 1885, in the area west of Chaboillez Square, everyone knew Tiquenne. He sold toffee, made, it was said, from a secret formula of his own. He was an old man, bent, half-blind, who looked down at his feet as he moved. Many people lived in that area then and he would go up and down the streets, selling his toffee at a cent a piece.

John Collins SKETCHBOOK

In the days of streetcars, running boards and Morgan's we had colorful Organ Grinders — including one who had his post at Morgan's corner

Old Tiquenne lived in St. Cunégonde. He would set out about 9 a.m. with a sort of wooden basket on his left arm. He carried a bell. Though his eyesight was poor, his hearing was keen. If anyone called out "Tiquenne," he would stop at once and make a sale. The sales were never great: one, two, or three pieces at a time. The way he rang his bell seemed to have a rhythm that sounded as though it was saying: "Tiquenne, Tiquenne, Toffee Tiquenne."

The old newspaper-sellers were among the best-known of the street characters. Greatest of them all in the 1870s was Old Hanavan. He sold his papers from a niche in the facade of the Medical Hall — the drugstore that was part of the great hotel, the St. Lawrence Hall, on the northwest corner of St. James and St. François Xavier. Old Hanavan was at his post every day till he was 85. He was a great favorite with the public, with his quaint sayings and his cheerfulness in all kinds of weather. Hanavan was friendly with the newsboys; they never tried to take advantage of him, old as he was. Even when they were jostling to get their supplies of papers, he would say, "Ah, now, boys, don't," and it was enough. Often, in stormy weather, they would let him get his supply first, to give him a "good show," and help him sell his papers.

The Montreal artist William Raphael, who was one of the original members of the Royal Canadian Academy, painted a portrait of Hanavan. It shows an old man with his hair fluffing out from under a shapeless cap. He wears a long coat, uneven at the hem, or almost having no hem at all. A pack of papers is under his arm and one is held out in his hand.

The perilous beauty of a Jersey Lily

"A beautiful woman is a disaster." So said the philosopher Epictetus 900 years ago. It was certainly true in the case of Lillie Langtry. Unquestionably, she was beautiful. And being so beautiful she brought disaster upon many who became involved with her. Yet she remained irresistible.

Montrealers learned how irresistible she was when she visited the city in 1883 and again in 1900. On these visits she appeared in Montreal theatres. Lillie Langtry had become an actress not because she loved the stage — but because she loved money. She needed money in great quantity to sustain the style of life to which she had made herself accustomed. The stage provided it. She was an actress who couldn't act. It did not matter. Her beauty and her notoriety combined to fill any theatre. She did not care what the drama critics might say about her. She was far more interested in the reports from the box office. These reports were invariably gratifying.

During her 1883 visit she appeared at the Academy of Music, the theatre on Victoria St., on land now covered by Eaton's. For the first night she chose a three-act comedy, *An Unequal Match*. Her performance was described by *The Gazette's* drama critic. He said that "outside the ability to play the lighter portions of the part very charmingly," Mrs. Langtry had not acquired "the strength and power" necessary for any serious claim to critical recognition. In the great dramatic scene, "Mrs. Langtry failed entirely to do justice to the situation . . . and lost her best opportunity."

Such criticism would have been enough to crush any other actress. It had no effect on Lillie Langtry's popularity. She appeared "before an audience which completely packed the house and rendered even standing room scarcely available." As for her acting, the critic had to admit, a little ruefully, that "the audience . . . was indulgent, and not only overlooked defects but applauded with an entire absence of discrimination." Not the play, or her way of performing it, but Lillie herself had proved irresistible.

Lillie Langtry was one of those women of the late Victorian era who were known as "professional beauties." Her beauty was far beyond the chorus-girl variety. Hers was classical, graceful, almost stately. It was the type that enabled her to take her place in the highest society of the day.

Lillie Langtry had respectable origins. Her father was the Anglican dean at St. Helier, Jersey, in the Channel Islands. She met her first husband, perhaps appropriately, in a storm. This rich yachtsman from Belfast, Edward Langtry, had sought shelter in St. Helier harbor. Lillie's father, Dean Le Breton, invited Edward Langtry to stay with him. He introduced him to his lovely daughter. Five months later she and the yachtsman were married. She was not interested in yachts, but she saw in her marriage a way of entering London society. She persuaded Langtry to acquire a fine London house, where they could entertain.

Her beauty attracted Sir John Millais, the most fashionable English artist of the day. He painted and exhibited her portrait. Sir John named the portrait *A Jersey Lily*. The name was soon generally adopted.

The Prince of Wales, later King Edward VII, always had an eye for a beautiful woman. He viewed the portrait and asked for an introduction to the "Jersey Lily." She soon took her place as one of the prince's favorites. Sir George Chetwyn and the Marquis of Lonsdale had a fistfight over her.

In 1899, Edward Langtry died and she then married a young heir, Hugo Gerald de Bathe. He was only 28; she was approaching 50. Hugo's father was Sir Henry Percival de Bathe, retired general and veteran of the Crimean War. The father, in a rage at what his son had done, threw all the young man's belongings out of the window. He then saw his lawyers, made a new will, and cut Hugo off without a penny.

When Lillie Langtry came to Montreal on her second visit in 1900, she chose a play that made the most of the notoriety that had now become her chief asset. The play was named *The Degenerates*. The playwright, Sydney Grundy, had written it specially for her. The public was wondering how far Grundy had gone in including incidents from Lillie's own past. Whatever her reputation had become, she still moved in high circles. When in Ottawa, she was invited to stay at Government House by the governor-general, Lord Minto, and Lady Minto.

JOHN COLLINS SKETCHBOOK

THE OLD ACADEMY of MUSIC located where the EATON store now stands

The "JERSEY LILY" LILLIE LANGTRY in one of her stage roles

Attending a dinner at Government House in her honor were the prime minister, Sir Wilfrid Laurier, and Lady Laurier.

In Montreal she stayed at the Windsor Hotel and performed at Her Majesty's Theatre (later His Majesty's), the celebrated playhouse on the east side of Guy St. a little above St. Catherine. On the evening of May 18, 1900, the theatre was filled by "a large and fashionable audience." Again the same distinction was made, as in 1883, between the actress and the woman: "The attraction was not the play. Rather, it was the fame, charm and personality of Mrs. Langtry, the 'Jersey Lily' . . . one of the most beautiful women on the English stage."

In the audience a mood of exhilaration prevailed. That very day good war news had reached Montreal. The town of Mafeking in South Africa, where Baden-Powell had been holding out for months against the besieging Boers, had been relieved by the oncoming British troops. Victory celebrations were surging in the streets outside the theatre. Lillie Langtry was quick to exploit the occasion. At the end of the play she was being recalled, again and again, by the applauding audience. In a brief interval between these appearances she rapidly dressed herself in a khaki uniform, placed a khaki-colored helmet on her head, and grasped a Union Jack in her hand.

The sudden change took the audience by surprise. Langtry stepped to the centre front of the stage. There she recited Rudyard Kipling's "The Absent-minded Beggar," his tribute to the British Tommy.

She then called for "three cheers for the Queen," and "three cheers for Baden-Powell."

The response was tremendous. Her audience cheered "with a lustiness that shook the house to the rafters."

The night the prince danced up a storm

"*O*nly *five weeks before the date fixed for the ball the cattle were grazing over the ground.*" So Nicholas Woods, the correspondent for the London Times, described the site of the tremendous wooden ballroom built in August 1860 for the visit of the Prince of Wales. The site was in the fields above St. Catherine St., near Peel. No ballroom in Montreal was nearly big enough for the thousands who wished to be present when the prince danced. A permanent building, of the size needed, would have been too costly. The solution was to put up a huge temporary building of wood, in the cow pasture that covered the area above St. Catherine.

It had been learned that the Prince of Wales, then only 18 years of age, preferred balls to any other kind of entertainment that could be offered him — a foreshadowing of the pleasure-loving life that was to be his through his many years as Prince of Wales and even through his later reign as King Edward VII. A committee was formed in Montreal to put up a ballroom which, temporary though it might be, would be as grand as anything he would encounter in his North American tour. The head of the committee was John Young, a redoubtable man known as "the father of the Montreal harbor," whose figure in bronze stands by the waterfront.

The pastureland round about was transformed into a sort of dreamland — a place of pleasure-grounds, fountains, groves and bowers, all brilliant with lights. No cost was spared, nor had anybody suggested that it should be. A little lake had been formed, probably by making use of one of the many streams that flowed through the farmlands between the city and the mountain. It was crossed by a rustic bridge. Lanterns hung from the branches of the trees. By some ingenious Victorian trick, even the water lilies in the pond were illuminated.

Attractive as the grounds might be, it might still have been thought that dignity and grandeur would be hard to give to the big wooden ballroom. The risk was that it might come to appear as something hastily thrown together, a sort of oversized barn. But all such associations were banished. The room was designed in one immense circle, with galleries big enough to hold 2,000 people. Yet the room was not really tent-like either. On the outside it was ornamented with battlements and turrets. And in the interior the decorators had made it sumptuous. The prevailing tone was a light rose, even for the ballroom floor itself. There was also a lavish use of ivory and gold. Rich drapery of scarlet and gold, and ornamented shields, hung from the pillars.

The night of the ball was Monday, Aug. 27. It rained. So much rain had followed the prince on his visit that some called him "the 'raining' prince."

But the excitement of the ball was not dampened. His Royal Highness was to arrive at 10 p.m. As it was not etiquette to come later, 4,000 to 5,000 people were crowding into the ballroom at about 9:30. Cab-drivers raised their fares to any price they wished. Worse still, many going to the ball could find no cabs to take them there. The horse-drawn buses used by the hotels to meet the boats were called into use. These buses, having much the appearance and three times the length of an ordinary English hearse, transported whole groups of city belles to the ballroom.

The Prince of Wales arrived exactly at 10 p.m. He was conducted to a dais, where the Duke of Newcastle (whom Queen Victoria had appointed to accompany the prince on his tour) presented the wife of John Young. At once the prince opened the ball with her. The first dance was a quadrille, danced to the music of the French-Canadian tune A la Claire Fontaine.

The report that the Prince of Wales liked dancing more than any other sort of entertainment proved quite true. Though under the scrutiny of thousands of eyes, "he danced and laughed away the time with perfect enjoyment and unconcern." Some twoscore dances were provided. He danced them all except the last. He never danced more than once with any of the ladies — but there was one exception. A Miss Napier appears early on his list of partners, and she reappears near the end. Hers must have been the triumph of the evening: to be the only one to dance twice with the Prince of Wales. It was nearly 5 a.m. when the prince left. He had danced so long and so late that he had only about two hours' sleep before starting out the next day for a trip through the rapids of the St. Lawrence.

The great ballroom was to be used once more

The temporary Ballroom In the fields

Erected above St. Catherine near Peel

The PRINCE of WALES in a Colonel's uniform

John Collins

SKETCHBOOK

during the prince's visit. On the evening of Thursday, Aug. 30, came "the People's Ball." Tickets were only $1; there were no restrictions as to dress; anyone could come. The weather was kinder to the people than it had been to society. That night the moon shone clear over the pleasure gardens. And fireworks soared and crackled at the foot of the mountain. The announcement of "no restrictions as to dress" was observed with careless freedom. It was interperted to mean corduroys, brown or gray shooting-jacket, yellow vest and scarlet necktie, with thick leather gloves or none at all. The women were there in bonnets and shawls. The $1 admission price made necessary a severe restriction of refreshments. The result was that everyone seemed bent on eating sandwiches before the prince came, in case none would be left later in the evening.

The prince and his party arrived in evening dress and were escorted to a box in the gallery. He was welcomed with tremendous cheering, but he was not tempted to descend to join the dancers. He remained little more than an hour. The fact that most of the people, instead of dancing, stood in a crowd staring at him seemed to hasten his departure. Many had doubted the prince would come at all to the People's Ball. They had been outside in the moonlight in the pleasure gardens, and came crowding in only when the word at last reached them that he had arrived. Many came too late, and found the prince had gone. However, once he was gone the dancing started in earnest.

When the prince left Montreal, the great wooden ballroom was taken down, the cows returned, and before long the grass was growing once more over the pathways of the pleasure gardens of August 1860.

A church born again when it was 63

In St. Laurent is a building that was 63 years old at the time it was put up. This building was erected in St. Laurent in 1931. But it dates from 1868.

There is an explanation. For different periods it has stood in two different places — places miles apart. It was first erected on Dorchester St. (which became Dorchester Blvd., which became René Lévesque). It was St. Paul's Presbyterian Church. This imposing church stood on the south side of Dorchester, across the street from where the south wing of the cruciform Place Ville Marie building stands today.

St. Paul's was taken down in 1930. It had been expropriated to make way for Central Station of the Canadian National Railways. As it turned out, the station did not quite extend over that site. At the time of the demolition of St. Paul's, scrupulous plans were made; every stone was numbered. The stones were then transported to St. Laurent. There the building was put together again. It became the chapel attached to the end of Collège St. Laurent, administered by a teaching order, the Congrégation de Ste. Croix.

Members of this order came from France to St. Laurent in 1848. For a number of years they carried on their teaching in a small two-storey stone building, later a grocery store. In 1852 construction was begun on the college building that is there today. Over the years, one addition was added to another. When the fathers of Ste. Croix heard that old St. Paul's on Dorchester St. was to be demolished, they saw their opportunity. The college needed a better chapel. If they could acquire the stone of St. Paul's, they could re-erect the church alongside their college.

The Presbyterians agreed to let them have the stones. By this arrangement, the Congrégation de Ste. Croix was able, at comparatively little cost, to have as its college chapel a building that had long been one of the most prominent architectural features of one of Montreal's principal streets.

At the time St. Paul's Church was built in 1868 its importance was described by a commentator: "The building is in the style known as the decorated Gothic . . . and its general appearance is such as to do credit to the city, and to entitle it to rank with the finest church edifices." It was a large building, seating 1,000 people. The internal dimensions of the nave were 102 feet by 62, with transepts of about 17 feet each. From the floor to the apex of the roof was 58 feet. In the high basement were lecture and schoolrooms. The church was as handsome as it was big. For all its ornamental parts sandstone had been imported from Ohio — a stone that lent itself well to carving.

The St. Paul's congregation could well afford a handsome church. It was becoming one of the richest in Canada. Among its members were the wealthy cousins Lord Strathcona and Lord Mount Stephen, who had been able, between them, to build the Royal Victoria Hospital.

The first St. Paul's Church had stood down near the waterfront on St. Hélène St., the little street below Notre Dame just east of McGill. This building, large for its day, also had architectural distinction. Its architect was John Wells, who had designed the Bank of Montreal on Place d'Armes. By the 1860s, however, the movement of Montreal's population was definitely northward — away from the waterfront and toward the mountain. The congregation decided to move with the times. The new site it bought on Dorchester was still an apple orchard. The trees had to be cut down before the church could be built. On this new location, at the edge of the town, the church, it was believed, would be in a position to command a rapid growth. So it proved, for many years.

Montreal's population movements, however, never ceased. About the time of World War I people were moving away from the Dorchester St. area, out to the new, far suburbs. The downtown congregations had to adjust themselves to changing realities. Nearby was St. Andrew's Church of the Church of Scotland. It stood on Beaver Hall Hill where the Bell Canada building is now. Both congregations saw it would be to their advantage to merge. In 1917 they agreed to unite as the Church of St. Andrew and St. Paul. They decided to close St. Andrew's Church and to worship together in St. Paul's.

Ten years later St. Andrew's was demolished. Not much of it was saved. Men with axes fragmented the pulpit and many other interior fittings. The stones of

ST. PAUL'S CHURCH — St. Laurent

John Collins SKETCHBOOK

its walls were tumbled down. Warning signs were posted round the church by the wreckers: "Safety First: If you wish to collect insurance on your car, or if you wish to collect insurance on your life, park here." Old St. Paul's might have met with the same fate in 1930, when it was expropriated and slated for demolition. But the agreement with the teaching order of Ste. Croix saved the historic building and gave it a new life in another municipality.

At St. Laurent the church was reopened as the college chapel in October 1931. Guy Panet-Raymond describes the day: "I was a boarder student at Collège St. Laurent and this Sunday morning we were shepherded into a brand new chapel that was to be dedicated this morn. As usual on Sundays we were in our clean uniforms: black double-breasted suits, white shirts, black ties, socks and shoes, trousers for the elders, knickerbockers for the younger. Without grasping the meaning of the event, we knew that this was to be a 'grand évènement.' As

we entered 'our' new chapel, which was still smelling of new plaster, cement and paint, lo and behold, we saw sitting in the first 10 pews English and Protestant guests. The guests were, of course, representatives of the congregation of St. Andrew and St. Paul who had sold their church for $1, as is and where is, to the Fathers of Ste. Croix."

The basement of the building was developed into an amphitheatre. There the "Compagnons de St. Laurent," under the direction of Rev. Emile Legault, staged plays for many years. A plaque on the building now reads: "Salle Emile Legault."

Old St. Paul's is no longer a college chapel. The college building as a whole has become a CEGEP. The chapel has come to serve various new uses, such as being a museum and a library.

But the born-again building is still there — still the same building, viewed from without, that was constructed in the apple orchard on Dorchester St. in 1868.

Bored soldiers on a 'miserable' little island

Those who visit Ile Ste. Hélène today see many reminders of the days when it was occupied by the Imperial Garrison. The old stone barracks, the powder magazine and other military buildings are still there, as is the little military cemetery.

What was life like for the officers of the Royal Artillery who had to spend several years on this little island? One of these officers, Lt. Francis Duncan, has left an account of his experiences there in the 1860s. His opinion was not favorable. To him, and his brother officers, Ile Ste. Hélène was a "miserable" little island. The monotony of long confinement in so small a space brought depression and dyspepsia. The officers began to feel that they were like caged animals in the Regent's Park Zoological Gardens.

Tempers wore themselves out. The officers grew taciturn and scowling. On parade every morning they would study the face of the commanding officer as he came upon the field. Often his skin would look muddy, his eyes yellow, his appearance bilious — and they might expect trouble. At the officers' mess the food was regularly criticized. Often they sat together with nothing to say in conversation, but ate and drank in a mingled solitude. Duncan soon learned how a few men kept apart from the rest of the world get to know everything that everyone in the group has to say. As he wrote: "for too early do we sound the depths of our respective minds, too soon do we know by heart — aye! even to loathing, our mutual witticisms, — too soon does that awful social hour arrive when during a whole meal we cannot raise among ourselves even the shadow of a laugh!"

This mood of weary boredom seemed to belong not only to themselves: it hung over the military buildings also. There was a decayed and trembling drawbridge. The gates — formidable in appearance, topped by spikes to make an attacker shiver — on closer inspection had missing hinges and broken locks, and would even swing to and fro, creaking and groaning in every breeze from the river. Platforms for guns had rotted and sagged, so that they could barely support themselves. The parapets were full of weeds.

The officers tried their best, in all manner of imaginative ways, to break the listless atmosphere by some kind of activity. But they found that after a brisk beginning, interest always waned. Despondency and apathy crept over them and they sank back into weariness. They began by passing the time writing letters to all their friends. They soon found that they had nothing more to write about: on the little island in the river, nothing ever happened.

They tried to get up games of cricket. A good hit sent the ball either into the river or into the treetops. No living batsman could make certain of a ball with such a background of dark stumps and fallen trees. Something more than restricted space and rugged surroundings made cricket seem a poor sport on the island; the officers who gathered to play had little spirit for the contest. If any batsman made a hit, the player who had to run for it would scowl and hate the batsman with a murderous hatred. No one's heart was in the game.

They tried fishing, but only caught "the most diminutive fish that ever existed," which also seemed to have "a most unnecessary abundance of bones." They tried duck shooting. But after prowling about the island, trying to conceal themselves with some discomfort, they only had to discharge their unused guns on their return. They took to gardening and raising fowl. Gardening, however, demanded more prolonged exertion than they were able to provide, and the fowl, seeming to share their depression, sickened and died.

Then in a fit of zeal they decided to pass the time by going in for watercolors. They went to Montreal and bought materials. They found a teacher, who agreed to come to the island regularly to give them instruction.

The teacher arrived according to the agreement. They got through their first lesson. They yawned through their second. On the morning of the third they sent him a message that on that day they were

Entrance
to the Fort -
St. Helen's
Island —

and a
Drummer
in Nineteenth
Century Uniform

John Collins SKETCHBOOK

engaged. His periodic visits made him come to appear as a merciless tyrant, a sort of Old Man of the Sea. The officers could not see how they could get rid of him. He was an excellent artist, quite good as a teacher, and they could scarcely say they had grown so proficient in the art that they no longer needed his services. At last, one day, there came a rumor that the Royal Artillery was to be moved to Quebec. Meeting in solemn conclave, they concocted an elaborate letter to him, stating that the preparations for their departure were so urgent that they feared they could not give him the attention that his valuable instruction merited.

Duncan discovered, however, that their "miserable little island," though inducing this enveloping mood of depression and uselessness, gave them all one undoubted consolation. At night it was transformed, to become a place of mystical beauty. At night the lieutenant would stand on the shore, or the green parapet, and watch the play of the merry stars in the hurrying river, or the grand white sheen of the patient moon spreading over its surface. The buzz of

some lazy insect, or the echo of distant oars on the St. Lawrence, with the cry, at stated intervals, of "all's well" from the sentry at his lonely post under the elms — these were the only sounds.

And as he would stand gazing, Duncan would see "the many lights of the great city come twinkling over the rippling water as if to cheer without interrupting one's solitude. Or one might hear, borne fitfully on the night air, the bells of the many churches sounding each passing hour, or inviting one to pray in a voice more solemn in the still island than in the crowded streets and thronging populace of a restless city."

At last the time came to leave Ile Ste. Hélène. On a bright September day a small steamer came and carried them away, to put them on their first stage to England.

The old lethargy lingered, for they marched on board with scarcely enough energy to cheer. But in the long nights at sea, and later in England, the image arose in their mind of the little island in the river with its strange, unearthly calm.

The big run on the City & District Bank

This bank had an unusual origin. It was proposed by a bishop — Msgr. Ignace Bourget, the Roman Catholic bishop of Montreal.

He wished to encourage thrift, through a bank that would welcome little savers, and protect them from the many failures that were occurring among Canadian banks at the time. His bank would be non-denominational. He wanted Catholic and Protestant businessmen, prominent in the community, to give some of their time to serving as directors and presidents.

By its charter, the bank would operate under certain restrictions to assure protection for those whose small savings were all they had in the world.

His intentions were carried into effect when the Montreal City & District Savings Bank was founded in 1846. From the start, those directing its affairs were aware that an institution of this kind would be unusually subject to "runs." Its customers, being largely those who had their all deposited in it, and not being well informed in financial matters, would be likely to become panicky at any rumor, however unfounded. Once a rumor got started, crowds of depositors would probably descend on the bank, demanding their money. The bank could expect these runs. It would always have a large amount of cash ready to meet any possible situation.

Eventually each of these runs would die out. Each time the bank would emerge stronger — for the good reason that it had dramatically demonstrated its stength beyond all doubt.

The runs did materialize. Many of them hit the bank like thunderbolts. The bank often had no idea how the rumors started. In the great run of 1913, however, it was able to trace the cause to its source. This time the rumor began with the chance conversation between two brokers in the cafe of a hotel. These "convivial spirits" were discussing the tightness of money in the market in general. One of them was having trouble trying to raise a loan. He had tried at the Montreal City & District Savings Bank but couldn't get a cent.

A bellboy happened to be nearby. He heard only the end of the conversation. What he had overheard, he thought, meant that the bank must be in bad shape. He telephoned a friend. At once the rumor began spreading.

Only rarely was a run predictable. Back in 1879 it seemed likely. Two Montreal banks — the Exchange Bank and the Ville Marie Bank — closed their doors in rapid succession. Though the Montreal City & District Savings Bank was in perfectly sound shape, many small depositors had come to think that no bank was any longer to be trusted.

Crowds gathered in front of the bank, jamming the stairs and swelling out over sidewalks and roadway. Those able to get inside became a struggling mass, fighting to get to the counters. One poor woman had her dress almost completely torn off. Another woman — in the heat, crush and stress — sank unconscious to the floor. When she recovered, she did not go home but insisted on staying until she got what she had come for.

Pickpockets and robbers were everywhere. A "hardworking" woman from Point St. Charles drew out her lifetime savings of $415. On McGill St. she was robbed of the whole amount.

Dr. William H. Hingston (later Sir William) arrived on the scene and climbed up on a counter. He was an eminent surgeon, recently mayor of Montreal, a director of the bank (and eventually its president). He spoke plainly. He was concerned that those who took out their money might have it stolen, or they would be tempted to go out and spend it all. "It is you timid people who will suffer," he said, "and the anxiety of the bank is for you. It has none for itself."

Little could be done by appeals to stop a run once it had begun. It had to be allowed to peter out by itself. Generally it took about three days. Runs would stop as suddenly as they began. When the run of 1879 was over, the bank's president, Edward Murphy, remarked: "Dull this afternoon, almost dull as hardware."

The bank found that the best way to bring a run to an end was to give depositors every facility to get their money out. The readiness of the bank to hand out the money was the best public assurance that it had it. During a run, normal banking hours were extended far into the evening. Additional tellers were mobilized; more wickets were opened. Money in

John Collins SKETCHBOOK

City and District
Savings Bank
St. James at St. John

bound packages was rushed to the branches from headquarters, and stacked up inside the tellers' cages for all to see.

In 1913 the bank's officials, including its distinguished directors, went about the branches. "We'll go on paying, don't be afraid," said president J. Aldéric Ouimet. "Any depositor who sees fit, notwithstanding the groundlessness of his fears . . . will have his wishes immediately complied with." A girl, a factory employee, did not know how to fill in the slip to withdraw her savings. Ouimet, seeing her perplexity, filled it in for her and she got her money. At the St. Timothée and St. Catherine branch a director, Senator Raoul Dandurand, declared: "If there is anyone present who would lose a moment's sleep because his money is in the bank, I advise him to take his money before he leaves. But there is no necessity for doing so."

Odd incidents took place. One man drew out all his money in $5 bills. Grasping his hoard in his hands, he made his way to the door. When he looked at the crowd outside, and knowing he would have to

push his way through it, he returned to the wicket, threw his bundle over to the teller, and asked him to take it back.

Another man called for all his money. He watched the teller counting it out. Then he refused to take it. "All I wanted to know," he explained, "was whether you had it or not."

Theft was as common in 1913 as it had been in 1879. It took various forms. A widow carried her money safely home. One of her boarders persuaded her to take a half-interest in a land deal. Next day the widow found she had lost both her money and her boarder.

In this run, as in the others, the bank observed that only its smaller depositors withdrew their money. In 1913 there was really no run at all at the bank's branch at Park and Laurier. It was in a comparatively affluent area, with better-informed customers. "No one would realize by a visit to the branch," remarked a commentator, "that there had been a run on the other branches of the bank in the city."

Emancipation on two wheels

A bicycle a woman could ride arrived with the 1890s. Its coming brought women a new measure of emancipation. At last they were free to move as they wished, no longer dependent on men for transportation. The new phenomenon appeared — "the Bicycle Girl." She was the image of liberation.

The joy of the new freedom burst at times into lyrical language, as in a Montreal comment of 1897: "The bicycle girl may . . . break loose in the glorious early morning. In easy tweed suit, cloth cap and low broad-toed shoes, with a substantial sandwich strapped to her handlebars, she may be miles away in no time, revelling in the glories of meadow, woods and waterfall and live and breathe as nature intended she should."

Bicycles, in one form or another, had been around for many years, but women had not wished, or had not been able, to make much use of them. The long era of the "pennyfarthings" left women as spectators. The pennyfarthing had a front wheel about five feet high. The back wheel was comparatively tiny, only about a foot in diameter. The "saddle" — seat — was not between the two wheels but perched on top of the towering front wheel. Getting on such a bicycle, without having it flop over, was a problem. Far worse was the risk that a stone or bump in the road would send the rider headfirst over the handlebars.

Women's day dawned when a new bicycle was unveiled on London's Victoria Embankment in 1885. An inventor, James Starley, introduced a bike with two wheels of equal size, each about 30 inches. The riding saddle was placed between the two. It was named the dwarf or safety bicycle. Mounting or dismounting was no longer a hazard, and the new bicycle was easier to propel.

At first even this new bike was unsuitable for women. The crossbar from front to back left no place for women's skirts. This drawback was eventually removed. The "drop frame" was introduced. Now women could ride a bicycle in the long skirts that seemliness required. Women turned to cycling with zest. By the end of the 1890s one of every three bicycles was being bought by a woman.

The Bicycle Girl, though emancipated, was still a young lady, observing grace and decorum. Advice was given on posture. A Bicycle Girl's neck should not be bent forward to keep her hat from blowing off. She must sit bolt upright. Handlebars must be sufficiently high to allow her to take a firm hold, with the forearm straight and the elbow in line with the waist. Gracefulness would be impossible, unless all unnecessary motion, particularly with the knees, was avoided. Pedalling, as much as possible, must be done with the ankles.

Women did not have to do their cycling by themselves. Some cycling clubs had male and female members. Mrs. Gordon R. (Olive A.) Langley recalled her mother's participation: "The bicycle was enjoying its heyday at the turn of the century. My mother was one of the first to acquire one of those exciting new rubber-tired wonders. When she became sufficiently proficient, she and my father joined a bicycle club. With friends they would ride forth in the evenings. A few years later my sister became the proud possessor of a 'wheel' — not only a wheel, but a bicycling costume. This consisted of a dust-colored suit, with a jaunty straw sailor hat."

Some Bicycle Girls set out together on long-distance trips, even between cities. But as late as 1916 it proved to be a rough experience. The two Coles sisters (Phyllis, later Mrs. G.B. Dorey, and Dorothy) set out to ride from Montreal to Ottawa. Roads were so bad, and bicycles or motorists so few, that people along the way thought they were doing it for a bet or because they were planning to write a book about their adventures.

They encountered only two motorists on the way up, only five on the way back. They saw almost no other cyclists. The road was so deep with ruts that they took, whenever they could, to cow paths along the side. Sandy patches in the road made hard going and loose stones were a threat to tires. On the way up, the rain came down in torrents. Though wearing waterproofs, they were drenched. They skidded from side to side in the clay.

In the end they decided to give up and take the train to Ottawa. The decision was made after they had sheltered for two hours in a woodshed with a pig and some hens for companions. They stayed in Ottawa for a week to allow roads to dry out. Then

JOHN COLLINS SKETCHBOOK

they set out for Montreal and home. This time the ruts in the road were like the furrows in a plowed field. Even following the cow paths was tedious. To get to the cow paths they had to jump ditches, dragging their bicycles with them. It was impossible to ride up hills. They walked up, pushing their bicycles beside them. At times they made no more than two miles an hour.

They were plagued by mosquitoes. Even after a week of drying, the roads were still damp clay in spots. The clay came up over their shoes. Riding from 9 o'clock in the morning till 7 at night, it took them 3½ days to get home. The nights they spent in villages along the way. After this inter-city trip the audacious Phyllis Coles remarked: "Personally, I would go again tomorrow to see the beautiful country — but unless you are unbreakable, or made of cast iron, take my advice and never venture by road from the commercial metropolis of Canada to the capital for some years to come, especially after a heavy rain."

The first careless rapture had pictured the Bicycle Girl in 1897 as being "miles away in no time, revelling in the glories of meadow, woods and waterfall." The reality did not quite correspond, certainly not on the furrowed road between Montreal and Ottawa.

The bicycle, nevertheless, was an emancipation. It gave the Bicycle Girl wheels of her own, even if the going might at times be rough.

A poet with a broom

"Would you like to know the secret of a charmed life?" Harry Barker used to ask students this question. The scene was ludicrous. Harry Barker was a janitor in the Arts Building at McGill. He was under 5 feet tall, but he was a sturdy little figure. And his head was magnificently large and well-shaped. His hair had receded sufficiently to disclose a truly noble brow.

Harry Barker was a poet. They called him McGill's poet laureate. Some called him Shakespeare Harry. He knew Shakespeare by heart: long passages were recited on the least invitation, and even without any.

Shakespeare Harry carried himself with unfailing dignity. Never had he regarded himself as merely a maintenance man in an office building. His years were spent in what he delighted to call "the halls of learning." He appreciated, even revered, his surroundings. Learning meant much to him. In other circumstances he might well have been a professor. In his limited situation he loved high thought and splendid words. He raised his work as janitor to an academic level of its own.

At first, not unnaturally, students would be amused that Harry was about to impart to them a secret that few, if any, had ever discovered. If, however, they showed the least interest, Harry Barker at once began to share his secret. He would pick up his broom and sweep together an empty cigarette package and the wrapping from a candy bar. "I like my work," he would tell them. "People coming in here might not think that what I do is at all important. But it is — very important. If I didn't keep sweeping things up here all day, the whole floor would be covered with litter. The dignity of this magnificent hall would be ruined. I am the one who keeps this building looking the way it ought to look. I know the value of what I'm doing. I never think of all this as just work. I regard it as my play." Then Harry would go on to summarize his secret: "Feel the significance of what you are doing, then make your work your play, and you'll have a charmed life."

Shakespeare Harry could apply a quotation to any occasion. One day he overheard a student in the college corridor asking another for a loan of 25 cents.

At once Harry interrupted him with Polonius's advice to Laertes:

Neither a borrower, nor a lender be;
For loan oft loses both itself and friend.

Another time when Dr. Cyrus Macmillan nodded to him as he was going by, Harry delivered a Shakespearean quotation. Macmillan paused and answered him with another quotation. Harry replied with still another. On they went, speaking and answering entirely with extracts from Shakespeare. It became a contest. Students overheard and gathered to listen. It was extraordinary to see a college janitor holding his own so well against the man who was the head of McGill's department of English and dean of the arts faculty.

Harry Barker was remarkable not only for his knowledge of Shakespeare but for his impressive manner of speaking the lines. Professor Frank R. Scott once heard him lean on his broom and say: "Professor Scott, 'To be or not to be, that IS the question.' " And Scott later remarked: "Suddenly the line, so flattened by constant repetition, took on a new significance. A quotation from Shakespeare became a challenge for today."

Shakespeare Harry's own poems used to be published in the McGill Daily. Invariably they were signed: "H.B. (Arts Year Unknown)." Twice the students raised enough money to print small collections of them in pamphlets. Both were titled: "Simple Rhymes for Simple Folk." At the front was a photograph of Shakespeare Harry standing on the Arts Building's steps. What Harry wrote was generally little better than doggerel, but most of it was inspired by a desire for the noble and elevated life. One poem had elements of strength and meaning: "How to Obtain True Beauty."

If thou wouldst be truly beautiful,
Work with the head, the heart, the hand,
Until the honest, pore-cleansing, and
skin-beautifying perspiration,
Rolls o'er your noble brow,
Covering the hills and valleys of your face,
With its soothing, healing, and beautifying balm.

Perhaps the best of his poems was one expressing his reverence for learning:

John Collins — Arts Building — SKETCHBOOK — mcgill

Books, medicine for the erring soul
Look out from the large shelves
And when you are calm and alone
Give a kind of solemn greeting.

Stephen Leacock was Barker's friend. The principal, Dr. F. Cyril James, thought highly of him. In his last years Harry was working as a janitor in the old east wing of the Arts Building. One of his duties was to bring James his afternoon tea. If no one else was in the office, he would ask the principal whether he'd like to hear his latest poem. James always said, "Yes, indeed." And James would say, recalling those twilight readings: "I enjoyed those poems."

The early details of Harry's life are obscure. He had been born in Dudley, England. Before coming to Canada in 1908 he had served in the British army, even (Frank Scott had heard) "to the limits of Afghanistan." He had been a janitor at McGill for nearly 30 years when he died in 1945. On one of his last days at work in a college corridor he paused in his sweeping to lift up the sleeve of his jacket. It was badly tattered. He looked at it solemnly, and quoted from *Macbeth:* "the ravel'd sleave of care." It was a quotation aptly applied to his sleeve.

But Harry Barker would never have implied that his work had made him careworn.

He had made his work his play.

He had discovered — and he had lived — the secret of a charmed life

The other island named Montreal

Canada has two Islands of Montreal. In addition to the one in the St. Lawrence, there's one in the Northwest Territories — where the Back River (formerly known as Great Fish River) flows into an inlet of the Arctic Ocean.

Why would an island so far away in northern Canada bear the same name as the one in the St. Lawrence? The story begins when Capt. George Back (later Sir George) arrived in the city of Montreal on April 9, 1833. He was a celebrity. Already he had won fame by his Arctic voyages. He was now to head for the far north on still another. This latest voyage was hailed not just as a new voyage of exploration but as an act of courageous benevolence.

Back was going in search of another explorer, Sir John Ross. Seven years earlier Sir John had sailed from England on his voyage of discovery. Not a word had been heard since of his whereabouts or his fate. An expedition of rescue had been organized. Private subscriptions were supplemented by a government grant. King William IV was the patron of the expedition. The Hudson's Bay Co. offered help. Back had been appointed commander.

He wrote: "No sooner was it known in Montreal that our little party was in one of the hotels than the commandant, Lt.-Col. Macdougall of the 79th regiment, and the officers of the garrison, as well as the principal inhabitants of the town, waited upon us, and vied with each other in administering to our comforts, and rendering as agreeable as possible the short time which remained to us for the enjoyment of civilized society."

Certainly Back's last few days before entering the rigors of the Arctic were a time of crowded luxury and sparkling entertainment. He stayed at one of the most elegant hotels in Montreal, the British American. For much of the entertainment provided, he did not have to leave the building — only to go from his own room to the dance or the banquet. On April 15 he and his second-in-command, Dr. Richard King, were invited to the Bachelors' Ball. For this annual event the bachelors sent out invitations to the most fashionable ladies and gentlemen of the town. It was a highlight of the social season. Back and King were seen that night in the hotel's ballroom mixing in the "hilarity and festivity."

On the evening of April 23 Back and King were the guests at a dinner given in their honor by a "very numerous" gathering, "comprising most of our merchants and respectable citizens." The hospitality was so lavish as to test the guests' endurance. Twenty-eight toasts were listed. Still others were added spontaneously, here and there. The chairman, Samuel Gerrard, prominent merchant and former president of the Bank of Montreal, proposed the toast to the guests. "Never has there been an expedition which has excited the feelings of the public as this has done," he said. Montrealers "could not but admire the intrepidity, courage and self-devotion of these travellers, in going upon such an arduous undertaking."

By about the 16th toast Back and King had received as much hospitality as they could prudently accept. They withdrew to their rooms in the hotel. Their departure was made the occasion for a supplementary toast: "Our guests who have left us."

In the evening of the next day Back and King were making ready for their departure. They were to set out from Lachine the following morning. Nearly all their baggage and equipment had been carried out of the British American Hotel. Then suddenly the hotel burst into flames. Lamps had hung suspended among boughs of "fir, spruce and other evergreens" — decorations put up for the Bachelors' Ball eight days before. An employee noticed flames running along a twig. He pulled it down. Flames had already spread. He only scattered them. In 40 minutes the grand hotel was in ruins. The sky, reflecting the flames, glowed red. In the darkness the church spires, the steamboats in the port, Ile Ste. Hélène, even the South Shore, glimmered in the glare.

Had Back delayed his departure for half an hour, all his equipment would have been consumed. As it was, he lost his only barometer — a serious loss for an Arctic explorer. The captain had more to worry about than his barometer. He had been recruiting in Montreal. From England he had brought only three men. The rest he had planned to find in Montreal or at northern posts of the Hudson's Bay Co.

SKETCHBOOK

John Collins

The OLD CANAL LACHINE

In Montreal he had enrolled voyageurs. These men, he knew, were extremely superstitious — a trait natural enough, considering the hazards of their trade. Back was afraid these men might look upon the fire, on the eve of his departure, as an evil omen. It might be enough to make them quit. Next morning he was at Lachine, his point of embarkation. He was relieved to find the voyageurs still there. They had been too busy enjoying their last chance to get drunk to care about anything that had happened to the British American Hotel.

People had come from Montreal to Lachine to see the expedition off. It put out from the little canal that still parallels the Lachine waterfront. Back described his departure: "We embarked amidst the most enthusiastic cheers, and firing of musketry. . . .

A few minutes brought us to the St. Lawrence, and, as we turned . . . our little vessels up that noble stream, one loud huzza bade us farewell." The search for the missing explorer, Sir John Ross, began.

About a year later a message reached Back by a Hudson's Bay Co. courier. Ross and some other surivors had been found. A whaler had seen them in the Barrow Strait. They had been taken to England.

Back was now instructed to carry out explorations and make maps. He added extensively to knowledge of the Great Fish River and its region. On Aug. 2, 1835, he discovered an island at the river's mouth. Back wrote in his journal, "I called the place Montreal Island in commemoration of the attention we had received from the public-spirited and hospitable inhabitants of that city."

Violence in the hotels

In the old hotels of Montreal, anything was likely to happen. And it did. In the lore of the hotels are many tales of strange occurrences. Such is a story about the St. Lawrence Hall, which stood on the north side of St. James St. just west of St. François Xavier.

The St. Lawrence Hall was noted for the number of its guests from the U.S., many of whom stayed for long periods. Among them was a Dr. Scitzinger of Philadelphia, described as "a wealthy gentleman." He had been at the Hall for the entire winter of 1866-67. In Boston in 1867 was a man named Edson who "took offence at some reprinted remarks of Dr. Scitzinger." Many Americans in those days believed in the old idea of hands-on justice. Edson set out for Montreal to deal with the doctor.

In Montreal Edson "provided himself with a heavy horsewhip." He concealed it in his pocket. At St. Lawrence Hall he asked the porter where Scitzinger could be found. The porter replied that he was out, but, looking across St. James St., he saw him. He pointed him out to Edson. At once Edson "prepared for action." He placed himself just inside the doorway. Scitzinger crossed over the threshhold, unsuspecting. He had scarcely entered the hotel when he received a heavy cut on the face from Edson's whiphandle. His cheek was bruised, an eyebrow lacerated. The blow stunned him. He was unable to defend himself. Edson struck again, then walked off.

The incident was reported to the police. That afternoon Edson was brought before W.H. Brehaut, the police magistrate. On the advice of his lawyer, Edson pleaded guilty. The magistrate fined him $4 and costs (altogether about $10). *The Gazette* deplored so light a sentence. "Cowardly assaults of this kind," it declared, "are eminently un-British, and it is to be regretted, notwithstanding the plea of guilty, that the police magistrate did not impose the full fine."

Another curious story is told about an older Montreal hotel. It is a story of a guest's being thrown out of a window — fortunately, it seems, a ground-floor window. The hotel was Rasco's, opened in 1836 and still standing on St. Paul St. opposite the Bonsecours Market. The proprietor was Francis Rasco, a most obliging Italian host, but with a fiery temper in reserve. Rasco had many military guests and patrons in the years when Montreal was one of the garrison cities of the British Empire. Some of the young officers were the sons of British aristocrats. A few brought with them "their follies, and insufferable arrogance."

One of these young officers rented a suite of rooms at Rasco's. There he entertained expensively, and, at times, uproariously. On this particular night the party, beginning in the early evening, went on into the early-morning hours. Everyone in the hotel was kept awake, even those in "the remote parts."

Rasco sent a polite note, asking the officer and his friends "to keep their mirth within bounds." His request was greeted "with cheers and shouts of derision." Rasco himself then went to the suite of rooms. His explosive temper had broken through his customary suavity. He spoke his mind: "I sent you a message to behave yourselves and make less noise but I was mistaken. I am looking at nothing but drunken brutes. Out of my house, every one of you." He pointed to the door. The officer lifted a heavy crystal goblet. He aimed it straight at Rasco's head. It skimmed past him, struck a mirror on the other side of the room, and shattered into fragments. "You'll go out first, my good fellow," said the officer. He raised the window, lifted Rasco off his feet and carried him to the window to toss him out.

Tom Pringle, a waiter, suddenly appeared. He had heard the crash of glass and came to see what had happened. Tom was large, young, tough. He laid hold of the officer, lifted him off his feet, carried him to the open window and flung him out. "Misery likes company," he said, as he seized one of the guests and sent him flying through the window. Leaning out, he shouted down, "Give Lord Fiddle-Daddle Tom Pringle's compliments."

The other guests in the room, preferring the door to the window, scurried out. On the street they picked up their host and carried him off to their quarters. Rasco, calming down, realized that he and his waiter had gone rather far in pitching guests out of a window. He expected they might be arrested next day. But that was the last they heard of the

SKETCHBOOK

John Collins

ST. JAMES
and
ST. FRANCOIS XAVIER

affair. He rewarded Tom Pringle "with a handsome silver watch, and a dainty little compass, suitable for the pocket."

In the days of duelling in Montreal any hotel that happened to be near a duelling-ground might become a sort of emergency hospital. In the 1830s one of the favored duelling spots was at the racetrack west of the city. No spot could be more deserted than a racetrack in the off-season, especially at 5 o'clock in the morning. Near this racetrack was a hotel, the Pavilion. It catered to the horsey men who came out for the races and to fishermen and duck-hunters. It stood on what today is LaSalle Blvd. in Verdun, a little west of de l'Eglise Ave.

About 5 o'clock in the morning of May 22, 1838, a farmer, J.B. Lanouette, was on his way to begin work in the nearby fields. He saw two men taking up positions to fight a duel. Lanouette heard the order to fire. He saw one of the duellists leap three or four feet into the air, then drop heavily to the ground. He came up and said to the man who had fired the shot, "That's a bad way to start your day." The man threw his pistol to the ground and began to sob.

Soon afterward the proprietor of the Pavilion Hotel was startled awake by a pounding at his door. He put his head out of an upstairs window. Men below called on him to open up. When he came down and opened the door, the body of an army officer, Major Henry John Warde of the Royal Regiment, was carried in. They laid down the body. A bullet dropped from the left arm. It rolled across the floor.

An English bishop in a strange city

"Upon the whole, I prefer Montreal, as a place of residence, to almost any town that I have ever seen." It was high praise. And it came from an Englishman who had never thought he would see the place, and never wanted to see it.

The great surprise of Canon Ashton Oxenden's life came one morning in 1869 while he and his wife were at breakfast in his "sweet Kentish rectory." The postman brought the "customary allowance of letters." He glanced through them. He found "amongst them one with the startling address: 'The Rev. Ashton Oxenden, Bishop Elect of Montreal'."

He couldn't imagine how Montrealers ever came to hear of him, much less why they would want him as bishop. The answer to the mystery was that he had written some religious tracts. Copies had somehow found their way to Montreal. The time had come when the Anglican Synod of Montreal had to choose a new bishop, the second in the history of the diocese.

The Montreal diocese favored Low Church principles. Canon Oxenden's tracts were written from the Low Church point of view. These Low Church Montrealers, the majority in the diocese, felt Canon Oxenden would be the man to uphold the principles they favored. He shuddered at the thought of being uprooted in his 60s, in his poor state of health, and set down in the rigorous conditions of life in Montreal. He could only ascribe what had happened to the strange ways of Providence. Being a devout man, he felt he must obey. But he was entering, late in life, with all his habits and attitudes formed, into strange, unfamiliar surroundings.

Being very English, he could not suppress the Old Countryman's tendency to make unfavorable comparisons. On his way to Montreal from Quebec he was displeased by the rail service on the Grand Trunk line. "The train was far less expeditious than those we had been accustomed to in England," he complained, "and the stoppages seemed to be needlessly prolonged." Stations were "miserable." When he saw the horses and carriages on the streets of Montreal, he had to say that "one misses the neat liveries to which we are accustomed in England; and the practice which prevails pretty generally of driving with one rein in each hand strikes one as a little awkward."

But a change soon came over the new bishop from overseas. He proved himself not only an excellent bishop in many ways, but an enthusiastic Montrealer. The city captivated him — a city "so beautifully situated," beginning at the shore of the "noble St. Lawrence and backed by a fine mountain-like hill." In his eyes it became "the youngest and beautiful Queen of the West." The residence provided for him on Drummond St. was "most comfortable and convenient." His cathedral, on St. Catherine St., completed only 10 years before his arrival, was "a very fine specimen of the Early Decorated style of Gothic architecture . . . very chaste and handsome."

As for foodstuffs, Montreal had a superb market — in the grand Bonsecours Market building on St. Paul St. At the market he found the meat "fairly good, but not perhaps first-rate." But he was astonished by the extraordinary range of game — partridges, prairie hens, quails, snow birds. Turkeys and fowl were "remarkably cheap and abundant."

It might have seemed that this elderly Englishman, who had fled every year from English winters to the south of France, would be appalled by winters in Montreal. On the contrary, he revelled in them. "I hardly know," he insisted, "a pleasanter place in which to pass the winter months than Montreal." He had advice: "And if anyone should contemplate a visit to Montreal, by all means, let him make it at this season, for he will then find it in all its glory."

Everything in winter was so novel, so cheerful. No carriages rumbled along the streets. Instead, sleighs glided "noiselessly over the snow." And they were so picturesque: "very handsomely got up, with an abundance of furs and other trappings." In a sleigh the motion was "most agreeable, and the pace delightful." The bishop had never enjoyed the cold so much in his life: "Even in the keenest weather, provided there is a tolerable absence of wind, one suffers little from cold. A fur coat and a hat with ear-pads completely protect one. We have sometimes been out at night in an open sleigh, when the thermometer has been considerably below zero, without feeling it so much as an ordinary cold night in England."

SKETCHBOOK
— MARCHÉ BONSECOURS

Everything about the Montreal winters seemed to delight him. He admired the rooftops, white with snow; the smooth road, nearly two miles long, over the St. Lawrence ice to the South Shore; the Victoria Skating Rink on Drummond St. where a fancy-dress ball on the ice "was one of the most beautiful sights" he "had ever beheld."

He and his wife became "the most persevering pedestrians in the place." They kept up their walks in winter. To prevent themselves from slipping, they equipped their shoes with "creepers," which he described as "something like the spikes which are attached to cricket shoes." He was sure such brisk and bracing winter walks "contributed not a little to their health." One thing about winter made him marvel most of all: "Few objects are more striking than a country church with a zinc spire glittering in the noon-day sun."

This aging Englishman had adjusted himself so well to Montreal that he might have remained bishop indefinitely. But he had begun late and found himself approaching 70. Duty had made him accept his bishopric in 1869; duty made him resign from it in 1878. He returned to England. But he now found the English type of winter too much for him. He died at Biarritz, in southwestern France, in 1892, in his 84th year.

To the end he dwelt in memory on those nine years in Montreal, when Providence had so strangely plucked a man in his 60s out of his seclusion in Kent, out of his "quiet and humble post," and set him down as a bishop in a faraway city. God, he felt, had been good to him in giving those unexpected Montreal years.

The hazards of St. Mary's current

The current still seethes and swirls in the narrow channel between Ile Ste. Hélène and Montreal. But as a result of dredging or other causes, it is not what it once was. Narratives of about 200 years ago picture the current as almost a rapids, curling and tumbling as it rushed by.

Professor Benjamin Silliman of Yale University, crossing the St. Lawrence in 1819, saw St. Mary's current dashing along "almost with the rapidity of water bursting through a flood-gate."

The current was the greatest obstacle for the harbor of Montreal. Sailing ships fought it in mounting the river. Isaac Weld, in 1796, saw ships "with all their sails set, and with a smart and favorable breeze, stationary for an hour together in the stream, unable to stem it, between the island of St. Helene and the main land." It was no uncommon sight to see fleets of sailing ships lying at anchor for days, even for weeks, at the foot of the current, waiting for the wind to veer in their favor.

The first steamboats on the St. Lawrence were even less able to mount St. Mary's current, in the channel between Ile Ste. Hélène and Montreal, than were the sailing ships. With favorable winds, the sailing ships could come up the channel to the harbor; but the early steamboats were towed up the current by long ropes, pulled by oxen or horses, on the shore.

The difficulties of early steamboats in the current are described by Philippe Aubert de Gaspé in his account of a voyage from Quebec to Montreal in 1818. On an October evening he left the Queen's Wharf at Quebec on board the steamboat Caledonia. Between 7 and 8 the next morning his travelling companion, Robert Christie, opened the window of the stateroom and cried out, "We are going famously." But as they neared St. Mary's current the river stiffened. It was then necessary "to have recourse to the united strength of forty-two oxen to assist . . . in ascending the current."

The merchants of Montreal had plans of their own. Like others in the 19th century, they had an almost mystic faith in the steam engine. It was the new man-made force that could conquer all obstacles and put nature itself in subjection. The steam engine was a marvel — a symbol of romance and liberation.

In 1823 a group of Montreal merchants came together to finance tugboats with engines strong enough to come up the current, even when towing a ship. These merchants employed Capt. George Brush, a Vermonter, with much experience in boat-building and navigation on Lake Champlain and the St. Lawrence. Under his supervision Munn's Shipyard in Montreal built the tug Hercules and fitted it with an engine of 100 horsepower, made by J.D. Ward at the Eagle Foundry in Montreal — an engine built on the Bolton and Watt low-pressure principle. The name Hercules expressed the hope of the merchants that the tug would have a giant's powers. Their hope was justified. Under Brush's command, in May 1824, the Hercules steamed up St. Mary's Current, with the ship Margaret of Liverpool in tow. The Industrial Revolution seemed at last to have broken the current's long tyranny in the river.

For many years, however, conquering St. Mary's current remained a struggle. Steamboats appeared on the river with engines strong enough to mount the current without needing any tug to haul them. But it was a slow ascent, so slow at times as to seem almost motionless. About 1841 Sir Richard Bonnycastle was aboard a steamboat mounting the current. It was a night voyage and the dark shoreline and the bright starlight gave a stage-like setting to the contest. It was interesting, he wrote, "to look on the high bank, covered with houses and foliage, in the bright starlight, whilst we were, though applying immense power, sometimes perfectly stationary, amid the silent swiftness of the mighty river. Art here strove against Nature, whose majestic powers, exerted without visible efforts, seem proudly to condemn the puny insignificance of the imaginary lord of creation. Such is the strength and volume with which the St. Lawrence rushes along the broad channel of its bed at this place."

The current was so swift that it had been used for waterpower. A mill had been rebuilt by Capt. David Alexander Grant of Blairfindie, who had married the last baroness of Longueuil and had come into the management of her huge properties, which included Ile Ste. Hélène. This mill stood at the northern point of the island at a spot known as l'Eperon, or the

SKETCHBOOK

John Collins

The
RIVER
at
ST. HELEN'S ISLAND

Spur. The current was made to turn the millstones that ground out a fine flour.

St. Mary's current, hurrying between Ile St. Hélène and Montreal, was a formidable moat in the years when the island was garrisoned and fortified. The British government began to erect military buildings on Ile Ste. Hélène about 1807 and acquired the entire island from the Longueuil family in 1818. A garrison was maintained there until 1870. Though the current was useful for defence, it made it awkward to maintain communication with Montreal.

The "garrison boat," setting out from the military wharf in Montreal, was first rowed upstream some distance, close to the shore. When it was turned into the current and headed for Ile Ste. Hélène, it would be carried quickly downstream, no matter how hard the soldiers pulled on their oars. The line of navigation took the form of a U; the boat would be carried down a long way before the current was crossed. Then it was rowed upstream, close to the shore of the island.

Rowing the garrison boat across the current was considered so strenuous that the crews were changed every month.

The garrison boat, making its regular and disciplined trips to and fro, was fairly safe. But irregular crossings made by officers or men were often calamitous.

From time to time items reporting losses would appear in the newspapers. In the military cemetery of Ile Ste. Hélène are many graves of the current's victims.

A hall that attracted disaster

St. Patrick's Hall had been in use less than two years when it made sensational news for the whole city. On the evening of Feb. 3, 1869, more than 1,000 people (nearly 2,000, some accounts say) attended a concert in the Grand Hall of St. Patrick. After the concert, the chairs were removed. Dancing began.

Suddenly a sound, like the boom of a cannon, echoed down from overhead. The dance went on. Five minutes passed. That sound boomed again — this time like three cannon, fired one after the other. Dancing ceased. Some cried "Fire!," although no smoke or other smell of burning had drifted into the Grand Hall. Still others suggested a gas explosion. The crowd panicked.

St. Patrick's Hall was one of Montreal's most imposing buildings. It stood on the east side of Victoria Square, covering the whole 140 feet from Fortification Lane to Craig St. (now part of St. Antoine). It was to be a building with a brief, dramatic history. Thomas D'Arcy McGee was one of the chief speakers at the meeting on Jan. 8, 1866, when an appeal for subscribers was made. McGee estimated the Montreal Irish at 25,000, or perhaps a thousand or two more — "the most numerous class, except for the French Canadians." It was time that they "ought to contribute something as a people to the embellishment of the city."

Nothing could serve the needs of the Irish better than a meeting place. "We have our useful and excellent societies of men," said McGee, "all of whom want the periodical use of a hall and the habitual use of a committee room; we have our charitable bazaars and fairs; we have our occasional lectures on literary subjects for all which we need a convenient and central place of meeting."

St. Patrick's Hall was all Irish. The architect, J.W. Hopkins, based his design on Cormack's Chapel on the Rock of Cashel, a chapel erected in the 12th century, in the Romanesque style, in the kingdom of Munster. Details of the hall were derived from "those still to be found in certain portions of Ireland among the ruins of monasteries and chapels distributed throughout that interesting and beautiful island."

The ground floor was planned to yield revenue: it had "eight first-class shops with show windows." The next floor was like a club, with a library, billiards room, and committee rooms. Occupying the whole of the third floor was the Grand Hall of St. Patrick. It claimed to be the biggest hall in town. It could be used as a theatre (having a large stage with dressing rooms on either side) or it could be a ballroom.

An image of St. Patrick himself presided over the new building. It stood outdoors in a niche at the top of the building, in a line above the main entrance. And to make the Irishness of the hall complete, its cornerstone was laid on March 18, 1867. (St. Patick's Day that year fell on a Sunday and the secular celebrations were held on the Monday.) The ceremony was performed by Rev. Patrick Dowd, pastor of St. Patrick's Church.

On that winter evening in 1869, when booming sounds loud as explosions came from the roof of Montreal's biggest hall, some people remained calm, but most ran for the exits. The architect, aware of the possibility of an emergency, had provided sufficient ways out. The hall was soon cleared. The crowd had not left on a false alarm. Twenty-five minutes after the first overhead boom, the sound returned. This time it was "long, deep and very heavy, making a species of roar which lasted about 10 seconds." People half a mile away heard it.

The roof gave way. Its boiler plates, riveted together and girded, burst apart. They crashed on the Grand Hall's floor, which gave way in places under the impact. The roof then spilled down into the second storey. Firemen with torches probed the debris. They found four women and a child. All had huddled near the walls, "utterly powerless from terror." None was seriously harmed.

More than a thousand people had narrowly escaped death.

A committee was formed to find out what had happened. At first it was conjectured that the roof had given way under the weight of snow. But the final conclusion was that the collapse had resulted from the action of frost on the iron girders.

St. Patrick's Hall was reconstructed. This time

John Collins SKETCHBOOK. Victoria Square and Fortification Lane

wooden beams replaced the girders. The reconstruction was an opportunity to improve acoustics. The former plaster ceiling was replaced by a false ceiling made of cotton stretched on thin boards and the stage was moved to the opposite end.

The hall on Victoria Square had three years of uninterrupted usefulness. But on Oct. 2, 1872, at 2:25 a.m., the firemen were called to Craig St. Just around the corner from St. Patrick's Hall stood a high brick building. It was used as H.J. Shaw's auction rooms and the boot and shoe factory of Messrs. Ronayne & Co. This building was on fire. St. Patrick's Hall was separated from it only by a lane 12 feet wide. From the northeast a stiff wind carried the flames across. Even before the firemen could get to work the roof of the hall was ablaze.

The Montreal Witness, always alert to a temperance angle in the news, hinted that St. Patrick's Hall might have been saved "had our firemen managed to keep dryer inside." *The Gazette* declared that the firemen "exhibited no signs

whatever of being in the slightest degree under the influence of liquor." The Witness, in a later edition, withdrew its charge. The trouble lay not with the firemen but with their equipment. Their hoses, especially at the couplings, were leaking: "almost as much water went on the street as on the fire."

In the dark, the fire assumed fierce grandeur. "At about 4 o'clock," said one eye-witness, "the conflagration presented a very brilliant spectacle. The whole interior of the hall was a sheet of fire. . . . The zinc-covered spires of adjacent churches reflected the glare, and though not a lamp was lit for fear the gas might explode, the surrounding streets were as light as at midday. Dense showers of burning embers were driven by each gust of wind . . . burning tiny holes into the wooden pavement."

St. Patrick's Hall was a total loss. A passer-by described "the ruins — gaunt and blackened, even on the sunniest day, and cold-looking and weird in the moonlight." After two such calamities in so brief a time, St. Patrick's Hall was not rebuilt.

North America's oldest swimming club

In the early 1950s Justice Joseph Archambault had an invigorating way of spending the lunchtime adjournment of his court. At noon he left his stuffy room in the old courthouse on Notre Dame St. and set out for Ile Ste. Hélène. In half an hour he would be at the Montreal Swimming Club. There he'd swim for half an hour, then bathe in the sun. He would have a light lunch at the club's canteen.

Archambault wasn't alone in spending the lunchtime recess at the Montreal Swimming Club. Men of all professions and occupations took advantage of the facilities during a sunny summer noon. Saturdays, Sundays and other holidays saw crowds at the club. On such days, said Archambault, it was not rare "to see at the club 1,500 swimmers taking advantage of the refreshing water and the pure air."

Until the formation of the Montreal Swimming Club, Montreal had been a big city on an island where swimmers had little access to the waterfront. A civic bylaw made waterfront swimming illegal. The club was founded in 1876. It had seen its chance. An ideal site had become available: the old military wharf, not far from the site of today's aquarium. This wharf was a relic of the days when the island had been a military station, fortified to defend Montreal from American invasion. In those days connection between Ile Ste. Hélène and Montreal was maintained by the garrison boat, a big rowboat with soldiers at the oars. The Montreal Swimming Club entered into direct negotiation with the federal Department of Militia, as the defence department was then known. Permission was granted on June 2, 1877, and confirmed in 1886 and 1888, to make use of the old wooden wharf and part of the adjacent ground.

This club ranked as the oldest swimming club in North America. From the 1870s till the 1960s it made the St. Lawrence available to Montrealers. It trained swimmers who became champions, record-setters, Olympic contestants. The club offered its facilities free to orphans and others in need, and held its fees so low that almost anybody, youngster or adult, could afford to join. And all its services were provided without any government grants or public campaigns. It was a public facility, privately provided for.

The Montreal Swimming Club put up a clubhouse — a plain, long wooden building. From time to time it sagged and leaned, and had to be straightened. At no time could the club be considered "posh." Facilities were sparse. But far from feeling itself underprivileged, the Montreal Swimming Club revelled in its plain, simple, almost primitive accommodations. It didn't wish to attract the fashionable and the idle. It was first and always a club for those who found exercise, relaxation and friendly competition in swimming.

At one end of the clubhouse was the changing area: only a wooden wall. It screened the members from the island side, but was exposed to the river. Members undressed in the open air. Senior members had certain privileges. Their changing area was separated by wooden bars; it was known as the "Bares' Cage." They all had full wooden lockers. Junior members or visitors used the "Basket Room." Here their clothes were put into baskets, instead of lockers, and the baskets were pulled up toward the ceiling.

The club's Spartan mood prevailed in other ways. Till the 1930s there was no running water in its clubhouse: facilities were of the "outdoor" type. It had no bar. Gambling was prohibited, though gin rummy could be played. There was no dining room. The concession, or canteen, had only a rudimentary stock — cigarettes, chocolate bars, and just enough for the plainest of lunches: sandwiches and coffee.

No discrimination was permitted as to race or creed. The club had anglophone and francophone founders, in more or less equal numbers. But the club didn't admit women. They had been admitted for a few years, in the 1880s and 1890s, but the cost of trying to accommodate their requirements led to a financial crisis. President and directors decided "to abolish the ladies' branch and to take strict measures of economy."

In all the club's history, from the 1870s to the 1960s, no one ever drowned. The record of safety came largely from the fact that the club considered itself an educational institution, a place for instruction in swimming. It engaged its first

John Collins SKETCHBOOK
Montreal Aquarium — St. Helen's Island

swimming master, Urgel Roussin, as far back as the 1870s.

Records were set by members. In 1889, C.E. Benedict swam 1,000 yards in 17 minutes, 58 seconds, beating the American record by 59½ seconds. George Vernot honored the club by coming second in the 1,500-metre freestyle Olympic race at Antwerp in 1920 and third in the 400-metre freestyle. In Canadian contests the club produced an amazing array of champions. Other members were innovators, such as Emile Bouchard, one of the first exponents of the crawl stroke in Canada.

The Montreal Swimming Club was among the first in the country to adopt water polo, introduced in 1887. Chris Goulden, the club's president and later honorary president, was one of the founders of the Canadian Aquatic Polo League and donated the Goulden Challenge Cup for the Canadian championship. The club's team won the Canadian water-polo championship for eight consecutive years, winning 51 games without a single defeat.

The time came, however, when the club could carry on no longer, victim of a changing way of life. Swimming pools were becoming common. Every community had them. Many people had them in their yards. The automobile age, with its better highways, had also given easy access to the lakes of the Laurentians, the Eastern Townships and elsewhere. Club membership had been dwindling. Then came the preparations for Expo 67. Ile Ronde was to be joined to Ile Ste. Hélène. The Montreal Swimming Club was in the path of the new project.

To Jack Steinberg, the last president, fell the obligation of disbanding the club and winding up its affairs. At the aquarium on Ile Ronde, now the club's approximate site, a tablet commemorates its history. The inscription reads:

MONTREAL SWIMMING CLUB
1876-1967
ON THIS SITE WAS LOCATED
THE OLDEST SWIMMING CLUB IN
NORTH AMERICA

Young Victorians just having fun

The Heather Bell Snow Shoe Club of the 1880s and 1890s was very unusual in Montreal: unusual in being a mixed club with male and female members. Nor did the women play secondary roles. They held many of the offices. Often one became president.

It was a young people's club — young people having a good time together under the winter moon. Unlike other clubs, it wasn't trying to prove anything. It was not competitive. It didn't run races against other clubs or try to become champions. It wasn't seriously athletic or strenuous. It existed only for the members' amusement, high-spirited, joking and carefree.

So noisy were its members at times that onlookers were startled. Returning from a tramp on the mountain, and coming down Peel St., "the club shouted and sang, causing numerous faces to look through window blinds to see what was the matter." Once the club had a run-in with authority. The minute book for Jan. 30, 1889, recorded: "Here, I am sorry to relate, we had our first altercation with outsiders. Bro. Essery was checked by a park ranger for shouting and making too much noise. The affair, however, ended without any serious results, which was just as well for the sake of the club's good name."

Members followed the customary snowshoers' route up Peel St., then along the pathway up the mountain — the path above Peel, just west of the stone wall of Sir Hugh Allan's old residence, Ravenscrag (now the Allan Memorial Institute). Unlike the other clubs, Heather Bell's members did not go over the mountain in their tramps. They went only as far as the toboggan slide, not far from what is now Beaver Lake. The pace was leisurely. If some members lagged behind, the others waited patiently till they came up. The last pair up were joked about. Why had they taken so long?

At the toboggan slide the tobogganers invited some of the girls to take a trip down. Generally they went down several times. Other members of the club tramped about to keep warm. In one of these waiting periods the secretary of the club ran into trouble. He wrote in his minutes: "Here I may mention the Sec was, to use a common phrase, 'set on' by the caretaker of the slide for going into the club room with his shoes on, for a glass of water for the ladies." On every tramp the members of Heather Bell were out to enjoy themselves. All were young, all lively. Everything about the tramp became fun. They laughed when heckled by idle bystanders as they made their way through the town on the way to the mountain. One of the men carried refreshments in the hood that was hanging down his back. From time to time the members stopped while these refreshments, peppermints or confectionery, were handed round.

They indulged in spontaneous antics. They tossed each other into the snow. On Jan. 30, 1889, they were tramping beside high drifts. "The members were not slow to avail themselves of this favorable opportunity," says the minute book, "and quite a number 'bit the snow'." Suddenly they might start dancing on snowshoes. On Dec. 6, 1889, the secretary wrote: "Everyone seems in the best of spirits. Dancing on snowshoes is a very difficult thing to do, but some of the members manage it, especially the polka."

At times, snowshoes were turned into toboggans, not for the park toboggan slide but for going down some of the mountain slopes, or down the long flights of wooden stairs leading back to the city. They slid down by crossing their snowshoes at the tail and sitting on them. Some girls went down in tandem. Sliding down the long stairs was easier than plodding down, one step at a time. But the wild descent was enough to "take the breath away." It also ended in something of a shock. "I must say," wrote one of the secretaries, "some were not altogether satisfied with the sensation produced by landing at the bottom."

The fun of the Heather Bell snowshoe tramps continued when the members, back in town, went on for a club meeting in one of the members' homes. These were "merry" evenings of "incessant laughter." Games, solos, duets, piano playing and refreshments were followed by a business meeting. The president would call for order, but order was hard to get. "The president called order," wrote the secretary on Nov. 17, 1890, "but no one seemed to hear the demand or pretended not to hear." The

president kept calling out: "Tom, keep quiet! Bert, sit down!" At another meeting, order at last prevailed and the business proceeded. Then Lily Camp "literally brought down the house" when she cried out: "Oh! mother, Katy has got her arms around Bertie!"

The records of the Heather Bell Snow Shoe Club show that young Victorians knew how to have fun.

To Kingston by coach and boat

On the morning of Aug. 3, 1838, Charles Kadwell stood in the courtyard of the Exchange Coffee House, Montreal's principal stagecoach inn, about to set out for Kingston in Upper Canada. The journey would be an adventure. He wouldn't reach Kingston for two days. On the way he would have to change, again and again, between stagecoaches and steamboats.

Four steamboats were used for travelling over the smooth stretches of the river and three coaches for the drives along the shore past the rapids. The journey to Kingston was so big an undertaking, and one bound to have so many picturesque incidents, that he decided to record it all, day by day, in a special diary.

The journey began from the court of the Exchange Coffee House, near the northeast corner of St. Paul and St. Pierre Sts. It was entered from both streets through long, narrow passageways. Kadwell's coach drove off through one of these passages. Kadwell noted the hour: half-past 10. First stop was the village of Les Tanneries, now St. Henri. When the horses had been watered, the coaches set out again. They moved through fine warm weather, by the farms on the way to Lachine. At Lachine the travellers left the stagecoach to go aboard the first of the steamboats.

It was the Henry Brougham, named for the lord chancellor of England. The Henry Brougham shot ahead in fine style over the broad waters of Lac St. Louis. Lunch was served aboard, for 50 cents. When the steamboat came to the Cascades, rapids prevented any further navigation. All passengers went ashore and into a stagecoach again. The coach went lurching and bumping along very rough roads. Kadwell had brought a mackintosh with him to protect him from rainy weather. In the coach he found another purpose for it. "My 'macintosh' I found very acceptable in another quality," he wrote in his diary; "indeed throughout the terra-firma part of my journeying its place was generally 'a posteriori'."

The stagecoach took the passengers past two furious rapids, the Cascades and the Cedars. At Coteau du Lac, above the Cedars, the steamboat Neptune was waiting for them at the wharf. The Neptune, being "a regular old tub," moved slowly. Night was setting in. Kadwell, walking the deck, saw fires along the shore, lighted to attract fish for spearing. The Neptune put in at Lancaster. Kadwell was now in the Glengarry country settled by the Highlanders. He was scarcely impressed, as his diary reveals: "Generally speaking, they are a rough uncouth set of fellows, conversing principally in the Gaelic dialect. . . . They pride themselves exceedingly in bedecking themselves in tartan and feathers, etc., which some of the 'ultras' carry to such an extent as almost to raise a blush with sober people for the true dignity of 'poor human nature'."

The Neptune steamed on to Cornwall. It arrived in the early morning. Kadwell had no time to see the town. Coaches were waiting. He hardly had time "to accomplish the necessary ablutions."

Sharp at 5 the coaches were rolling through Cornwall's streets by dawn's white light. In the prevailing silence the wheels made an odd hollow echo. Only when the shutter of some house happened to open, as the coaches moved by, was assurance given that the procession was not passing through a deserted village. The road ran close by the river. Passengers had entrancing glimpses of the Long Sault rapids, "naught else than a sheet of dancing foam." At the wharf at Dickinson's Landing, above the Long Sault, lay two steamboats. They competed for the passengers from the stagecoaches. Some went aboard the steamboat Dolphin, others the Brockville. The two boats put out about the same time, with the Dolphin ahead. Kadwell had chosen the Dolphin. It was a pleasant August day on the river, with attractive farmhouses along the shore and small neat churches, with plover and snipe fluttering into view, and with other boats, their flags streaming in the strong warm wind, saluting the Dolphin with the ringing of their bells.

The keen air of the morning had made the passengers hungry as hunters. When they were called to dinner, Kadwell "made havoc among the good things which graced the table," especially a huge joint of roast beef. He did not linger among the wine-bibbers but went back to the deck.

The Dolphin put in at Prescott. This time, when the passengers went ashore, they did not board

JOHN COLLINS SKETCHBOOK, St. Paul and St. Peter

stagecoaches. That part of their journey was over. They would be taken the rest of the way by another steamboat, the William IV — a far bigger and stronger boat. It would go not only to Kingston but to Toronto, and would have to contend with the rough water of Lake Ontario.

Everyone went aboard the William IV. It went on to Brockville, then put out again at 6 o'clock in the evening. As it entered the Thousand Islands the moon rose over the river. For Charles Kadwell it was a scene of brooding but spirited romance like something pictured in the poems and novels of Sir Walter Scott. At times deer were seen moving about the islands or swimming from one to another. Kadwell wrote in his diary that the islands, with all their richness of foliage, seemed "floating as it were upon the surface of a mirror."

Morning dawned in a changed mood. The air was bitter; the deck was wet with dew; a dull fog dropped over the river. Penetrating dampness drove Kadwell indoors for the warmth of the engine room. His journey was nearing its end. Already Lake Ontario was in view. Back on deck he had his first glimpse of Kingston's fortifications through a spyglass borrowed from the sailing master. At 10 to 8 that morning, the William IV was in Kingston harbor.

Charles Kadwell's journey up the St. Lawrence was over. It was just two days since he had set out from the courtyard of Montreal's Exchange Coffee House. Repeated changes from stagecoaches to steamboats had made the journey slow and often uncomfortable. But signs of changing conditions were evident. Above Cornwall a canal was under construction. The era of slow journeys up the St. Lawrence, with their picturesque hardships, was already beginning to draw to its close.

When the river's ice held Montreal captive

Beginning in the 1840s, the captain of the first ocean vessel to reach Montreal in the spring was awarded a top hat. The gold-headed cane didn't come till later. The top hat was almost always awarded in May — the month when the port of Montreal was opened to ships from overseas. Today, with the port open the year round, it seems strange to think that in earlier times nearly half the year was over before the first sea vessel arrived.

Only twice during the two decades from 1829 to 1849 did overseas ships arrive earlier than May. In both cases they came very late in April — on April 27 and 30. Not till the 1890s did April displace May as the earliest month for port openings. Not till the early 1960s did March replace April. By 1964 the great leap forward took place, when the first overseas ship reached Montreal in January — the beginning of Montreal as a port that would never be closed.

The long delay in lengthening the period of navigation is explained mainly by the ice problem. The formation and persistence of the ice were natural phenomena. Men could do little, but had to wait upon nature every year. Every year Mother Nature closed the port, and every year she released it. She did it in her own way and in her own time.

The natural process of opening the port, known as the "Ice Shove," was one of the most powerful spectacles of its kind to be seen anywhere in the world. Montrealers crowded the waterfront to look on. Visitors who happened to be in the city were urged not to miss it. The Ice Shove generally came in March. Sometimes it was delayed until April. In 1855 the ice didn't begin to break up till St. George's Day, April 23.

The annual Ice Shove was awesome in its "stupendous power and irresistible force." Huge blocks of ice were tossed upward by an unseen force below. Twisted and curled, they mounted, one on top of the other, till they toppled and crashed upon the surrounding ice. It was a wild, massive struggle, always in movement, always with a voice. One observer described the mingled sounds: "Sometimes it is a noise as of grinding machinery . . . sometimes it is like the whirr of a humming-top; sometimes it is as the discharge of distant artillery; sometimes like all these combined."

The first ocean vessels that arrived in Montreal early in May had adventurous owners and captains. Their ships came with their sides scraped and battered by ice. The anxiety of passengers aboard these early ships is seen in a diary kept by Charles Kadwell. He sailed from Gravesend to Montreal in the spring of 1832 to take a position in the mercantile house of Gillespie and Moffatt. On May 2, while his ship was trying to enter the Gulf of St. Lawrence, he wrote: "Enclosed with ice nearly all round and obliged to keep sailing out to sea as far as we can and then into land again, but cannot help now and then having a knock, which makes a noise resembling thunder against the ship's sides, and is very unpleasant when in one's berth."

The year 1854 was one of the worst for ships on their way to Quebec or Montreal. In the gulf, ice smashed through the bow of the Marion on May 26, while it sailed westward of the Bird Rocks. Passengers were praised by Capt. Borland "for assisting in pumping the ship, as she made a great deal of water." Twenty-seven incoming ships found themselves, near the end of May, frozen in the ice.

"It looked as though we were in the Arctic regions we had heard so much about," wrote Donald Campbell, one of the passengers. Children from the ships went out to play on the ice and throw snowballs. Passengers visited from one ship to another. Provisions, though shared, ran low. Tea and biscuits were all that was left. One ship was crushed by the ice and sank. No passengers were aboard. The crew escaped to the ice, but fog had come on. They groped about for four days until it lifted, disclosing the position of the other ships. They went aboard for refuge. However, one of the men had died before the fog lifted. Altogether seven weeks went by before the ice broke and the ships escaped into clear water.

At Montreal the arrival of the first ships from overseas revived business after half a year of icy stagnation. Montreal merchants held sales to get rid

John Collins SKETCHBOOK HARBOR IN WINTER

of old stock and make room for the new. Additional clerks were hired, ready for the rush of trade when the new stock came in.

The coming of the first ship was cheered by crowds on the wharves. One ship, the Great Britain, set a record never equalled since. Its Montreal agents, Peter McGill & Co., advertised in 1843 that the Great Britain's master, Capt. Swinburn, would, "as usual," have the ship off to Canada in the spring ahead of all the others. The boast was justified. Between 1840 and 1850 the Great Britain came in first six times. (Only on the last voyage was Swinburn not the master.) Top hats were awarded for about 40 years. Gold-headed canes replaced them about 1880.

On Jan. 4, 1964, everything was suddenly changed. The Helga Dan, a small Danish merchant ship, sailed into port. It was the first ship to arrive so early in the New Year, yet for that 1963-64 season the port had never been closed. It would never be closed again. Montreal had become a year-round port.

This revolution in navigation seemed sudden. Actually it was the final result of years of innovation. The Canadian Coast Guard's icebreakers had been conquering the ice more and more effectively. New types of merchant ships had reinforced hulls. An elaborate system of navigational aids had become available.

Major works controlled the ice at strategic locations along the river.

The annual custom of awarding a gold-headed cane, however, has been continued. Though this ceremonial presentation no longer marks the opening of the shipping season, it has now become a means of repeatedly reminding the world that the port of Montreal, though far inland, has become open to the sea in all seasons.

The bishop who rescued Irish orphans

One day in 1847 a strange and sad procession moved through the streets of Montreal — a procession of carriages. In the first of them sat Msgr. Ignace Bourget, the French-Canadian Roman Catholic bishop. In the carriages following were nuns, Sisters of Charity of Providence. All the carriages, from first to last, were crowded with orphans.

These orphans weren't French Canadian, but Irish. All had become orphans within the last few months, weeks or days. Recalling that procession, Bourget was later to say: "One of the sweetest moments of my life was, when, at the head of this crowded family of little orphans, I moved through the streets of the city, to take them to the refuges prepared for them." These hundreds of Irish children had found themselves orphans in a strange land, thousands of miles from home. Help had to come from strangers. They were being rescued by a French-Canadian bishop, aided by French-Canadian nuns.

Before they were driven away in carriages, the orphans had been herded together in sheds at Point St. Charles, near the Montreal waterfront. "This scene in the children's sheds was beyond description," says one account. "Their wailing was heard far and wide." Ireland in 1847 and 1848 had been gripped by the Great Potato Famine and by the Great Pestilence. Failure of the potato crop had left thousands to starve. Then came typhus. Port towns were crowded by thousands seeking escape over the Atlantic.

Immigrant ships soon became "fever ships." Many passengers were buried at sea. Others, arriving sick, were taken ashore to die on Grosse Ile, the quarantine station in the St. Lawrence below Quebec. The "seemingly well" were sent on. By the time they reached Montreal, thousands more were stricken with typhus.

Everything done at Point St. Charles to receive this oncoming tide of the sick was hasty and makeshift. The beds were wooden bunks. The sick were carried to them, two or three to a bunk. Many died quickly. Dead and living sometimes lay side by side for a long time. Children clung to dead parents. Gradually some order was established. Children were gathered together in separate sheds. There Bishop Bourget saw them: "The spectacle of hundreds of children, famishing with hunger, covered with rags and in danger of succumbing to the attack of that terrible disease, which had deprived them of their parents, was so poignant that it can never be forgotten."

The sheds were visted by Lord Mark Kerr, aide-de-camp to the governor-general, Lord Elgin. He wrote in his journal on June 27, 1847: "It is a most melancholy sight. They bury about 25 a day. I saw the burials going on in a piece of ground railed off. . . . The coffins everywhere, and women lying on them, and crying and embracing them before they are buried; one girl, alone on her father's or mother's coffin, was a most affecting picture."

The Irish community of Montreal was doing what it could to help. But it was as yet a new community, mostly immigrants recently arrived. It still lacked the resources and institutions to deal with an emergency of such dimensions. The needs had to be met mainly by the French-Canadian bishop and the orders of nuns in his diocese. The Grey Nuns went to the sheds; so did the Sisters of Providence. The bishop even released the nuns of the Hôtel Dieu from their vows of cloistered life, so they could serve also. He himself worked in the sheds, along with Sulpicians, Jesuits and other clergy.

Faced with the problem of hundreds of Irish orphans, Bourget appealed to Mother Gamelin, who had founded the Sisters of Charity in Montreal. These were the sisters who had joined with the bishop in the procession of carriages he led through the streets of Montreal, as the orphans were taken to the refuges Mother Gamelin had made ready.

Bourget realized that crowding these orphans into institutions wasn't the answer. They needed the warmth of home life; they needed new parents; they needed to feel they belonged to families. In March 1848 the bishop wrote a pastoral letter and commanded that it be read by the priests in all parishes of his diocese. It was an appeal to their parishioners to take "these poor orphans" into their homes: "Receive them, without considering either, that they may be a burden to you; for you know very well that charity, to have any merit, means thinking of others more than of yourself."

THE IRISH STONE

SKETCHBOOK

Collins *on the approach to Victoria Bridge*

Some people had already come to adopt orphans. He had seen "with what emotion" the children watched the faces of these visitors, "in the hope of being fortunate enough to be chosen." The bishop appealed in his pastoral letter: "Receive, pious and charitable laymen, and adopt these helpless children with that cordial joy that is the characteristic of true charity. . . . Is this not the time, if ever, to put into practice these touching words of Our Lord: 'As you would that men should do to you, do also to them in like manner.'?"

The response was prompt and openhearted. Parishioners from the country districts joined with Montrealers in coming to take Irish orphans into their homes.

In the desperate confusion of the sheds, no records could be kept of the dead. All were buried unnamed in common graves in the middle of Bridge St. near the entrance to the Victoria Bridge:

TO
PRESERVE FROM DESECRATION
THE REMAINS OF 6,000
IMMIGRANTS
WHO DIED OF SHIP FEVER
A.D. 1847-48

Most of the Irish orphans were brought up as French Canadians. As Bourget had said, "brought up in our midst," they would "make common cause with us." They married French Canadians. Among the thousands of French Canadians today with Irish blood are descendants of these orphans rescued by Bishop Bourget from the fever sheds in the 1840s.

Boys would be boys – and usually bad

"Even to those who enjoy the use of vigorous and agile limbs, it is a considerable annoyance to have to skip and pirouette and display all kinds of improvised gymnastics." The Gazette made this complaint on Dec. 10, 1870. It was condemning boys who came down Montreal's hills on their sleds. For the sake of their own safety, these boys were using the sidewalks. Any pedestrian might have to leap out of the way.

The pedestrians' anger came not only from the danger of being sent flying; it came also from the insolence of the boys. They would ride "exultingly by." Angry pedestrians, escaping injury, were in a mood to inflict their own immediate vengeance. "But vengeance is the policeman's," said The Gazette. "Let him only raise the baton, or his voice, and this nuisance will soon disappear. We would also recommend that offenders should be punished according to age — on a 'sliding scale,' this is. The sight of an overgrown youth indulging in the streets in this amusement is absolutely intolerable." The trouble was that the police did little to protect the pedestrian. "Policemen wink at it all," The Gazette deplored, "and the city foot passengers expostulate in vain."

At times, however, the police caught a culprit in the act. The recorder viewed the offence seriously in his court at city hall, where he dealt with offences against the bylaws. One boy, John Murphy, was brought to court after a night in jail. He had been sidewalk-sledding down Beaver Hall Hill. The recorder lectured him. Sliding on sidewalks was prohibited by law because it "might be the cause of mischief to others."

A few days earlier a merchant, walking down the hill, came to a stretch of sidewalk where the ice had been polished "by the sleighs of boys rushing down." The merchant slipped. Ever since this fall he had been in bed, lying on his back. The recorder warned the boy that if he were ever caught again sliding on the sidewalk of Beaver Hall Hill, he would "be very severely punished." The boy was dismissed, "very glad to get away."

Troubles with boys who became public nuisances appear in the records even before the municipal government was established — in the days when

Montreal was administered by magistrates. The magistrates met from time to time to consider the city's problems. As far back as 1787 they had to do something about the broken pump in Place d'Armes. At that time Montreal had no regular water supply. Many citizens had pumps in their back yards; public pumps were provided at convenient locations, where any citizen could draw water.

The problem was that boys had been playing with the Place d'Armes pump and "abusing" it. They had ended by putting it out of order. Even if it were repaired, it could not be watched at all times. The only way to protect the pump was to build a fence around it. A chain and lock would be fixed to the pump's handle. Anyone wishing to use the pump would have to get a key made at his own expense. It was all bothersome, but something had to be done to keep the boys away.

Boys were troublesome with other antics. They made the streets noisy. This was bad enough on weekdays, but they were as noisy on Sundays. In 1799, and again in 1803, the magistrates deplored that boys and other idle persons were gathering "in numbers on Sundays for the purpose of play and amusement in the streets, squares and other places of the town." They had been making so much noise in Place d'Armes on Sundays in 1799 that worshippers in Notre Dame Church were disturbed. Constables with staves were stationed in Place d'Armes to disperse the culprits. In 1803 such disturbances in any part of town on a Sunday were penalized with a fine of 10 shillings for each offence.

Boys even misbehaved in a manner shocking to the ladies. They were swimming in the river in front of the town, "stripping themselves naked upon the beach." The magistrates deplored their behavior, saying: "This practice has not been confined to the dark of any evening or to an early hour of the morning but at every hour of the day to the great scandal of His Majesty's well disposed subjects whose houses front the river or who may be inclined to enjoy the benefit of a walk and fresh air of the evening." This practice was condemned as "tending to shock the delicacy of the female character in particular." In future any boys caught bathing nude on the waterfront would be fined five shillings.

SKETCHBOOK

John Collins

PERILS
of a
VICTORIAN
WINTER

Perhaps the most dangerous public annoyance came when the boys played with catapults. Stones could be catapulted almost as dangerously as bullets could be fired. Police had orders to arrest catapulters and confiscate their weapons. The danger was seen in 1856, when some boys gathered at the corner of Notre Dame and St. François Xavier. Another boy appeared, wearing a tall straw hat known as a "cheo." Such a hat was an attractive target. A piece of gravel was adjusted in a catapult and sent flying. The aim was too high. It missed the hat and struck the plate-glass window of Wilson's boot and shoe store. Plate glass was still unusual at that time. George Wilson was proud when it had been installed in his shop. He came outdoors from time to time just to stand in the street and admire it.

The piece of gravel from the catapult hit the window in the middle. It did not go through but sent cracks spreading out in all directions. Wilson was out in a moment. He stared at his window, "amazed, speechless, aghast." No boys were to be seen. None had lingered to find out what had happened. The sound of glass was enough for them. They were off in a moment.

The culprit who fired the stone had the "awful experience" of being a fugitive from justice. When sent on errands to the post office, not far from Wilson's shop, he came and went by the back door. He felt shadowed, never knowing when he might feel a firm hand gripping his shoulder. He was never caught, but he had learned a lesson. His catapulting days were over. His friends observed that "though mischief was inseparable from him," the catapult had no part in his later adventures.

Watching the ships come in

A century ago Montrealers came down to the port in thousands as spectators. Sundays, in particular, brought the crowds. They came to enjoy the waterfront, the sight of the river and the coming and going of the ships.

Provision had been made for these spectators. They could view the port to best advantage from a waterfront boardwalk built along the top of the high revetment wall — the heavy stone wall built to hold back the river when it overflowed its banks, especially when the ice floating downsteam in the spring piled up against Ile Ste. Hélène or Ile Ronde and formed a dam.

This wall ran the whole length of the harbor, all the way from the mouth of the Lachine Canal to Hochelaga, a distance of 1½ miles. The wharves where the ships were loaded and unloaded were 10 feet below the wall. A guidebook of 1884 said that spectators "leaning against the protecting rail" could "see at a glance the whole business of the port spread out below them."

The variety of vessels made a fascinating show: from the great transatlantic steamers to such small river craft as barges for hay or wood. Ships were there from many faraway countries — from the ports of the British Isles, France, Germany, Holland. From the Mediterranean came cargos of wines, from China tea. Flags flew of all colors and designs. The age of sail had by no means ended.

Three-masted vessels were still arriving, many of them from Scandinavia. Masts towered beside smokestacks. Variety was increased by Canadian craft — the sailing ships from the Maritimes and from the St. Lawrence River below Montreal. Among them were the oyster schooners. When they arrived in port, they became floating oyster bars. Anyone with 25 cents was welcomed aboard. Oysters were in barrels. They were also shovelled up from the ship's hold and heaped on deck. Heavy planks were laid across barrels. There the oyster eaters stood and "literally dug into the heaps of bivalves."

The boardwalk along the harbor presented an intensely varied and active scene to the spectator at all times of the day. As he leaned on the railing, and saw it all taking place before his eyes, he might find himself in dreamy reveries. As Alfred Sandham wrote in one of his books, *Picturesque Montreal,* in 1876: "A tour around the waterfront is full of charms; the scenes and incidents have no uncommon fascination."

Though the scene was fascinating at all times, Sandham believed that it was most memorable at dawn. The harbor was then awakening. The rising sun brought into clearer relief the clusters of masts and rigging "woven against the receding night clouds." The desert-like stillness broke suddenly into a fretful roar. Shutters at the warehouses were thrust aside, doors opened. The river smoothly lapping the piers in darkness broke into a surfy tumult as it was beaten by ships' paddlewheels. Gangways were opened to the vessels. Men began carrying boxes from deck to wharf. Again appeared the heavy drays drawn by powerful horses and laden with tons of merchandise. The harbor was aroused and awake and busy with movement.

The same awakening of the port, seen every morning through the season, was seen on an even grander scale at the end of April or the beginning of May. Then the port, after the long winter closing, made ready for its annual reopening. The earliest seen in the port of Montral, and the last to leave, were the river steamboats — the ferries and the ships sailing to nearby points down the St. Lawrence or up the Ottawa. Long before the first ocean steamer arrived in port, the river boats made their appearance. As far back as 1821 they were arriving in a dramatic burst.

The Montreal Herald for May 2, 1821, reported: "On Saturday last our harbor presented a gay and animated spectacle, in the arrival of no less a number than eight steamboats, with flags flying from their wintering station at William Henry [now Sorel]. The air of novelty and bustle thus given to a scene, where all had been dull and dormant during the winter months, attracted to the beach a long line of spectators." Later many Montrealers came to the waterfront to watch for the first ship from across the ocean.

A character regularly seen in the 1890s was an old sea captain wearing a peaked cap. He had long been ashore and was now spending his time down by the river, watching the life of the harbor. He knew all

SKETCHBOOK

The Boardwalk along the waterfront

about everything that was going on. He knew the waterfront workers — who they were, who they had been, what might become of them. The workers he had learned about included a former English clergyman. For several seasons one of London's most brilliant barristers was employed on the Montreal wharves as a stevedore, at the roughest, hardest work. The captain replied, when asked what had happened to this man: "Oh, drink, or a woman, as usual, I suppose."

Of a very different class were the young students, working on the waterfront to pay their college expenses. "Why, not 100 miles from this city today," the captain would say, "there is a brilliant young doctor who worked hereabouts as a common laborer at the most menial task. He was a farmer's son from the backwoods with plenty of ambition and very little money, and he did what he set out to do."

Though others thought anything seen in the distance must be the first ship from overseas, the old captain never erred. In the end, when a speck appeared in the far distance and none of the other watchers could even be sure whether it was a ship or not, he would announce its name, then leave the crowd with a wave of the hand, and hurry to the wharf where the ship would berth.

Overcrowding and uproars on steamboats

Maintaining order was sometimes a problem for captains aboard steamboats on the St. Lawrence. The boats often had steerage, where hundreds of passengers, mostly immigrants, crowded together in great discomfort. Conditions in the steerage favored quarrels and fights.

Many ocean ships did not come upstream to Montreal. They did better to put their passengers ashore at Quebec and get out to sea again, to make as many transatlantic voyages as possible. Passengers were taken up the river to Montreal in the paddle-wheeled steamboats. Those who travelled on first- or second-class tickets were generally comfortable and satisfied. Those herded into the steerage were soon in a mood to quarrel among themselves or even to rise in a riot. Discord was all the more likely when immigrants of many races and languages mixed uncomfortably in close quarters.

Conditions were made still worse when a steamboat proprietor engaged in the practice of increasing profits by opening a bar in the steerage. Before a boat had gone many miles the steerage was in an uproar of "swearing, fighting and scuffling." Generally the captain and his officers ignored what went on in the steerage. The immigrants down there were left to settle their own quarrels as best they could. But from time to time, the roar from below became so loud that something had to be done.

What was done was sometimes drastic. Dr. J.J. Bigsby, travelling by steamboat to Montreal, witnessed an incident, pathetic in its way, when an Irishman, fighting drunk, was put ashore: "Having been, and continuing to be, extremely troublesome, he was forcibly set on shore, ignorant both of the people and the language. As we paddled off I saw him, shillelagh in hand — for it had been thrown to him — vaporing away alone on the beach, by the side of his little bundle."

Not only immigrants travelling in the steerage might threaten the peace and order of a river steamboat. The raftsmen were a tough lot, hard to handle when they went wild. They came down the Ottawa River with timber rafts, then down the St. Lawrence to Quebec. Having delivered the rafts, they took passage back in the river steamboats. One gang of about 20 raftsmen came aboard a steamboat at Quebec on June 28, 1858. As the boat moved toward Montreal they came up from the steerage and surged into the area of the cabin passengers. They demanded liquor from the steward. He refused. A gigantic raftsman, leader of the gang, snatched up a chair. He hurled it at the steward's head. Then he called on his followers to seize the ship and kill the captain.

Capt. A.M. Rudolf, told of what was going on, came down from his cabin. He found the raftsmen already driving passengers and crew to the boat's bow. The raftsman then made himself a barricade on the deck. Rudolf reappeared. Alone he stepped up to the barricade and spoke to the menacing giant, urging him to be sensible. But the giant, towering over the captain, muttered vengeance and murder.

The captain ordered his crew to encircle the barricade. They obeyed, feeling it would be safe so long as the giant did not burst through the only opening he had left for himself. This, however, was the first thing he did. The crew scurried off. The captain stood deserted. He turned to the passengers who were looking down from the promenade deck above. He pleaded for someone to support him.

One passenger — only one — volunteered. He came down from the promenade deck, armed himself with a handpike, and stood beside the captain. Rudolf again spoke to the raftsman, ordering him to drop the big bowie knife. But the raftsman raised the knife and plunged forward. The one passenger stood his ground. When the raftsman was only a few inches away, he hit him hard on the arm with the handpike. The arm broke under the blow and flopped, useless, at his side. The riot was over.

The passengers who had held back now came forward. One of them spoke for all: "I think I speak the opinion of all passengers when I say Capt. Rudolf deserves our thanks for the manner in which, at the peril of his own life, he restored and maintained order under the most trying circumstances."

Passengers on steamboats who paid the higher fares were rarely troubled on their upper deck by such wild surges from the steerage passengers down

PADDLE-WHEEL STEAMBOATS
IN THE PORT OF MONTREAL

IN THE LAST CENTURY
THEY CARRIED THE CITY'S
PRODUCTS and PEOPLE UP
AND DOWN THE RIVER

John Collins SKETCHBOOK

below. And over the years the amenities for first-class passengers increased. The Scottish publisher William Chambers, travelling by steamboat from Quebec to Montreal in 1853, exclaimed: "A person accustomed to the river vessels of England would be startled with the first view of the magnificent apartment." He saw Persian carpets, elegant armchairs and sofas, cut-glass chandeliers, vases of flowers, door handles of gilt porcelain or ivory. The staterooms were "rigorously clean and commodious." There was even an elegant barbershop.

As the publisher was "wandering over the vessel" he came upon the steerage. It was "an unpleasant spectacle" — crowded, a confused jumble, gin being rapidly sold, "a fight among several men, and all sorts of disagreeable noises." Chambers concluded: "I was fain to retreat, pitying the unfortunate beings who were condemned to pass a night within its fetid precincts."

Remembering 1799

Few men have had a longer life than William Henderson. He lived to be 100. As late as 1883 he could look back on his coming to Montreal in 1799.

His journey over the Atlantic in a sailing ship was made unusually rapid by favorable winds. It took only seven weeks. Henderson, a Scot from the Shetland Islands, was 16 at that time. He was coming to Montreal as an articled clerk to a wholesale merchant. When he arrived, there were no wharves. The ship anchored in the river as near as possible to the bank. Passengers were taken ashore in the ship's boats. Cargo was unloaded on rafts. In wet weather the shore was deep in mud.

Henderson had taken passage in the Eweretta (a name that appears in many spellings), a ship held in unique esteem by Montrealers. No other ship could be counted on to come to Montreal every year without fail. That voyage was the only one it made each season. It came every spring — so early that the timbers of its sides were scarred by the ice still floating in the river.

After unloading, the Eweretta lay all summer in the river near the foot of St. Sulpice St. (then called St. Joseph). It sailed for London every autumn, on Oct. 28. On that day business transactions for the year were closed. The ship left laden with furs. Many fur-traders left also. They spent the winter in England or Scotland. In the Eweretta they came back to Montreal in the spring.

The Eweretta was so much the Montrealers' ship, said Henderson, that "it would not be deemed safe to venture across the ocean in any other — at all events it would have been most unpatriotic." Captains of the Eweretta, Henderson said, were always "well-bred, gentlemanly men." They frequented the best society in Montreal. They were invited to the banquets of the exclusive club of the fur traders, the Beaver Club. They returned such hospitality by giving dinners and dances aboard the ship.

Henderson himself had "the honor and distinction" of being invited to the Beaver Club. There he saw James McGill, the fur-trader who founded McGill University. In 1860 the principal of McGill, William (later Sir William) Dawson, was preparing an article on the university's founder. As McGill had died in 1813, Dawson could find no one who had ever seen him — no one except William Henderson. Henderson described McGill as he had seen him at the Beaver Club — "a very old man, at one of the meetings, singing a voyageur's song with accurate ear and sonorous voice, and imitating, paddle in hand, the action of the bow-man in a 'North canoe' in ascending a rapid." He said McGill's " 'Indian haloos' (the war whoops) at the close of each stanza" were "never to be forgotten."

The Montreal that Henderson had known in 1799 was still enclosed by the old stone fortifications built during the French régime. They confined the town (roughly speaking) within what is now McGill St. on the west to Berri St. on the east, and from Commissioners St. on the south to about Fortifications Lane on the north. Outside the walls were straggling suburbs. There the houses (with some notable exceptions) were mainly built of wood.

Henderson remembered when the whole large area from Beaver Hall Hill to St. Lawrence was still countrified: "It was laid out in small lanes, with here and there huts occupied by laborers and carters. These lanes were cul-de-sacs, terminating at different orchards below the mountain." Within the walls many of the old houses of the French régime still stood on the narrow streets. Seasoned mortar had been used to join the fieldstones. Mortar and stones had combined "to render the walls as indestructible as a solid rock throughout." Such houses were spacious. Ceilings were lofty. Rooms were well lighted. Often they were panelled in the Louis XIV style.

Every effort had been made to protect houses from fire. Stone walls were immune to sparks or flames. Iron shutters could be closed to protect windows. Roofs generally were fireproofed with tin or sheet metal. Even if attics took fire, the rooms below remained safe. Flagstones, like those used in footpaths, had been laid beneath the attic floors. Such stones may still be seen under the attic flooring of the old Château Ramezay on Notre Dame St. Such precautions were all the more necessary at a time when the means of fighting fires were primitive. Montreal had no civic fire brigade. It had no

SKETCHBOOK

JOHN COLLINS

MONTREAL IN 1803 —
A VIEW FROM ILE STE. HÉLÈNE

effective water supply.

Henderson described the firefighting methods. When a fire broke out, the alarm (a church bell) kept sounding furiously till every man turned out. They formed long lines. Buckets were passed to and from the St. Lawrence or the little Rivière St. Martin (commonly called "the creek"), which flowed along Craig St. (now part of St. Antoine). In this way the fire engines were, mainly, supplied with water.

Another source of supply: the water carts that carried puncheons of water from the St. Lawrence to be sold by the bucket to Montreal householders. In case of fire the cart drivers received payment for every puncheon they brought to serve the fire engines. To encourage the water-cart men to get to the scene of a fire as quickly as possible, an extra payment was made to the first to arrive. Water-cart men, eager to get that premium, would refill their puncheons at the end of every day. They wanted to be ready to start at the first sound of an alarm during the night. Henderson remembered hearing the water carts "thundering along the streets, all wishing to get the prize."

William Henderson used to wonder at times why he took such pleasure in looking back and telling others what life was like in the long ago. He gave this explanation: "Oblivious of recent events, the memory of the aged seems to revert to the scenes of their youth with redoubled force. The pleasures of hope are reversed: while the present and future are gloomy and dark, the past is all beauty and sunshine. With the garrulousness of age, I could scribble volumes of ancient reminiscences."

Such were the charms of retrospection for William Henderson, a man who had so much more past than future to survey.

Professor Pepper's patented phantom

Early in 1873 Montrealers were presented with a most unusual kind of entertainment. Professor Pepper advertised that he would produce a ghost for all to see — and at an appointed hour. The scene of his demonstration was to be the stage of one of Montreal's chief theatres, the Queen's Hall on St. Catherine St., where Eaton's stands today.

The audience was not disappointed. The theatre was darkened. The stage showed a student pondering at his desk by the light of a lamp, a pile of books before him. Bookshelves stood in the background, and the moonlight streamed through two tall Gothic windows. It was a setting that suggested lonely speculations in the student's mind about the problems of life and death, and the strange realms of the supernatural. The sombre quietness of his room and the delicate moonlight all suggested that the rest of mankind was fast asleep, while he burned his midnight oil, seeking to penetrate the veil of life's mystery.

Suddenly there was a gasp from the audience. A ghost appeared on the stage, standing near the window, in the pale moonlight. It was the ghost of a young woman, wearing a long robe. In her hands she held a scrap of paper — a letter, it seemed — which she was anxiously reading, as if this had been a letter of great meaning in the last days, perhaps the last hours, of her life. That she seemed a veritable ghost, nobody could deny.

Clearly visible as she was to everyone, she was yet transparent and spectral. As she moved, she did not conceal the windows behind her, so that even the panes of glass could be seen clearly through her ghostly form. On the stage the student drew back in amazement, nearly overturning his lamp. He thrust back his chair, knocking a book to the floor. Then the ghost vanished as silently as she had come. And as the audience stared at the spot where she had been a moment before, she suddenly reappeared, still reading her letter as she moved in the gentle moonlight.

John Henry Pepper, FCS, had been producing such ghosts for many years. At first he made the ghost appear in a room that he had built in London for the purpose, the directors of the Polytechnic Joint Stock Co. putting up the money to finance the demonstration. It proved a most attractive venture. During the first year it was exhibited it brought in 12,000 pounds, though the directors reaped the benefit and the professor received only about 200 pounds.

Pepper's ghost must be one of the few in history that have been patented. Acting under this patent, the professor found that he no longer needed a special room for the performances but could cause the ghost to appear and disappear on the stage of any theatre. Pepper's ghost walked the celebrated boards of Drury Lane, as well as those of the Adelphi and Britannia theatres.

Then Professor Pepper took his ghost abroad. He caused it to appear on the stages of Paris. He brought it back to England and toured the theatres of the provinces. But the inevitable happened. Others intruded upon the professor's patent. The ghost found its way, without the permission of the patent owner, to Germany, Spain, India, Russia and the U.S. By their illegal efforts these exhibitors, in Pepper's estimate, realized at least a quarter of a million sterling. The professor, however, was able to defend his sole right to the ghost in the courts of his own country. The case of the ghost was brought by trial before the lord chancellor, Lord Westbury. The judgment was favorable, and Pepper was left in undisputed possession of his ghost, at least in Britain.

The purpose of this remarkable performance was scientific. The ghost was used only as a special means of attraction to induce audiences to attend lectures on general science. It was Pepper's philanthropic and educational purpose to bridge the gulf that lay between the remote work of the scientists and the popular mind.

At the Royal Polytechnic Institute in London he gave popular lectures in chemistry and mineralogy. The fees were very low, and some special evening lectures were given "working men at half-price." His work was under the special patronage of the prince consort, husband of Queen Victoria. He also was a visiting lecturer at boys' schools and mechanics' institutes.

It appears he was in Montreal on more than one

John Collins SKETCHBOOK

PROF. PEPPER'S GHOST

From a drawing made in 1873 showing the scene on the stage of the Queen's Hall on St. Catherine street when Prof. Pepper made a ghost appear before his audience

occasion, and may have lectured and demonstrated his ghost not only in the Queen's Hall but also in the Mechanics' Institute on St. James St. When he spoke in the Queen's Hall in the winter of 1873, the ghost was only part of his performance. He also lectured on "noise, sound, harmony and music," and "coal and coal mines." The ghost was a very clever way of stimulating attention and interest in the subject of popular science. And as such it worked extremely well.

Nor was Pepper like a magician, leaving his audience in doubt and mystery as to how the ghost was produced. He would, later in the evening, give an explanation. It was all a trick of reflected light. Anyone walking or standing in front of a sheet of glass, with a light behind (even the daylight), will see a reflection — a transparent reflection that does not conceal whatever is behind the glass. "When we walk past large plate-glass windows in shops," he

explained, "we may see our own 'ghosts' walking among the silks and satins, or hams, cheeses, butter, etc. within."

On his stage Pepper had simply set up a large sheet of glass in front of the Gothic windows. While concealing the girl in the long robe from the audience, he threw a strong light behind her. Her reflection on the glass turned her into a transparent spectre, whether standing or moving. When the light was turned off, she disappeared.

The lecturer went on to speak about the whole phenomenon of light, its effect upon clouds, and the many wonders of nature. It was all a kind of showmanship. Yet it was showmanship in a good cause. The hundreds who crowded the Queen's Hall to see Pepper make a ghost walk in the stage moonlight began to learn far more about the laws of natural science than they might have learned in any other way.

Fires in the night

Fire in the night has always been dramatic. So it was in Montreal in the summer of 1832. Asiatic cholera had come with immigrant ships. It spread rapidly through the city. Death lurked everywhere, and fear deepened with the dark.

The nights in 1832 were made all the more eerie by flames. At that time tar was believed to be a purifier of the air. Barrels of it were kept burning in squares and streets.

Among the immigrants arriving in Montreal that summer were the Perry family. One of the children in that family, Alfred Perry, was later to recall the scene that night: "The city . . . wore an appearance of horror and gloom beyond imagination. In the centre of Place d'Armes arose a huge bonfire of tar barrels, the dense black smoke from it filled the narrow streets like a pall of doom. There was little movement save the rumble of the dead carts" — carts gathering the dead and carrying them away for burial in the cholera trenches at Point St. Charles.

The Perrys found shelter in a building at the corner of Commissioners and St. Sulpice Sts. used for the temporary accommodation of immigrants. Several families were in one large room. Crowding during an epidemic only spread the disease. A number of the immigrants in the building fell ill. One of them was the father of the Perry family.

Mrs. Perry was determined that her husband would not be taken to the cholera trenches at Point St. Charles. By giving the driver of the dead cart one of her husband's suits, she induced him to take her to the Protestant cemetery on Papineau Rd. (now Papineau Ave., where Logan St. crosses). By then it was about 8 o'clock in the evening. She was able to get a blanket and a quilt from the lodging. She wrapped the body in them. They set out. She sat with her husband's head on her lap. Her son, Alfred, wrote, "Tar barrel fires were blazing at intervals . . . presenting with their glare and huge clouds of smoke, seen through the drizzling rain, a scene of almost infernal horror. Along the dreadful avenue my mother rode with her lifeless burden out to the cemetery."

Fires in the night were never without their drama. When a great fire was seen from a distance, its pulsating light in the sky might have an irresistible attraction. Such attraction appears in William Kingsford's account of the red glare in the city seen from the mountain slope high on Côte des Neiges Rd. On that evening of April 25, 1849, Kingsford was a dinner guest at the house of a Mr. Derbyshire. Toward the end of the meal a report reached the table that a big fire had broken out somewhere in the city. Host and guests alike were curious to know what and where it might be. All went out on the terrace behind the house. For a while Derbyshire looked on in silence. Then he remarked that the fire seemed to be where the parliament building stood on St. Ann's Market (now Place d'Youville).

At that time Montreal was the capital of Canada — Canada consisting of Upper and Lower Canada (now Ontario and Quebec), which had been united under one government. Derbyshire recalled that a mass meeting had been due to take place that evening on the Champ de Mars. Political feeling was angry. Could the crowd have surged from the Champ de Mars to attack the parliament building? All went back to the table. But restlessness had settled over the whole company. The party soon broke up. Kingsford and his wife, with Derbyshire, walked down the slope from Côte des Neiges and into the city. It was as Derbyshire had guessed. The parliament building had been attacked and set on fire. By the time the group from Côte des Neiges reached the scene, the building seemed one gigantic flame that leaped skyward, swaying and flapping in the gusty April night.

At times flames at night have not been fearful or awesome at all, but only pleasantly picturesque. Such was the campfire seen by Mrs. John Graves Simcoe on coming into Montreal about 11 o'clock in the evening of Sept. 13, 1792. The wife of the first lieutenant-governor of Upper Canada, she was on her way from Quebec to join her husband at York (now Toronto). In her diary she wrote: "On the road we passed a group of Indians sitting around a fire near the river, which in this dark night afforded a good subject for a picture."

Perhaps the most pleasingly dramatic of flames in darkness were the torches carried on special occasions by snowshoe clubs on Mount Royal. The

NOTRE DAME CHURCH and the SEMINARY of the SULPICIANS The ONLY BUILDINGS ON PLACE D'ARMES THAT WERE THERE DURING THE CHOLERA EPIDEMIC OF 1832

John Collins SKETCHBOOK

snowshoers, following one another in Indian file, gave the torchlight a serpentine quality. A torchlight procession greeted the governor-general and his wife, Lord and Lady Dufferin, on their visit to Montreal in January 1873. Lady Dufferin wrote in her journal: "This evening we attended a snowshoe torchlight procession given in our honor. The procession walked up the mountain, and we drove round it, watching the fiery serpent winding among the trees."

There was nothing awesome or fearful about these flames at night: "The sight really was very picturesque and very Canadian. The snow-covered ground . . . the torches, and the gaiety of the whole scene, were delightful."

A confectioner with a difference

Joyce Park is at the southwest corner of Lajoie and Rockland in Outremont. Here Alfred Joyce, the Montreal confectioner, once lived.

Joyce played a prominent part in the life and development of the community. He was an Outremont alderman from 1896 to 1907 and mayor from 1905 to 1907. In 1921 a school on Durocher Ave. was named Alfred Joyce School in his honor.

Joyce Park once had associations with the Hudson's Bay Co. In a stone house, Beaver Lodge, lived John Clarke, a chief factor of the company and at one time a business partner of John Jacob Astor. After a lifetime of travel, hardship, adventure and trading in the wilderness, John Clarke spent his last years in Beaver Lodge. One summer Clarke sent an invitation to the chiefs and Indians at the reserve on the Lake of Two Mountains. Forty tents were set up in his large orchard at Beaver Lodge.

Clarke's daughter, Adèle, described the scene: "It was a novel sight. Perfect order was kept. The squaws worked at their beadwork and made good sales. They went away with plenty of money. . . . At night they had lighted lanterns on the trees and crowds of people came out of town to visit the encampment. Beaver Lodge was opened [by the Clarkes] to their friends that week and all enjoyed themselves."

By the time Alfred Joyce bought the property it was rocky and overgrown by weeds. As the years passed the grounds changed wonderfully. He had cleared the rocks and weeds away and planted bank after bank of flowers — asters, zinnias, begonias, roses and other varieties, all growing between bordering plants. The grounds became a showplace. They were open to anyone who wished to visit them. Visitors would ask him how he became so interested in flowers. He explained that he came from Dunmow in England, where everyone had flower gardens. There he had learned the value of beautiful surroundings. He ascribed his excellent health (he lived till he was 95) to the peace-giving recreation of gardening.

If there was one thing Joyce liked even more than his flowers, it was his work in town. He had kept on working in his confectionery shop till he was in his 83rd year. After retirement he would admit: "I miss

my old work very much. Even the beautiful surroundings hardly seem to take the place of the interests that kept me in touch with the general business world."

Alfred Joyce came to Montreal in 1857. Four years later he set up in business for himself. At first his shop was in the old downtown area near Notre Dame Church. He was the first businessman in Montreal to foresee that the retail street of the future would be St. Catherine. There he moved in the 1860s to the corner of City Councillors, the corner where the Orpheum Theatre was later to stand. This shop, claimed to be the first on St. Catherine St., was very little — one storey high, renting for $10 a month.

From this small beginning Joyce prospered. He knew how to invest his money to make it grow. The same foresight that had made him the retail pioneer on St. Catherine St. led him to buy properties while they were still cheap. He bought much of the land on Phillips Square. He invested in properties on Dorchester. His large property in Outremont was bought at a time when the area was far away and countrified. While all his real estate increased in value, his confectionery business was growing also. He eventually moved his shop to the south side of Phillips Square, where the Canada Cement building is today. It was a handsome stone store designed for him by one of the leading architectural firms of Montreal — A.C. Hutchison and his partners, also the architects of the Peter Redpath Museum at McGill University and the Erskine Presbyterian Church (now Erskine and American United) on Sherbrooke St.

Joyce's confectionery shop had the carriage trade. In his day these customers really did arrive at his door in carriages. He was not just another confectioner: all his services and products had a special status. Among his regular and profitable customers was the prestigious Montreal Hunt Club. He catered for its balls.

One Montrealer, Mrs. S. Wright Jewett (Lucy Potter) spoke of the prestige of a little gift ordered from Joyce's: "Joyce's had the most wonderful candy always and their prices were much higher than the other confectioners but the gift of a box from

ALFRED JOYCE'S CONFECTIONERY STORE — on Phillips Square

John Collins SKETCHBOOK

'Joyce's' was considered something special." Joyce could be generously thoughtful in making gifts of his own. Mrs. Jewett recalled: "Mr. Joyce and his wife (who was with him in the shop) were both very friendly and kind to me as a little girl, and many a box of lovely chocolates came my way with Alfred Joyce's compliments."

While Joyce was pleased to make gifts, he was severe with customers who picked cakes or candies off his counter displays and ate them while they were looking things over. At such times Joyce would come out from behind his counter and present them with a bill for what they had taken. They were often indignant but he always insisted on being paid.

Joyce was always ready to divulge the secret of his success in business: "I began working with my father when I was very young, and he trained me to be precise and regular in my habits and to keep working." With a touch of sarcasm he spoke of the young people of a later day: "What we want today is a little more of the thoroughness of the old days."

Joyce postponed his retirement until 1918. For about half a century he had been on Phillips Square. He sold his business to R. de Goroq, chief of the victualling department of the Canadian Pacific Ocean Services. While he kept busy in his garden and conservatory in Outremont, he missed his old shop.

"But I can't complain," he would say, "for in summer I have my flowers, and in winter, my books." He died on a July day in 1931 — a midsummer day when his flowers were at their best.

Happy days in jail

Being in jail in Old Montreal could be a happy experience. Though behind bars, a prisoner could enjoy all the comforts of home — and sometimes many more. If he had enough influence and friends in the outside world, he could enjoy lavish and lively parties and crowds of visitors.

Jail authorities, respectful of influence, raised no objections. In the years while the Nor'Westers dominated Montreal, any partner in jail lived from feast to feast. The North West Co., with its Montreal headquarters, conducted the fur trade by way of the Ottawa River and through the network of waterways leading deep into the northwest. Its aggressive energy challenged the old Hudson's Bay Co. The companies, bitter rivals, often clashed in the wilderness.

In 1817 the Hudson's Bay Co. charged some of the Nor'Westers with criminal acts. Several were arrested. They were shut up in the old jail on Notre Dame St. But the lordly North West Co., whose rich partners were called "the nabobs of the North," saw to it that those imprisoned enjoyed their stay. When an officer of the Hudson's Bay Co., Colin Robertson, came to Montreal in 1817, he was astonished to see the jail lit up at night as if for some patriotic celebration. Robertson was well aware that nobody in authority in Montreal could be expected to interfere with this roistering in jail. The Nor'Westers' "ostentatious wealth," he realized, had won "the friendship of the legal authorities."

The biggest celebration in jail in Montreal's history came in 1849. By that time the city had a new jail, opened in 1836. It stood much farther east on Notre Dame St., at the northeast corner of de Lorimier Ave. This building still stands, though it ceased to be a jail in 1913, a year after Bordeaux was opened. Here, in the spring of 1849, those suspected of burning down the parliament building were confined. At that time Montreal was the capital of Canada (in those pre-Confederation times, Ontario and Quebec). This parliament building, converted from the old St. Ann's Market, stood on what is now Place d'Youville. The Tories were furious. On the afternoon of April 25, a bill they opposed (the Rebellion Losses Bill) had become law, when signed in the parliament building by the governor-general, Lord Elgin. Tories claimed it would recompense rebels from the public treasury.

That evening the Tories gathered in an outdoor mass meeting on the Champ de Mars. The meeting, beginning with moderation, soon burst out of control. Shouts were heard: "To the parliament building!" The crowd surged toward Place d'Youville, its torches bobbing ominously. The mob burst into the parliament building. Members, at a night sitting, were scattered into the streets. The building, inside and out, was soon in flames. By morning it stood in ruins. Many prominent Tories were arrested. They were lodged in the jail on Notre Dame St. E. (then called St. Mary). But before long "Dolly" arrived. "Dolly" was Robert Isaacson, whose chop house was one of the choicest dining places in town. Dolly, a Tory, came with two of his waiters. They brought roasts, sweets, wines. For the prisoners "the night passed pleasantly."

Through the following days pleasures increased. Dolly took care that they wanted for nothing in food or drink, both of superb quality. As many of the prisoners were Scottish, the Scots of Montreal came crowding to visit them. Alfred Perry, one of the prisoners, described those days: "Our life while in prison was anything but a time of sorrow. We were more than abundantly supplied with all the necessities and luxuries our hearts could desire."

Visitors jammed the prisoners' quarters. Tom McGinn, "a jovial fellow," was jailer. He provided larger accommodation, as if he were the manager of a convention hotel. He assigned the ground floor of a prison wing as a reception area. There the prisoners could entertain their guests with greater ease. The party spirit prevailed. "All were full of excitement and enthusiasm," said Perry, "and soon became fuller of whisky. I never saw such a time. I was the only sober man in the crowd."

The floor of the jail wing assigned to these prisoners had been the female prisoners' quarters. The women had been moved upstairs. Through a grating in the ceiling they could see and hear much of what was going on below. One day a woman upstairs shouted down through the grating: "Hello! Can't you send us a drop?" Down came a line of garters tied together. At the end was part of a woolen stocking. Perry at once saw what was intended. The

SKETCHBOOK
John Collins

Notre Dame Street in the 19th Century with the Old Jail facing Nelson's Monument

stocking was soaked in whisky. Up it went through the grating. Soon the line descended again. "This movement was repeated," said Perry, "till fully the contents of two bottles had disappeared."

Before long the government decided to set the prisoners free, afraid a mob of their supporters might start a riot. The released prisoners were escorted from the jail by thousands, "cheering all along the way."

Another example of the comforts of jail for those with influence came in 1864. This time the prisoners were not Montrealers but Confederate soldiers. In the American Civil War neutral Montreal had a nest of Confederate agents. Here they plotted terrorist moves against the northern states. On Oct. 19, 1864, about 25 Confederate soldiers left Canada for a raid

on St. Albans, Vt. They robbed the banks of $200,000, set the town afire and killed a man in their escape. On complaints from Washington a number of the raiders were arrested and tried in Montreal.

Confederate agents in Montreal, well provided with cash, saw that the prisoners had all comforts. These prisoners, in fact, were not really imprisoned at all. They were accommodated in the jailer's own quarters, almost as if they were boarders. Lt. Bennett H. Young, commander of the St. Albans raiders, played friendly games of chess with the jailer. Other Confederates in Montreal, and Montrealers who were Confederate sympathizers, sang songs for them in the street. It was even said that "those who felt the need had the solace of feminine company at night." After two trials, all the prisoners were released.

Strathcona the enigma

Lord Strathcona, one of Montreal's richest, most generous and most prominent citizens, remained an enigma all his life. He considered himself the only man in whom his confidence might be safely placed. No one knew what he might be thinking or what his conclusions might be till he chose to disclose them, if ever. By his absolute self-reliance he assured his absolute independence.

This inner core of detached self-command in no way limited his social life. He entertained on the grand scale. His Montreal house at the northeast corner of Dorchester and Fort Sts. would be crowded with guests. He was attentive to every one of them. Yet he remained inwardly apart.

Professor John Macnaughton of McGill University, one of Strathcona's chief admirers, had a feeling that Strathcona's unusually courteous manners were some sort of defence. Many, he says, found "his really fine manners" were "more impenetrable and isolating in their lubricant defensiveness than crocodile's scales. . . . He loved the solitude of a crowd, a privacy of mild light, from which he shone benevolently on all alike and upon no one in particular."

Those who worked under him while he was governor of the Hudson's Bay Co. were at times baffled by his reticence. To his great house on Dorchester he might summon Clarence Chipman, one of the company's chief officers, from great distances, perhaps a thousand miles away. Chipman would arrive at the mansion convinced that the governor must have reached some radical decision about the company's management. For about nine days Strathcona would entertain him. Conversation would be always interesting and delightful, if rambling and general. Chipman might be given no hint why he had suddenly been called from far away, and in haste. He would leave the mansion, with his host in the porch, or even at his door, bidding him a most gracious farewell, with every good wish.

On his way back to the northwest Chipman would ponder the mystery. Obviously, Strathcona had been near to saying something important; the meeting had been arranged for significant business. But Strathcona's thoughts had meanwhile been flowing in their secretive channels. By the time Chipman arrived Strathcona had other ideas; he had changed or delayed his decision. As no explanation was ever offered, Chipman never knew what it was all about.

Strathcona's enigmatic character was felt even by those who were playing important roles in institutions he had founded. Among his large gifts to McGill University was the Royal Victoria College. Ethel Hurlbatt, warden of the college, was always aware of the invariable remoteness that lay beyond all his courtesy and interest. "I knew him only as a very old man, always with a certain detachment of manner," she remarked, "as if he had already passed some boundaries of time and space beyond his fellows, and while occupied and keenly interested and ceaselessly concerned with work and duty and service, really alone with himself. Perhaps he was always like this — utterly master of himself and his fate. The early years of discipline and loneliness may have worked this in him."

Strathcona was never rude, but his evasions were smoothly effective. It happened, for example, at Windsor Station in 1896. That was the year of a Canadian general election. Tory fortunes were on the wane. The party was urgently seeking funds. William Watson Ogilvie, of the Ogilvie flour mills, had been looking for an opportunity to get a donation from Strathcona for the Tory war chest. Strathcona had been busy and elusive. There was one last chance. Ogilvie learned he was in his private car at the station. Train time was near. Ogilvie hurried to the station, found the car and clambered aboard. What he saw dismayed him. Strathcona was there, chatting with John Redpath Dougall, editor of the Montreal Witness, a Liberal paper.

Still Ogilvie hoped. "The train will not leave for 20 minutes," he thought to himself, "and as Dougall will leave in the meantime, I shall have time to talk 'business' with my man." Hope seemed about to be fulfilled. Soon Dougall got up from his chair. He said he must be going. "Sit down, Mr. Dougall, sit down," said Strathcona. "There is never anything private between Mr. Ogilvie and myself." Five minutes later Dougall got up again. At once Strathcona repeated, "Sit down, Mr. Dougall, sit down." About half a dozen times Dougall made ready to leave, but every time he was told to remain.

PORTRAIT OF LORD STRATHCONA HANGING IN THE LOBBY OF THE ROYAL VICTORIA HOSPITAL

The Hospital given to the city by Strathcona and his cousin Lord Mount Stephen

John Collins

SKETCHBOOK

Suddenly the bell began to ring. Conductors were shouting "All aboard!"

Ogilvie and Dougall hurried out of the car together. They stood on the platform as the train moved slowly out. At one of the windows they saw Lord Strathcona. He was waving pleasantly as he disappeared into the distance, out of reach of them both.

Lord Strathcona's skilful evasiveness was experienced by Rev. W.D. Reid, superintendent of missions in Alberta and later the minister of Stanley Presbyterian Church in Westmount. He went to see Lord Strathcona in the office in London where he was the Canadian high commissioner. The object was to solicit Strathcona's help to build a ladies' college at Red Deer, Alta. Strathcona received him with his customary good manners, with his habitual affability. Reid raised the question of the college. But the conversation soon went off to other topics. When Reid was able to get back to the question of the ladies' college, Strathcona said: 'Yes, I will give you a contribution, but not today. I have been giving a great deal away, and I want to see how my account stands."

When Reid judged it was time to leave, Strathcona said: "Don't go yet, I have enjoyed this talk about dear Canada."

Finally, when Reid left, he shook hands sitting behind his desk. Then he got up and shook hands at the office door. Following Reid to the elevator, he gave another hearty handshake. "If you are ever in London again," he said, "and I am here, be sure to come in again."

Reid adds: "But the donation never came."

Montreal's first railroad

The first railroad on the island of Montreal ran for only eight miles. It was the little line that connected Montreal with Lachine. Like a number of other railroads in Canada, it was a sort of portage on rails, built to carry passengers past the Lachine Rapids.

Yet the opening of the Montreal and Lachine Railroad on Friday, Nov. 19, 1847, was observed with dignity and hope. It had brought the railroad age to Montreal. At the banquet following the inaugural ceremony the governor-general, the Earl of Elgin, saw it as only the beginning of greater things. "I trust that the time is not too distant," he prophesied, "when this railroad will be but a link in the chain, which, if it does not bind together the two oceans, will, at least, unite the various dependencies of Great Britain in North America."

Short as the Montreal and Lachine Railroad was, it had been difficult to build, for part of it had to be laid through a swamp. That swamp has long since been forgotten, but was once a feature of the Montreal landscape. Samuel de Champlain, on his visit to Montreal in 1611, marked on his map, as covered with water, a large portion of the flats below the Lachine Rapids, near Côte St. Paul. It was particularly bad where the little St. Pierre River meandered through Ste. Cunégonde and St. Henri.

Finding a bottom firm enough to run trains across was a grim problem for the engineering skills of the 1840s. Everything that was dumped into it to build the roadbed seemed to disappear. One day an engine being used in the construction was run too far from the firm part of the line. It toppled into the swamp. The railroad-builders had no equipment for raising it. The ooze closed over. Later another engine was lost in the same way. To this day they might be lying somewhere in that area.

The right-of-way of the railroad itself is below the level of today's streets. Not many years ago excavations beside the fruit warehouse of the Canadian National Railways, near Guy St., uncovered a portion of the original right-of-way fence of the Montreal and Lachine line. It was six feet below the present ground level.

When dumping earth into the swamp did not have much effect, the engineers had to make a roadbed by driving in wooden piles. As late as the 1890s these piles could still be seen.

The first locomotive was built in Philadelphia and came to Montreal by steamer. It weighed about 18 tons; the wheels were five feet in diameter. Eighteen horses hauled it along St. Antoine St. The carriages were made in Canada, on the English plan. The first-class carriages were furnished luxuriously — satin hangings, softest cushions, silk blinds. The second-class carriages were "substantial." They had "comfortable leather seats." Though the windows had no silk blinds, they at least could be said "to protect the inmates against the inclemency of the weather." The third-class carriages were open.

The railroad was also provided with two Scottish engines — Kinmond engines. P.L. Kinmond recalled his experiences many years later when the engines were tested on the line. The directors of the railroad and three engineers from the U.S. came to see how the Scottish engines would work. Alexander Miller, the foreman, decided to show them all just what a Scottish locomotive could do. He said nothing when the directors told him to go slowly; they were afraid of the swamp. Kinmond sat in the box with Miller and was surprised when Miller at once gave the locomotive full steam. In three first-class carriages behind, the directors and their American friends were shaken like dice. One moment their high hats were almost going through the roof, the next moment they landed on a seat or were thrown against the side.

In 11 minutes the train drew into Lachine. It was an extraordinary feat in the 1840s to take a train eight miles in 11 minutes. But the directors were furious. They came to Kinmond and told him that if there were to be any more experiments of this kind, they would order horses and carriages to take them back to Montreal.

Miller promised that he would not do the like again. But this time he refused to allow Kinmond to join him in the locomotive. He gave an excuse: the locomotive was too small and he needed more room. Then he spoke the truth. "With some strong words," he told Kinmond: "These directors will find out now that this is a Scotch engine and that we can go even at a quicker rate. We will show them what we can do

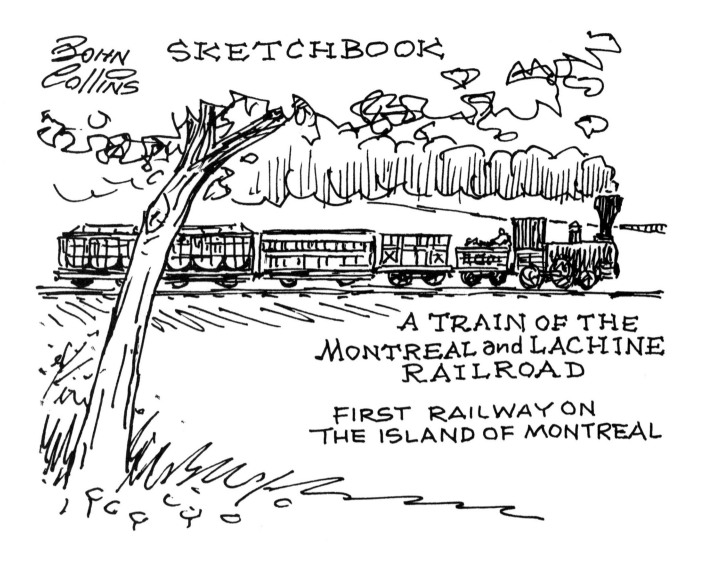

SKETCHBOOK

John Collins

A TRAIN OF THE
MONTREAL and LACHINE
RAILROAD

FIRST RAILWAY ON
THE ISLAND OF MONTREAL

now when we have them." He told Kinmond to get into the third coach: "If there is anyone's neck to be broken, let it be mine. You are not coming up here."

The train put out from Lachine. At once Miller gave it full steam. Once more the directors rattled like dice in their first-class carriages. Just outside the windows they could see the black ooze of the swamp and knew the mad Scot in the locomotive might send them all leaping into it, to sink out from the light forever. Miller had done even better on the way back than on the way out. This time he covered the eight miles in nine minutes.

Of what happened, Kinmond wrote: "If the directors were startled with the speed shown . . . when they went out in eleven minutes, you may be sure that they were nonetheless so when they came back. They had been on the point of asking our firm [of locomotive manufacturers] to let Mr. Miller stay with them and manage the road, but now the

president came to me very much ruffled and told me he would discharge Miller in the morning. I did not go near the directors for some days. In the meantime the feat of the Scotch engine so surpassed the Americans and had got to be so much talked of that the directors began to take pride in the performance. They had recovered their breath, and their commonsense came uppermost. Most of them, and the shareholders, too, were Scotchmen. They did not discharge Miller, but asked him to become manager of the road. That was his triumph, and, of course, ours, too."

The words used by the governor-general in 1847, when the Montreal and Lachine Railroad was opened, proved to be true. This little line was to become a link in a great chain.

It was leased to the Grand Trunk Railway in 1854 and sold to it in 1872. It is now merged in the CNR system.

The Tom Moore house at Ste. Anne's

One event made Ste. Anne de Bellevue known to the world for generations. It happened when the Irish poet Thomas Moore wrote about "the evening chime" of its little Roman Catholic church. An immensely popular song, with its wistful appeal:

Faintly as tolls the evening chime
Our voices keep tune and our oars keep time.
Soon as the woods on shore look dim,
We'll sing at St. Ann's our parting hymn.
Row, brothers, row, the stream runs fast,
The Rapids are near and the daylight's past.

Visitors to Canada made pilgrimages to Ste. Anne's to see the village made famous by Moore; they hoped to hear the chime he had heard in 1804. Ste. Anne's, by passing into literature, had become real to thousands who had never seen it.

What was the Irish poet Thomas Moore doing as far away from home as Ste. Anne's in 1804? The answer lies in an appointment he had received only a few months earlier. Influential and admiring friends wished to do something to give him relief from the usual financial uncertainties of authorship. They arranged to have him appointed registrar of the Admiralty Court in Bermuda. Moore went out to Bermuda to assume his office. But he was only 25 and did not have the patient, resigned temperament to spend his days in regular business routines. Soon he grew bored, restless. And he did what many other office-holders used to do in those days. He did not give up his lucrative appointment; he hired a deputy to do the work for him.

Moore, in a happy mood, left Bermuda. Instead of going directly home, he decided first to make a tour of the U.S. and Canada. Like many travellers of the time, he entered Canada at Niagara and then came down the St. Lawrence. That voyage gave him the experiences immortalized in A Canadian Boat Song. No steamboats were then on the river. Moore came down in a big, wooden bateau, rowed by voyageurs. All this was picturesque enough. But what charmed Moore most was the songs of the voyageurs as they pulled on their oars:

"Our 'voyageurs' had good voices, and sung perfectly in tune together. . . . I remember when we have entered at sunset, upon one of those beautiful lakes, into which the St. Lawrence so grandly and unexpectedly opens, I have heard this simple air with a pleasure which the finest compositions of the first masters have never given me; and there is not a note of it which does not recall to my memory the dip of our oars, the flight of our boat down the Rapids."

No other church meant as much to the voyageurs as the little church at Ste. Anne's (which some believe survives as part of the convent). Its spire was the last they saw, its bell the last they heard, before leaving the island of Montreal behind. Voyageurs employed in the fur trade, who left Montreal for a journey up the Ottawa and on to Lake Superior, or beyond, ran the greatest risk of death. Clusters of little crosses stood on the shore by every rapids on the long route. They were a reminder of voyageurs drowned on earlier journeys.

Anne was the voyageurs' patron saint. At the village the voyageurs went ashore to say a last prayer in the church and to leave some offering. Even when they had gone into the wilderness, away from all civilization, they would think of this church.

Long tradition has claimed the poem was written in a stone house still standing in Ste. Anne's. It is now 153 Ste. Anne St., facing the waterfront, only a few feet from the nearby and overshadowing bridge. The tradition that Thomas Moore stayed at this house is certainly not a modern invention. It appeared in print at least as early as the 1860s, and was said to be an old tradition even then. No documentary evidence exists to confirm it. It is a tradition that has long lingered, though unproven. The house belonged to Simon Fraser — not the Simon Fraser who discovered the Fraser River, but a local fur-trader. In Ste. Anne's in 1804 this Simon Fraser was one of the principal residents. As Moore was being entertained along the route, it would not be unlikely that he stayed at Fraser's house (if this house was in fact where Fraser was living in 1804). It is said that Moore was later at Lachine, and known that he was in Montreal.

Some evidence, however, suggests the poem was not written anywhere on shore, but on the river. Moore himself, in publishing his poem, placed under the title the words: "written on the River St. Lawrence." One day in Dublin in 1835 Moore was

John Collins SKETCHBOOK *Simon Fraser House* — Ste Anne de Bellevue

told that a barrister, Charles Richard Weld, had a book with A Canadian Boat Song and the music written on a flyleaf. Weld would like to show it to Moore to see whether he would recognize the writing as his own. Next day Moore and Weld met by appointment. When Moore took the book into his hands, he at once recognized his handwriting. The book was Joseph Priestley's *Lectures on History*. Moore remembered he had taken that book with him on his Canadian travels in 1804. He recalled that he had made a present of the book to his fellow traveller, Hackness, the son of a Dublin merchant. Now Hackness, he believed, was dead.

The contradiction between the statement by Moore that this poem was written on the St. Lawrence and the tradition that it was written in the Fraser house at Ste. Anne's may still be reconciled. The clue could lie in words written by Charles Richard Weld in 1855. Weld said that the version of the poem on the flyleaf of the book and the version as later published differ in a number of ways.

Weld added that Moore, though writing the lines in the book while journeying on the river, "transcribed them at night." These details Weld presumably heard in his conversation with Moore in Dublin in 1835.

This might be the answer to the contradiction. Moore might have written the first version on the river and the revised, final version that night in Ste. Anne's.

An actor on a sinking ship

Early Friday morning, May 29, 1914, an actor played his most dramatic farewell performance on the deck of a sinking ship. It was not a scene contrived for a stage. It was all real.

The ship was the Empress of Ireland, sinking in the Lower St. Lawrence a little below Father Point. It would carry more than 1,000 people to their deaths, the actor and his wife among them.

The actor was Laurence Irving, younger son of Sir Henry Irving, one of the greatest actors of all time. Something sombre, doomful hung over Laurence Irving, a gloomy shadow. Another actor of the day, Sir Herbert Beerbohm Tree, remarked: "One feels that his end is in tragic harmony with his being." Irving had come to Canada on a theatrical tour. He had appeared with his wife on the stage of Montreal's His Majesty's Theatre, the ornate playhouse on the east side of Guy St. a little above St. Catherine. *The Gazette's* critic described him as "a force to be reckoned with among the leaders of the English stage." But success was coming to him just before his end.

Irving's life had been clouded. His father and mother quarrelled and separated shortly before he was born. Henry Irving refused to attend Laurence's christening. Laurence and his elder brother, Harry, lived with their mother. They had a dismal childhood. Their mother was a woman venomously bitter toward her absent husband. Their father, the few times they met him, was sardonic and chilling. Both sons persisted in becoming actors. Their father wanted little to do with them. He was fearful that they would make fools of themselves, and of him. He doubted that they had sufficient talent. When Laurence went on the stage, Sir Henry refused to have him in his own theatrical company. He placed him in another company, where he was restricted to insignificant roles.

Laurence sank into depression. After a visit to his father he wrote: "He was so icy and obnoxious, I was glad to leave him." Not long afterward Laurence shot himself with a pistol at lodgings in Belfast. He recovered. Relations with his father gradually improved. He was admitted into his father's company, where he met Mabel Hackney, the actress who became his wife. Toward the end, his father toured with Laurence as his understudy.

After Sir Henry Irving died in 1905, Laurence was still in difficulty. His father's greatness continued to overshadow him. For years he seemed only his father's son, struggling in vain to make a place for himself on the stage. Gradually he broke through into a life of his own. His talent, maturing slowly, was winning recognition.

While in Montreal he was invited to address the Women's Canadian Club in the hall of the Royal Victoria College. The topic of his lecture was the drama as a factor in social progress. Members assembled, ready for a serious, instructive lecture. But he ignored the announced topic. An hour was spent in rambling talk about theatrical experiences.

If his remarks to the clubwomen were eccentric, his performances in His Majesty's Theatre were triumphant. Characteristically, the plays he had selected were both deep, dark tragedies. The first was Dostoevski's *Crime and Punishment* in the stage adaptation named *The Unwritten.* Irving's last play in His Majesty's Theatre — his last appearance on the stage in Montreal — was another tragedy, *Typhoon.* Here he played Dr. Takeramon, a Japanese diplomat in Paris, trying to pry out secret information to enable Japan to wrest Tonkin from France. Failing in his mission, because of his infatuation with the French girl Hélène (played by Mabel Hackney) he calls his companions together and commits hara-kiri — an act approved by the other Japanese as worthy of his rank.

Irving's acting was acclaimed. Persistent calls after the final curtain brought him back to the stage. "The unhesitating verdict of last night's discriminating audience was that Laurence Irving was an actor of undoubted power, authority and intellect in his own right," *The Gazette* concluded.

At this crest of his success, Irving and his wife set out for England aboard the Empress of Ireland. The early morning of May 29, 1914, was cold and foggy. Below Father Point the Norwegian collier Storstad was sighted two miles away. In a confusion of signals (the Storstad was blamed in the official inquiry) the collier rammed the starboard side of the Empress, penetrating the hull for about 12 feet. Water tumbled

The EMPRESS

and the ship's
lifeboats
picked up at sea
after the collision

John SKETCHBOOK
Collins The Empress of Ireland

in. Only a few lifeboats could be launched in the 14 minutes between the crash and the sinking.

Irving and his wife were last seen alive by a Toronto passenger, F.E. Abbott. "I met him first in the passageway," said Abbott, "and he asked calmly, 'Is the boat going down?' I said that it looked like it. 'Dearie,' Irving then said to his wife, 'hurry, there is no time to lose.' Mrs. Irving began to cry and, as the actor reached for a lifebelt, the boat suddenly lurched forward and he was thrown against the door of his cabin. His face was bloody and Mrs. Irving became frantic. 'Keep cool,' he warned her, but she persisted in holding her arms around him. He forced the lifebelt over her and pushed her out of the door.

He then practically carried her upstairs."

Abbott went on deck. He dived overboard. Gripping a piece of timber, he kept afloat. Looking around, he saw that Irving by this time was on deck. He was kissing his wife. As the Empress of Ireland sank they remained in each other's arms.

Laurence Irving had not intended to sail in the Empress of Ireland. He had booked passage home on the Corsican. Sir John Martin-Harvey, a fellow actor, had recently made a happy and comfortable crossing in the Empress of Ireland. He advised Irving to change from the Corsican.

"He did so," said Sir John, "with the terrible result everyone knows."

The philanthropist with the umbrella

A strange procession, "long and motley," made its slow way along St. Paul St. Very old men and women, many infirm and scarcely able to walk, struggled along as best they could. In the procession were children who had once been abandoned and rescued and were now being shepherded along. Others were insane persons who did not know where they were or why.

These were the people Mother d'Youville and her Grey Nuns had been sheltering and caring for in the Hôpital Général. She had made herself the mother of the homeless and the unwanted. She never closed the door of the Hôpital to anyone who came to her. In the afternoon of May 18, 1765, all these needy people had lost the roof over their heads. Already helpless, they had become suddenly homeless as well.

A wealthy man named Levington had caused a fire that destroyed a quarter of Montreal. Levington hated to waste anything. He stored the ashes from his fireplace in a corner of his attic. From time to time he used them in making soap. On that May day in 1765, embers still in the ashes burst into flame. Soon Levington's whole house seethed with fire.

A blustering wind drove the flames westward. Mother d'Youville saw the blaze and smoke. She was not alarmed. Her Hôpital Général seemed to her too far off to be threatened. It was close to the waterfront, near what is now Place d'Youville. In this confidence she sent all the personnel she could spare to help at the scene of the fire. But the same wind that was driving flames westward was carrying sparks faster and farther.

Sparks settled on the Hôpital's roof. Before anything could be done, it was a sheet of flame.

The aim now was to get the inmates of the Hôpital out to safety. When that had been done, she did her best to salvage the building's contents. People came hurrying to help. Some arrived with carts. They carried away 40 loads of linen, beds and other furniture. The helpers turned out to be bold thieves. Mother d'Youville never saw those 40 loads of property again.

Even much of what her nuns, and some able-bodied inmates, had saved was lost. In the hurry and excitement goods carried from the building were piled too near. They caught fire and were lost. A big bale of good clothing and more than 20 chests were burned outside, not far from the door. Mother d'Youville realized what the disaster meant. There she stood with her nuns and those who had been sheltered by the Hôpital — 118 of them. Now nothing was over their heads but the sky.

When she had first seen the distant fire, she had felt sure, she said, that God would protect the building — the refuge of *les misérables*. But he had permitted the disaster. It was, in her belief, a test of her resignation and her faith. She repeated aloud the words from the Bible: "The Lord gave and the Lord hath taken away; as it hath pleased the Lord, so it is done: Blessed be the name of the Lord."

Mother d'Youville then invited all around her to go down on their knees and sing together the Te Deum, the great hymn of thanksgiving. One of the nuns thought that thanking God for a disaster was going too far. She said something to the effect that it was a fine time to be singing Te Deums. She recovered herself, however, and knelt with the others.

All those driven out of the Hôpital needed to be fed and sheltered. Evening was coming on. Something had to be done before dark. Then the superior of the Sulpicians, M. Montgolfier, arrived on the scene. He had arranged with the sisters of the Hôtel Dieu for accommodation in their building on St. Paul St. at the corner of St. Joseph (now St. Sulpice).

The procession was formed for its slow progress eastward along St. Paul. At the Hôtel Dieu they were received with the utmost sympathy, though it was not easy to find room all at once for so many. Temporary accommodation was no real answer to the problem. A new Hôpital Général had to be built.

The fire had come at a bad time. Montreal was in a financial recession. The Sulpicians were generous. Many smaller contributions came from other sources. The Indians of Caughnawaga and Lake of Two Mountains remembered the nuns' many kindnesses. As well as money, they gave up some of their cherished possessions: silver pins, porcelain beads, wool blankets, goat-skin shoes, linen, sugar. But even when everything was put together, the total fell far short of the cost of building and equipping a

SKETCH BOOK

John Collins

Site of the
Hôpital Général
on
Normant Street

new Hôpital Général.

Mother d'Youville's problem was beginning to appear unsolvable. The crowd of people from the Hôpital Général had congested the Hôtel Dieu and were interfering with its work.

It was at this moment that the needed aid came, from far away — largely from the man with the umbrella. He was Jonas Hanway of London, for whom carrying an umbrella was philanthropy. Carrying an umbrella had needed courage. No one, it was said, had ever carried one in London before. Everywhere Hanway went people pointed at him, hooted and laughed. But Hanway carried an umbrella for the purpose of benefiting Londoners: he was teaching them that they could walk protected, even on rainy days.

Hanway had previously launched charitable campaigns in London for the protection of chimney sweeps against the hazards of their work, for the reform of prisons, for the guidance of farm girls coming to town to be servants. When Hanway heard of the great fire in Montreal, he at once headed a campaign to raise funds for relief. First he saw the

need for publicity. He wrote and circulated a pamphlet describing the extent of the calamity. He named it The Case of the Canadians at Montreal, Distressed by Fire.

Hanway called for a general response from the English. The French inhabitants of Montreal were new citizens of the Empire. This was a time to show them charity and succor. Hanway gave practical details. Those wishing to subscribe to the fund were informed just how they could do it. He and other trustees met at a London coffee house every Thursday and would "be glad to be favored with the assistance of any subscribers." He also listed 20 "firms of merchants and others who would take subscriptions."

In the meantime, others in London were raising money for the same purpose. A great part of the money subscribed in England was assigned to Mother d'Youville for the reconstruction of her Hôpital Général.

"If we had not been helped," she wrote, "by the charities of London . . . we would never have been able to recover from our fire."

The tuque: ideal headgear for the winter

The tuque seems to be a French-Canadian creation. In dictionaries it is one of the very few words identified as French-Canadian in origin. One dictionary defines a tuque as "a cap consisting of a knitted cylindrical bag with tapered ends, worn by thrusting one end inside the other."

Early visitors to Montreal from other countries had never seen a tuque before, and were at a loss to describe it. They groped after something they knew that might seem comparable. Often they called it a nightcap. The comparison was not unreasonable. Many men wore nightcaps in bed to protect their heads in cold and drafty bedrooms.

The tuque, like every other article of the rural French Canadian's winter clothing, was homemade. French-Canadian households, with their family industries, were almost entirely self-sufficient. Wool for tuques was provided by sheep on the farm. It was made into yarn on the family's spinning wheel. From this yarn tuques were knitted, and cloth was woven for the long winter coats. Hides from cattle were tanned and made into moccasins or high boots.

Another household product for winter wear was the sash — the "ceinture fléchée." These sashes, in brilliant colors, were often many feet long. They were tightly wound around the waist, two or three times, with the fringe falling down to one side.

These winter costumes were made by the women of the household. Much of the work was done in the summer, in preparation for the inevitable winter. The homemade winter costume, with its tuque, was so well adapted to the needs of the winter that it became almost a national costume. It was standardized into a sort of winter uniform. These winter costumes continued to be made in French-Canadian homes even into the 20th century.

Such family industries, however, had survived only in more remote areas, as in the north country or along the Lower St. Lawrence. By the 1870s many French Canadians living near cities had been giving up homemade clothing for the machine-made products of the big factories. The change was noted in 1871 by a writer in the American magazine *Scribner's Monthly:* "Home-made clothing has given away considerably to the cheapness of mill manufacture; the growing taste for finery and colors tempts a more frequent visit to the village or city shops; and with the growth and development of the country, the French-Canadian family imbibe a love for better apparel than their own humble ingenuity and industry can produce."

The French-Canadian winter costume found a new future when it was adopted by Montreal's snowshoers. For snowshoe clubs it was the ideal costume for long snowy tramps on cold winter nights, when they went over Mount Royal and back, or on long-distance tramps to Lachine or Sault au Récollet. The Montreal Show Shoe Club, oldest of them all, became known as "the Tuques Bleues." It was founded as early as 1840. What its costume was in its early years is uncertain; but at the annual meeting on Dec. 4, 1869, it adopted "a uniform cap . . . viz., blue 'tuque' with scarlet tassel." The showshoe club costume (though generally machine-made) was closely modelled on the old French-Canadian pattern — the "blanket coat," the moccasins, the sash. But the chief symbol and identification was the club's blue tuque.

As other snowshoe clubs were formed in Montreal, they, too, adopted tuques, but the tuque of each club had its distinctive color. Tuques of the St. George's Snowshoe Club were white with purple tassels; those of the Emerald Snowshoe Club (mostly young men of the St. Patrick's Association) were green; YMCA Club's were cardinal. When the Snowshoe Union was formed in 1908, its 34 clubs displayed tuques of 34 different colors or combinations of colors. Members of the Montreal Snow Shoe Club, with the prestige of their seniority, had become not only the "Tuques Bleues," but the "Old Tuques Bleues." In all the club's hearty snowshoe songs its tuques were extolled. One chorus went:

Now chant a rhyme, while the words keep time
To the tramp of our swift snow shoe
And we'll sing a song, as we march along
In praise of our old Tuque Bleue.

From time to time the Montreal Snow Shoe Club gave a concert in one of the city's principal halls, with the proceeds going to charity. The halls would be crowded to their "utmost capacity." Ushers were members in the club's costume, with their "tuques

SKETCHBOOK — John Collins

Most of us remember that most Canadian of headgear — THE TUQUE and the pulled-up scarf with only the eyes visible

But it was most famous as the symbol of the well-known Snowshoe Clubs of Montreal

bleues." They went "flitting about, imparting a variety and brilliancy to the scene never surpassed."

At one of these concerts members filed onto the stage and opened with a solo by one of the group, with everyone joining in the chorus of the "Tuque Bleue" song. The audience demanded an encore. During the last chorus, "Hurrah for the wearing of the bright tuque bleue," all the snowshoers took off their tuques and waved them — a crescendo of music and motion.

Even when snowshoeing in Montreal declined as a sport, the tuque found ways of survival. It was often preferred by skiers, skaters, tobogganers and those who worked outdoors or did winter walking.

This endurance of the ancient tuque, through all changes of time and fashion, was far more than evidence of a taste for tradition and the picturesque. The tuque, functional from its beginnings, remained so.

The natural suitability of the old tuque for the rigorous Canadian winters was commended by one of the most prominent Montreal doctors of the 19th century, Sir William Hingston. He praised it in an address on "The Climate of Canada" delivered to the Montreal Natural History Society about 1870. The rural French Canadian, he said, was always comfortably and suitably clothed, in his homemade apparel. Above all, he did well to wear the traditional tuque: it was "light and porous," keeping the head "sufficiently covered and warm and, at the same time, dry." It was far preferable to some other types of headgear that keep the head "hot and moist."

Members of the old Montreal Snow Shoe Club would have agreed. They had put their tuques to severest tests in the worst of storms. When the club gave its concerts, W.B. Maltby, the member with the best voice, would appear on the stage to sing a solo, as if grandly defying a blizzard on the slope of Mount Royal:

We love the blustering storm that blasts
Upon our bright tuque bleue.

Settling arguments: a hands-on approach

For many years in Montreal, men settled grievances with their fists. They might do it privately, in a lane. More often, they did not wait, but fought it out at once, in the street. Usually there were only a few onlookers on hand when the dispute began. Soon a crowd of outsiders would gather. They'd have no idea what it was all about, but it was a good show, unexpected and exciting.

As the crowd grew, so would the risk of attracting the police. A constable walking his beat could spot a crowd in the distance. He'd hurry to the scene and work his way through to the inner circle. In the name of the law, he'd lay a hand on each of the fighters. Sometimes the fighters would respect the law and give up. At other times they'd join in pummeling the constable to the pavement. When this happened, the crowd would make a quick opening for their escape. When the constable regained his feet, the fighters would have vanished. Nobody, of course, would say who they were or where they had gone. The crowd would disperse, leaving the constable to attend to his own cuts and bruises.

For a while, in the 1830s, some of the ceremonious ways of duelling were adopted by some of the fistfighters. They did not fight in the streets, but in the distant fields and pastures of Côte à Baron — the name given to the vast open countryside lying east of the mountain and largely below Sherbrooke St. The time was appointed. Each combatant drove out to Côte à Baron in a calèche, the clumsy-looking carriage with two big wheels. Beside each sat the friend who would be his second.

The fisticuffs at Côte à Baron were far from secret. Word soon spread in town that such a fight was going to take place. The two contestants in their calèches might be followed by 50 or 60 other calèches in one long procession. These carriages were jammed with sports enthusiasts (especially boxing fanciers), professional men, many butchers (which seemed appropriate), idlers and street-corner characters of all kinds.

At the appointed spot at Côte à Baron the spectators formed a ring. The fighters stripped to the waist. What followed was no impulsive brawl. Fair play was enforced by the seconds.

Although these fights took place in the open countryside, the coming of the police was still feared. Somebody only had to cry "Police!" to bring the contest to an immediate end. Although collusion was suspected at times, it was hard to prove. In any case, it was actually less an end than a postponement. It provided a sort of intermission. The fight had to be renewed the next day. It went on until one of the combatants really gave up and conceded defeat.

The formalized fisticuffs at Côte à Baron were unusual. Most fights in Montreal were spontaneous, unregulated. They broke out suddenly in the streets or squares of the town. Such street fighting was not always angry. It could be good-natured — just friendly encounters and tests of strength. This was not to say, however, that they were mild and considerate, with punches pulled. Strength could not be tested except with hard blows.

Fights of this kind took place every spring in the old market near the waterfront, now Place Royale. The voyageurs were beginning, at that time of year, to get ready for the long canoe journeys they would soon be making from Lachine to Lake Superior, often even to the farther west and northwest. These journeys for the fur trade were hard and danger-filled. Voyageurs challenged one another to prove their toughness before setting out. The market was a natural place for such contests — an open space near the waterfront, in the neighborhood of many taverns.

Voyageur fights of this kind were described by Thomas Storrow Brown, who came to Montreal when a boy in 1818: "Rare sport it was for the boys to see the whole square filled with these people — a dozen fights going on at the same time — fresh men stepping into the ring, as the vanquished in their blood were led off — all as if it were merely a dance." Nobody interfered, "as it was all among themselves and good natured, for even the fighting was without ill-will, only to give proof of strength and endurance."

Street fighting in Montreal, whatever its various origins, was evidently frequent. Reference to it keeps appearing in what was written about quite different matters. It is seen in the instructions drawn up by the Sulpician teachers at the Collège de Montréal

SKETCHBOOK

John Collins

NARROW STREET
OFF PLACE ROYALE

(the Petit Séminaire). This boys' school then stood on what is now St. Paul St., west of McGill. Every year the boys were given a summer holiday at the Priests' Farm, the Sulpician estate on Sherbrooke St. They were marched up the slope from the Collège, led by a school band. They went in disciplined ranks. The Sulpician teachers at the Collège did not want the boys to break ranks and run off to see anything that happened to attract their attention along the way. The instructions particularly emphasized they must not go running off to watch street fights.

Not often, of course, but on rare occasions, some of Montreal's most eminent citizens might use their fists in the street, if felt compelled to do so. One of them was William Henry Drummond, the Montreal physician and poet. Drummond was a powerful Irishman, son of an officer in the Royal Irish Constabulary. He was an athlete in snowshoeing,

hammer-throwing, putting the shot. He was the Canadian amateur champion in fast-walking competitions.

One day, not long before his death in 1907, he was going along a Montreal street when he saw a carter flogging his horse without mercy. Drummond shouted to him to stop it. The carter laughed and hit the quivering horse harder than ever. All his life Drummond hated bullies. He saw the carter as a bully who had to be stopped. He could not bring himself to walk away and allow the cruelty to go on. He did what he felt he had to do, when no one else was on hand to do it. He took off his coat and "came in swinging."

The carter put up a fight. It became a real street battle. But the doctor was determined to win — and he did. Drummond had raised a street fight into an affair of honor.

Goodwill among the churches

Montreal, in past years, suffered much from religious prejudice and bitterness. Intolerance incited harsh words, even violence. But charitable gleams often shone through the strife.

A gracious gesture as far back as the 18th century had a lasting influence on history. At that time one of the prominent ceremonies of the Roman Catholic Church in Montreal was the Corpus Christi procession. The Sacred Host (the "blessed sacrament") was carried through the streets. Devout Catholics knelt in adoration as the priest carried it by. Soon after the beginning of British rule, the commandant of the garrison in Montreal was instructed by the governor to provide an escort of soldiers to accompany the Corpus Christi procession. It would be an act of courtesy and respect. At times troops lined the route. When the Host was borne by, they presented arms in salute.

The Roman Catholic clergy appreciated this consideration. They remembered it during the American Revolution when an army of Americans invaded the province, captured Montreal and went on to besiege Quebec. The American Congress, then with headquarters at Philadelphia, sent diplomats to Montreal. Benjamin Franklin led a special commission in the early spring of 1776. He brought with him a distinguished Jesuit priest, John Carroll, later the first Roman Catholic bishop in the U.S. Carroll, bilingual, was to try to persuade the Catholic clergy of Montreal to exert their influence in favor of the revolution.

But Father Carroll's best arguments had no effect. The French-Canadian clergy told him they were well satisfied under British rule. The rights of the church had been guaranteed; religious liberty had been assured. When Carroll was told that the Protestant governor even provided military honors for the Corpus Christi procession, he was astonished. In the end, he gave up his attempt at persuasion. He had come to doubt the morality of trying to stir up discontent among clergy who were so evidently satisfied with the protection and respect the government had given the church. Carroll soon left Montreal with the Franklin commission. The retreating American army followed.

In Montreal the Roman Catholics made gestures of respect to the Protestants. The early Anglicans in the town had no church to hold their services in. They were accommodated in the handsome chapel of the Récollets (the French Franciscans) at their monastery on Notre Dame St., a little east of where McGill St. is today. In the Récollet chapel the Montreal Anglicans worshipped for more than 20 years, till 1789.

After the Anglicans left for a church of their own, the Presbyterians applied to the Récollets for the use of the chapel. The monks consented. On Sept. 18, 1791, "the Sacrament of the Lord's Supper was administered . . . in accordance with the usages of the Church of Scotland." Next year the Presbyterians moved into a church they had built on St. Gabriel St. As the Récollets refused to accept any payment, the Presbyterians expressed their gratitude with a gift. It took the form of two hogsheads of Spanish wine (containing about 60 gallons each), and a box of candles.

Another example of gracious accommodation came in Victorian times. The Unitarian church on Beaver Hall Hill (the Church of the Messiah) was severely damaged by fire in the early Sunday morning of Oct. 24, 1869. Only a few hours later the president of the St. Patrick's Society, F.B. McNamee, called on the Unitarian minister, John Cordner. He offered the Unitarians accommodation in St. Patrick's Hall on nearby Victoria Square, a building erected as the social and cultural centre of Montreal's Roman Catholic Irish. The offer had been prompted by Rev. Patrick Dowd, pastor of St. Patrick's Church. The room offered in St. Patrick's Hall would be provided with seats for 300, as well as gas, light and heat — all free of any charge.

The offer was gratefully accepted. For four months the Unitarians worshipped in St. Patrick's Hall, till the schoolroom in their own church had been repaired. The congregation expressed its thanks to the St. Patrick's Society for its "great kindness and liberality."

The spirit of interdenominational goodwill was advanced by the first Anglican bishop of Montreal, Rt. Rev. Francis Fulford. He was an Englishman, appointed by the Crown in 1850 as bishop of the

SKETCHBOOK
John Collins

The
OLD RECOLLET CHURCH
ON NOTRE DAME
JUST EAST OF
McGILL STREET

newly created Montreal diocese, and consecrated in Westminster Abbey. Fulford had never seen his Montreal diocese. He knew little of conditions there. Many wondered what attitude he would take toward the Roman Catholic majority or the nonconformist Protestant denominations.

From the start, Fulford made his attitude clear. He would claim in Canada none of the privileges enjoyed by Anglicanism as the established church of England. In Montreal the Church of England would "exist but as one of many religious bodies." His aim would be "to cultivate the spirit of chivalry to all around." He looked with no favor on any attempts to interfere with the Roman Catholic church or to try to convert Roman Catholics to Anglicanism. "Be careful," he warned, "how you destroy the hereditary religion of a people." He had observed that those who move from one faith to another often end up with none.

With this tolerant spirit he administered the Anglican diocese of Montreal, as its first bishop, until his death in 1868. At his funeral it was reported: "The tolling of the great bell of the Anglican cathedral was answered by the tolling of the great bell of the Roman Catholic church of Notre Dame . . . and . . . many gentlemen of French descent were noticed in the procession which followed his remains to the grave."

Bishop Fulford had defined the difference between religious goodwill and religious ill-feeling as being the difference between much religion and a little of it. "A little religion," he said, "is very apt to engender a violent spirit of partisanship; a larger measure of grace and knowledge . . . teaches us . . . more correctly in what way we ought to act towards others."

Lively times in Bonsecours market

Some farmers used to arrive at 4 a.m. They wanted to be sure of as good a place as possible in the outdoor Bonsecours Market. Some would even come to the market the evening before, sleep in their wagons, and be ready to do business with the dawn.

The market's management had its "collectors" at the market by 4 a.m. They charged each farmer 50 cents (later $1) for a parking space. To save farmers the need to get up so early on market days, Tuesdays and Fridays, the management offered season tickets. For a lump sum, a farmer could rent a spot of his own choosing. During that season no other farmer, no matter how early he came, would be allowed to park there. Most farmers, however, still preferred to pay the one-day fee. Market carts filled the whole of Place Jacques Cartier southward from around Nelson's Monument on Notre Dame St. When carts began to overflow the market, additional accommodation was provided on the nearby Champ de Mars.

The outdoor buying and selling made up only part of Bonsecours Market. It was really an expansion outdoors from the massive Bonsecours Market building still standing west of Bonsecours St. between St. Paul St. to the north and de la Commune on the south. Even today (though no longer serving marketing purposes) it looms, with its great dome, as one of the most imposing buildings in the city. When built in the 1840s, it was regarded as awesome.

"This is a magnificent . . . building in the Doric style," wrote one commentator, "erected at a cost of $280,000." In part of this building stalls or shops were rented to butchers; sellers of farm produce had another part. The rest of the building was occupied by the city hall, the municipal (recorder's) court, the chief police station, a concert hall and a headquarters for militia. Gradually, however, more and more of the building came to be used for marketing, as the other activities were accommodated elsewhere.

This indoor marketing had an atmosphere of its own. It was described by Mrs. R.E. MacDougall: "Inside the Bonsecours building was a long, wide alley, with butchers' shops, not stalls, on both sides.

Here serious men, of dignified mien, gave their customers undivided attention, hauling from the cold storage huge quarters of beef, lamb, etc. . . . In the winter there was different and equal interest; the ice and snow melting on men's woollen clothes . . . smoke from Canadian tobacco, the smell of heat from tiny stoves in each booth — this made a rich aroma of true Quebec, never to be forgotten."

The interior of the great market building, however, never equalled the atmosphere of the market outdoors. Those selling outside were the hawkers and hucksters. Their shops were their carts. They were offering produce from their own farms. These were not at all the "serious men of dignified mien" as Mrs. MacDougall described the merchants inside the market building. Doing business outdoors from the wagons meant brisk and excited bargaining, a babbling squabble, a loud and lively struggle. Prices first asked were never taken seriously. A final price could be reached only after a few dramatic gestures of turning away.

Yet it was not a rancorous dispute. It was vigorous giving and taking, ending in a cheerful sale. Over the years friendly relations developed between the same customers and farmers. Pleasant inquiries were made about each other's families. All the same, the shrewd bargaining went on. Friendship was friendship, but business was still business.

A bilingualism of sorts served both buyer and seller. Many of the farmers spoke scarcely any English, many of the buyers scarcely any French. Yet they got along and negotiated their bargains. How it was done was noted by an English visitor: "A curious sort of jargon is carried on in the marketplace between the French, who do not understand English, and the English who do not understand French. Each endeavors to meet the other half way in his own tongue; by which means they contrive to understand one another, by broken phrases, for the common French marketing terms are soon picked up."

Housewives of the Victorian period, and in the early 20th century, bought the family foodstuffs largely in bulk. Meat was bought in huge pieces, often a quarter of a carcass. Butter was bought in wooden tubs known as "tinnets," rendered fat came in pails. Partridge were bought by the brace, often

When I first started sketching Montreal Bonsecours Market included the large building with its conspicuous dome....

...and Jacques Cartier Square plus the area next to the Chateau de Ramezay now a parking lot....

...all a colorful mixture of horses, carts, trucks, produce and people...

JOHN COLLINS SKETCHBOOK

several brace at one time. Today's home refrigerators, even in their deep-freeze compartments, are insignificant in size compared with the larder and cellars of the Victorians and Edwardians.

Mothers took their daughters, especially the eldest, with them on their visits to Bonsecours Market. The daughters had to learn the art of household purchasing. When foodstuffs were bought in bulk, a mistake or poor bargaining might mean a serious loss. The farmers at the Bonsecours Market had much to sell besides food. They brought handicrafts in their wagons: baskets, rugs, quilts, moccasins. Mitts hung from the carts in bunches. Tobacco was plentiful, the true "tabac Canadien." It came in long bunches of greenish and yellow-brown leaves, knotted together at one end.

Bonsecours Market maintained much of its active and picturesque scene until after World War II. Then it dwindled — and quickly. The new way of life was against it. Once the market was near to where people lived. It became remote as they moved away to new areas to the north, west and northwest.

In these new areas (above all in the suburbs) people had the shopping centres. Methods of marketing were changing. The demand no longer was for food in bulk but for food in small packages, often just enough for one meal, and already processed.

Bonsecours Market, remote among the narrow, traffic-choked streets of Old Montreal, belonged more and more to a receding world. By the end of the 1950s Bonsecours had almost lost its battle with modern food-processing and more convenient regional marketing.

Also, the great market building was failing. Damaged by fire, it had become almost derelict. Demolition seemed likely.

It was saved just because it had become outdated. It took on new value as a heritage building, part of the city's past. It was restored and used again as municipal offices, as it had been, in part, when it was new. And the copies of the old gas lamps along St. Paul St. have restored something of the glimmering ambience of its past.

Black magic in a judge's garden

Judge Joseph-Charles Coursol was worried over strange goings-on in his garden. He had a large property below Dorchester St., east of Atwater. He took pride in his garden. But trespassers were coming in at night, treading on his flower beds and cutting up his paths. A circle had been drawn on one of his lawns, and the earth within the circle broken up as if a squadron of cavalry had been carrying out manoeuvres.

In April 1878 Judge Coursol called in the police. Detective Lafond was stationed in the garden. At midnight he saw two men coming in through the gate. One had an enormous rosary around his neck and hanging down his back. From the end of the rosary hung a crucifix, from the crucifix a watch. This man drew a sword from its scabbard and stabbed the earth.

"Entrails of the earth, open!" he commanded, invoking the spirits of evil. He sprinkled the earth with water from a sponge and ripped it with the sword. In the middle of the lawn a large circle was drawn with the sword's point. The two men walked round and round this circle, intoning mysterious incantations.

Lafond leaped out of hiding and seized the sorcerers. At the police station they gave their names: Paul Boone, native of Belgium, and Jean Sudan, a Swiss immigrant. Police examined the mystic paraphernalia: a two-edged sword, a rod, a whip, vials and flasks of magic liquors. There were also two old books about dealings with the devil. One was published in Cologne in 1626, the other (with illuminated pictures of demons) dated from the beginning of the 18th century. One of the prisoners said he had been practicing black magic for years. They had chosen Judge Coursol's garden because they had heard treasure lay hidden there.

Coursol didn't lay charges against them for taking liberties with his garden. He looked on them less as criminals than as "poor fools." The police released the prisoners, but the books on black magic were handed over to the "ecclesiastical authorities." These authorities were seriously concerned with any evidence that black magic was being practiced. To turn from the worship of God to the worship of the devil was heresy in its most appalling form. The Roman Catholic bishop of Montreal, Msgr. Ignace Bourget, had issued a warning to his whole diocese to beware of all such evil practices.

The struggle against such practices had gone on for many years. One of the early instances occurred in 1676. This case was particularly serious in that a priest had become impressed by sorcery. He was Abbé Guillaume Bailly, a Sulpician from France, who had been placed in charge of the Indian mission the Sulpicians had established on the mountainside in the area later known as the Priests' Farm. Bailly, in many ways, was a good man, devoted to his work and talented in languages. Then the strange thing happened. He was not only influencing the Indians, but was being influenced by them.

Bailly was awed by their sorcerers and fascinated by their procedures. The Sulpicians had to take action. The superior of the Sulpicians in Paris felt nothing could be done with a man once he had fallen under such hallucinations. He was recalled from the mission on the mountainside and eventually left the society altogether. From Paris the Sulpician superior wrote: "I am sending you this year a person who is firmly immune to such Devil's tricks." He was M. de Belmont — a remarkable man who later became the superior of the Sulpicians in Montreal.

The story of a soldier, Charles-François Havart de Beaufort, is an example of the serious view taken of black magic in any form. This bright and fluent man was also something of a wag and prankster. In June 1742 a 20-year-old shoemaker in Montreal, Charles Robidou, had money stolen from him. Havart de Beaufort offered, for a fee, to find out who the thief was. He would use black magic. Robidou agreed. That night the soldier went to the shoemaker's house with all his magic equipment. The chief item was a crucifix. He set the crucifix on a table and proceeded with a great display of hocus-pocus. Havart de Beaufort was no sorcerer; he was in reality only playing a trick on the shoemaker. But by doing so he was exposing himself to serious charges. Word of what he had done got about town. He was brought to trial. Accusations were under three headings — sorcery, magic and sacrilege.

He was sentenced to be taken "in his shirt" before the great door of the old parish church in Place

SKETCHBOOK

John Collins

The
GARDEN OF THE HOUSE OF
JUDGE JOSEPH-CHARLES COURSOL
ON ST. ANTOINE STREET

d'Armes (the building that preceded the Notre Dame Basilica there today). According to his sentence he would have to hold a torch of burning wax weighing two pounds. A rope would hang around his neck, together with placards, front and back, condemning him as a "Profaner of Holy things." At the church door he was to kneel and loudly declare his crime.

Then he was to be taken through "the squares and the public thoroughfare," whipped all the way. After this punishment he was to serve as "a convict in the galleys of the King" for five years.

This sentence was entirely carried out, except for the time in the galleys. The five years were reduced to one.

The Montreal lawyer Sidney Bellingham told a story of Jean Bilodeau, who lived in the parish of St. Lazare in the 1840s. He was "a man of position, living on his means," in a house close to the church. Despite his means, Bilodeau was far from comfortable. He suffered the pains of the devil ("les douleurs du diable") from rheumatic gout in the knee.

In the 5th Range of St. Lazare lived a celebrated sorcerer who practiced some kind of black magic. The curé of the church condemned him as an agent of the devil. Bilodeau's friends, however, urged him to seek help from this sorcerer. Others in the parish were said to have been cured by his mystic methods.

Bilodeau was a regular attender at the village church. But he could stand the pain in his knee no longer. He would not go to the sorcerer himself. He sent his relatives on his behalf. When they called on the sorcerer, he told them they could return home and would find that Bilodeau was cured. They found he was right. Bilodeau's pain had ceased at the very moment the sorcerer had said it would.

Yet Bilodeau had gained little. A visitor found him much disturbed "because the church strongly condemned these superstitions." Bilodeau had had dealings (however indirectly) with the devil's agent. He got the pain out of his knee — but would he ever get the guilt out of his soul?

Excursions to a Back River village

In the 1890s the Montreal Park & Island Railway, which provided tramway services to the suburbs, decided to build a line northward right across the island, out to Sault au Récollet on the Rivière des Prairies (the "Back River"). The purpose of this line, six or seven miles long, was not to serve commuters, if any, between Montreal and Sault au Récollet, a small country village. It was to transport Montrealers and tourists who wanted to get away from the city for the day, for a change of scenery, and to enjoy the picturesque charm and peace of an unspoiled French-Canadian village.

The idea of excursions from Montreal to Sault au Récollet didn't originate with the Montreal Park & Island Railway. Back in 1867 a guidebook said: "Another beautiful drive is out to the Back River by the Mile-end road, to the village of . . . Sault au Recollet . . . a lovely spot . . . for picnics, well-wooded and close to a picturesque old mill."

Excursions flourished in summer, and did not cease in winter. It was a pleasant destination for a sleighride over the snow, as it was for carriage drives in summer. One Montrealer, Florence Mary Ramsden, recalled in 1955 "the splendid high-stepping horses, the musk ox, buffalo or bearskin robes edged with scarlet or blue or green, the flashing harness and silver bells . . . dashing along the snowy packed road out to Péloquin's."

M.J. Péloquin, proprietor of the local hotel, had been well trained at the St. Lawrence Hall on St. James St. in the days when its proprietor was Henry Hogan, one of the best-known hotelmen in North America. The Hotel Péloquin at Sault au Récollet was far from the typical village establishment. It was impressive, three storeys high with a four-storey tower. Two balconies ran round three sides of it — at the first- and second-floor levels. Flags, at least four of them, were always flying. Péloquin was expansive, affable, full of little courtesies and tactful compliments, a man meant to be the host in a hotel of his own.

"The views from the verandahs of the hotel are superb," one visitor said. "On one side Mount Royal comes against the horizon, its dark mass distinctly showing against the white cloud-wreaths." The veranda on the other side gave a view of the river winding through the trees. One of the sights at Péloquin's was the timber rafts swirling downstream and seething through the rapids. Sometimes visitors could see as many as 15 or 20 of them, their timbers lashed together with ropes, the men on them working at gigantic oars to hold the rafts in the right channel.

Altogether, Sault au Récollet had many attractions: good fishing, good hunting, picturesque walks and "unlimited sunsets." Péloquin catered not only to persons or parties but to clubs and societies. They would arrive by scores, even hundreds. Péloquin could handle any number, even when they wanted banquets. On some winter days the Montreal Tandem Club would meet on Dominion Square and drive in an elegant procession to Sault au Récollet.

Montreal's snowshoe clubs sometimes made Péloquin's the destination of their long-distance tramps. In the 1890s bicycling became the craze. Bicycle clubs wheeled the six miles to Péloquin's, sometimes returning after dark with Japanese lanterns attached to the handlebars, a long line of swaying lights moving along the country road to Montreal.

The Montreal Hunt Club was one of Péloquin's most profitable customers. Its members were the Montreal aristocrats, often members also of the Tandem Club. Farmlands at the Back River were excellent hunting country where wild foxes might soon be scented by the pack of hounds. Farmers of the area welcomed the coming of the Hunt. They made money by boarding horses, providing feed, doing blacksmithing. If members of the Hunt damaged fences or trampled crops, compensation was fully and promptly forthcoming.

The Hunt Club, realizing the importance of good relations with the farmers, held a picnic or fair for them in the exhibition grounds near Park Ave. The farmers responded with a dinner for members of the Hunt at Péloquin's on Jan. 17, 1884. Péloquin rose to the occasion. About 200 were present. The dining room "was most prettily decorated and the tables laid out with the greatest taste." The great figures of the Montreal Hunt Club were there. The farmers were on hand to welcome their guests.

At the dinner the chairman was Joseph Brosseau, president of the County of Hochelaga Agricultural

The Montreal Park and Island Railway gave trips to Sault-au-Récollet to see this typical French Canadian village with little houses and old-fashioned gardens.

John Collins

SKETCHBOOK

Society. He proposed the toast to the Montreal Hunt Club. Before the evening was over, a member of the Hunt offered the farmers of the Back River a gold medal worth $50. It was to be competed for in a plowing match between the farmers of Hochelaga and Jacques Cartier counties.

Excursions to Sault au Récollet became easier when the Montreal Park & Island Railway built its line to the Back River in the 1890s. Every 30 minutes a car left the corner of St. Lawrence and Craig Sts. Cash fare was 10 cents; 50 tickets were $3. The railway pictured the charms of the trip in one of its promotional brochures: "The sweep of verdant pastures and cultivated fields, sprinkled with stately elms and maple groves, with picturesque farm buildings and church steeples rising here and there, and the silver sheen of the river in the far distance, makes a notable landscape scene."

Such outlying communities as Sault au Récollet retained something of their remote character till after World War II. Suddenly a network of modern streets seemed to spread over the island. The charm of isolation was no longer possible.

Gone are the days when excursionists went by carriage or sleigh, by snowshoes, bicycles or tramcars to visit Péloquin's or to see (as the Park & Island Railway said) this "typical French-Canadian village" with "its little houses, its French ovens, its old wayside crosses and its old-fashioned gardens."

Caughnawaga on the Nile

Caughnawaga on the St. Lawrence is a long way from Egypt on the Nile. But in 1884, 56 Indians from the Caughnawaga reserve were hurried to the Nile to take boats upstream against the rapids. Their special skill as voyageurs, acquired on the rough rivers of the Canadian northwest, had made them invaluable in a sudden Egyptian emergency.

The British government had a deep-vested interest in Egypt, after Prime Minister Benjamin Disraeli (with the secret backing of the Rothschilds) had purchased for Great Britain a controlling interest in the Suez Canal, then regarded as the lifeline of the British Empire. Its security meant protecting Egypt against all menace or disturbance.

In the early 1880s, Mohammed Ahmed, nephew of a Nile boatbuilder, proclaimed himself the messiah. His aim was to conquer the world. This fanatic (who called himself the Mahdi) defeated the Egyptian army, under its English commander, Hicks Pasha. The Sudan seemed likely to fall into his hands. By this time Disraeli had been turned out of office by William Ewart Gladstone. Gladstone, as a Liberal, hated imperial entanglements. He would have liked to get England out of Egypt. This, however, would appear politically as a retreat. He was persuaded to send "Chinese" Gordon into the Sudan. This British general had demonstrated an almost mystical influence over native peoples. Gladstone hoped that Gordon would somehow solve Egypt's problems without requiring the British government to send in troops.

But Gordon found himself cut off in Khartoum, in a country dominated by the Mahdi's fanatics. A cry arose in Britain to send an expedition to rescue him. This was the last thing Gladstone wanted to do, but in the end he had to take action. The call went out for volunteer voyageurs from Canada.

The idea of using Canadian voyageurs had come from a British officer, Lord Wolseley. He had seen voyageurs perform when he served in Canada and led the expedition to the Red River in the Riel Rebellion of 1870. Volunteers came from different parts of the country. Many were French Canadians. Among the Indians the greatest number was from Caughnawaga (now known as Kahnawake). They had

an able leader in Louis Jackson. From Alexandria to Assiout, Jackson and his men jolted along in crowded railway cars. Sand drifted in on them. It was a strange, arid land for men whose very names — like Peter Canoe and James Deer — recalled the life of the Canadian streams and forests.

At Assiout they changed railway cars for barges. Side-wheeled steamboats took them in tow. It was a procession of curious sights. They laughed at a cow and a small camel harnessed together to draw a plow. They were awed by the ancient figures, carved from immense stones, some standing, some sitting in stone chairs, some looking toward the river with huge impassive faces. And there were things of rare beauty. Distant temples and high towers looked white, airy, unreal. About four miles above Wady Halfa the Nile became impassable for steamboats. The Indians went ashore to camp.

The Caughnawaga Indians were paraded for inspection. Though they were not told, they were to make an experimental journey: to determine whether the Nile was a feasible route to follow in rescuing Gordon. A British officer, Colonel Alleyne, was appointed to go with them, examine the route and make reports.

A series of cataracts lay ahead, each with problems and hazards. In the Semneh Cataract they had to keep to a 20-foot channel in a river 1,000 feet wide. The Ambigol Cataract was a mile long, with a channel not only crooked but swift; the combined strength of 35 men was needed to pull one boat with its load. The Tangur Cataract was tortuously broken by rocks and islands. In the Akaska they fortunately found a smooth channel in the middle of the river. But in the Dal Cataract they were unable to follow the channel on one side because it was too shallow, or the channel on the other side because it boiled and seethed. They were saved by an Arab swimmer; he carried a line through the rough water to the shore.

All that the Indians had learned in Canada was put to effective use. They were in a different land, but they were acquainted with rough, swift, rocky water. By the time they reached the head of the last of the Nile's cataracts, all six of the boats were still in service. They had had rough use, running aground

SKETCHBOOK

John Collins

STREET IN
CAUGHNAWAGA

on sand bars and grazing rocks. They had been dragged on shore from time to time for repairs. But they had been brought through, although one of the men drowned.

When they reached the head of the last cataract, they had accomplished their mission: proving the rapids could be mounted. Now they were called upon to prove that the hazards of shooting the rapids on the way back could be overcome also. If the force sent to rescue Gordon could get up the Nile but could not get back again, it might find itself cut off. Shooting the rapids was an old, familiar skill with the Caughnawaga Indians. But it was a wild, exciting sight. The Egyptians came running out of their huts. All lined the shore to see the Indians plunge by.

The Indians accomplished their second mission as successfully as the first. All boats were brought down safely into the quiet water below the Semneh Cataract. There an impressive British force and many whaleboats had been assembled. Alleyne reported that the Caughnawaga Indians had proved that the route up and down the Nile, though difficult, was passable. With this information the movement of the expedition to rescue Chinese Gordon began.

For several months longer the Caughnawaga force remained in Egypt. They served as guides for the fleets of whaleboats mounting the river; they instructed the native Dongalese in the skills of the voyageur. But early in 1885 their active service in the Nile expedition ended and they returned from the Nile to the St. Lawrence. The expedition had failed. Gordon was killed two days before the rescue expedition arrived. The effort to save him had been made too late. Indignation surged against Gladstone for his procrastination. It was one of the reasons he and his government were swept out of office.

Old Josiah Eaton's amazing walk

In the hot days of 1846, sporting persons were anxious about the thermometer. "Do you think he can do it?" and "Have you heard how old Eaton is today?" were questions repeatedly asked. Out at Caledonia Springs, a favorite summer resort for fashionable Montrealers, the thermometer registered 81 in the shade, and seemed more likely to go up than down. But "Old Eaton" (Josiah Eaton, a 76-year-old baker at the Canada House hotel) was bearing up.

Years before, in Suffolk, Josiah Eaton had won renown as a walker. When he was in his 40s, he had attracted attention by walking a mile every consecutive hour for 1,000 hours. In Canada, in 1846, people had hardly credited the old man who claimed that once he had been famous as a champion walker. One of them, however, was willing to try him out, admittedly for his own ends. Henry Clifton, who ran the Canada House, at Caledonia Springs, employed Eaton as a baker. Perhaps it was understood that he would also provide some of the organized entertainment for the guests, although Eaton felt it necessary to publish a denial that he had been forced in any way to take on anything beyond his strength.

Maybe it was nothing more than the longing of an aging and forgotten celebrity to achieve fame again that led Eaton, at 76, to attempt a repetition of the triumph of his youth. This method was called the "Barclay Plan," after a Captain Barclay, another Englishman who in the early years of the 19th century had set himself the task of walking 1,000 miles in 1,000 consecutive hours. It was said that 100,000 pounds had been staked on the issue.

Only 500 pounds was said to be backing Eaton in 1846 and he himself had offered a modest wager of $25. A suitable track was laid out at Caledonia Springs, and it was announced that the old man would begin his "Herculean feat" on July 2. Unfortunately, Eaton caught a bad cold. Not till July 15 was he well enough to begin walking.

At first few people seemed to give much for his chances of finishing the course, but as July drew to a close, interest mounted. "Never since walking was fashionable has there been such excitement," wrote one correspondent from Caledonia Springs. "The old

veteran, while we are writing, is going his fiftieth trip. . . . He is in full view of the visitors from the Canada House and all other hotels. The tinkling of a bell announces his departure and arrival every hour. Respectable persons are engaged to attend him, by night and by day, to see that he performs his mile every hour, and to note the time occupied and to enter it in a timebook kept for the purpose. Many others occupy themselves doing the same thing."

Even at this stage, most people still felt that he was unlikely to be able to complete his undertaking. Visitors to the hotels in Caledonia Springs, their holidays over, would return to Montreal giving the latest news of Josiah Eaton to interested inquirers, not a few of whom had probably a wager or two at stake. One report was to the effect that old Eaton did not seem to hurry himself, but took, on the average, 24 minutes to the mile. For the remainder of the hour he could rest. His mile walked, he would lie down. The old account says: "The moment he lays his head on the pillow he is fast asleep, and as yet a touch arouses him, and then there is no stretching and yawning, but starting up, he slips on his shoes and instantly *WALKS* into his walk."

So the days wore on, and Josiah Eaton continued to pace off one mile every hour. At last, on Aug. 26, Eaton proved that in old age he was even more worthy of fame than in his youth. He completed his feat of pedestrianism of 1,000 miles in 1,000 successive hours. In a young man this Barclay Plan of Walking was considered "a wonderful undertaking;" in the case of Josiah Eaton, "considering his age and other contingencies," its successful completion was regarded as "the most remarkable undertaking ever accomplished." The "hearty cheers of the assembled multitude" were no more than his due. But there was compassion for his age, and he was allowed to retire to rest immediately.

It had been said, more than 30 years earlier, when Barclay had walked his 1,000 miles in 1,000 consecutive hours, that "the pain undergone by the gallant captain" had been "excessive." He had often to be lifted when the hour had struck for his next mile. But Josiah Eaton, four hours after he had done the 1,000 miles in 1,000 hours in his old age, was on hand for a celebration in his honor. The first sight

IN THIS AGE OF THE AUTOMOBILE IT IS HARD TO IMAGINE JOSIAH EATON THE GREAT WALKER

IN HIS OLD AGE HE WON FOR ENDURANCE IN A "PEDESTRIAN" CONTEST

John Collins

SKETCHBOOK

that met his eyes as he stepped out from the hotel, to the accompaniment of cheers, was a chair.

While Eaton had been sleeping, the lady guests at the hotel had been busy. The chair was decorated with flags and ribbons, with flowers and with wreaths of evergreen. And as the old man sat down on the chair, he felt it being raised high in the air. Once again Eaton went his mile but this time he was carried around the course. In front of him marched a man bearing a banner inscribed "One Thousand Miles in One Thousand Hours." Following him was a crowd of people, while the air was filled with cheers and the martial strains of Highland bagpipes. The ladies fluttered their handkerchiefs.

And they had still another surprise for him: when the procession completed the "beat" and returned to the Canada House, they presented him with "a crown of flowers fashioned by their own hands." "Two fair damsels" placed this crown "upon the veteran's head," and "he wore it with all the dignity of a victor in the Olympic Games."

Eaton had lost 12 pounds, bringing his weight down to a mere 116. Although it was noticed that his spirits had never failed, his health and strength had seemed to be "fast giving away." But he soon began to pick up again, and four days after his feat was accomplished, this "perfect miracle" of a man who had "walked his way to everlasting fame" had put on eight pounds. It was proposed at once to set out the facts of the story in a pamphlet to be sold "for the sole and exclusive benefit of Mr. Eaton."

When Buffalo Bill came to Montreal

"Buffalo Bill" is a name out of the far past — the name of the renowned buffalo-hunter and scout in the days of the Wild West on the American plains, the days of settlers in their covered wagons and the Indian raids. Yet in the 1950s lived a Montrealer who had seen and met Buffalo Bill — in Montreal. He was a Montreal lawyer, H.J. Hague, then in his 90s and living in retirement in the Château apartments.

Buffalo Bill — William Cody — had found a new occupation after his hunting and scouting days were over. A born showman, he then organized Buffalo Bill's Wild West Show. It was a spectacular re-enactment of his earlier western adventures. In the show were cowboys and Indians. He even had the original Deadwood Coach — which had gone over prairie trails in the days before roads, and had had running fights with galloping Indians.

Buffalo Bill first brought his show to Montreal in 1885. He camped with all members of his troupe in the Driving Park at Point St. Charles. H.J. Hague went there with his father. As his father, George Hague, was general manager of the Merchants' Bank (later amalgamated with the Bank of Montreal) they were given VIP treatment and introduced to the great Buffalo Bill himself.

However, it wasn't a day for seeing him to best advantage. Conversation was mostly confined to his complaints. He had just got an attack of "fever and ague." It would prevent him from doing full justice to the show. Yet the Wild West show, despite that, was superb. Hague remembered that it went "with wonderful vim from the beginning to the end."

Buffalo Bill made a dramatic entry at the start, coming in on a "magnificent horse" at the end of the procession. Nor had the fever and ague impaired his marksmanship. During the show an Indian rode in front of him, carrying a basketful of glass balls. One by one he tossed them into the air. Buffalo Bill, firing from the saddle, hit all except one, and the Indian tossed about 20.

Astonishing marksmanship was also displayed by a member of his team, little Annie Oakley. At that time she was 25 years old and had just joined the show. She was tiny, dressed in a cowgirl's tunic, very short skirt, calf-high boots and a flopping sombrero.

Among her accomplishments was shooting holes through playing cards tossed into the air. A 50-cent coin was held in a man's hand. She shot it out from between his thumb and forefinger.

The climax of the show was the Indian attack on the Deadwood Coach. When the coach first went out into the American west in 1875, Indians blasted its driver with buckshot. Later Buffalo Bill went out to search for it, brought it back and repaired it. In the re-enactment a desperate, galloping fight was performed. The Indians gave up and rode off. The coach was saved. It was a display of frenzied excitement and confusion, completely planned in advance.

Another feature of the show was Chief Sitting Bull in person. It was he who trapped and slaughtered General George Custer at the battle of the Little Big Horn in 1876. H.J. Hague and his father were presented to him.

"He was squatting in his wigwam," Hague recalled, "looking very dignified, with an Indian standing behind him who acted as interpreter. The conversation was naturally very brief. Indeed, I remember that my father was rather at his wits' end what to say."

Hague recalled other events of his Victorian days, and the different way of life. He had his memories of the great Montreal floods of the 1880s. Boats moved about the flooded streets. Hague remembered "seeing two girls standing at the edge of the water, and watching the boats for hire that were moving about. One said to the other, 'I think I'll pay a dollar and go and see Pa and Ma'."

After the flood had receded Hague walked along Commissioners St. He noted the line left by the water — "bags of meal half wet and half dry." At Custom House Square (now Place Royale) the planks of the wooden sidewalks, which had floated loose, lay in heaps.

The happiest of Hague's memories seemed to be associated with the Victoria Skating Rink. It was a huge building with an iron-beamed ceiling that stood on Drummond St., a little above Dorchester. "I remember it during the 1880s," he wrote, "when one constantly heard, 'Goodbye, see you at the rink,' for at the rink one was almost certain to meet everyone

JOHN COLLINS

SKETCHBOOK

SITTING BULL

The SIOUX VICTOR OF THE BATTLE OF THE " LITTLE BIGHORN "

"BUFFALO BILL" CODY

PONY EXPRESS RIDER, SCOUT, HUNTER and SHOWMAN

you know." People went to the Victoria Rink whether they intended to go on the ice or not. A wide promenade, about a foot higher than the ice, ran all around the rink.

A band (often the band of the Victoria Rifles) played on Saturdays, and on most weekday evenings. Hague would dwell in his memories on the fancy-dress carnivals at the Victoria Rink: "The fancy dress carnivals justify everything that can be said about them. . . . The wonderful effects of colors in the fancy dresses, the constant movement of the skaters, for it was not a cause of looking at a performance — everybody was in it, either on the ice or strolling round the promenade. . . . I always have a nostalgic feeling . . . remembering the old days and the throngs of young people coming through the central door. . . . It would be hard for anyone to realize who had not actually been 'in it'."

The mail takes wings

"*It is difficult indeed to exactly analyze one's feelings as the great motors which will haul us through the skies begin to roar, and we know then that history, vibrant and pulsating, is being made.*"

So wrote an aviation correspondent, H.A. Somerville, on Oct. 1, 1928. He was on a plane taking off from Albany, N.Y., for the St. Hubert airport near Montreal. The flight was history-making because it was inaugurating the first airmail service between the U.S. and Canada — the first international airmail service on the American continent. The naive tone of the dispatch (even though it was written by an aviation correspondent for the Montreal Herald) came as a reminder that flight in the 1920s could still be a startling novelty.

While this correspondent was thrilled with the rise of the airplane, thousands of spectators were converging on St. Hubert. Automobiles jammed the Chambly road. All those coming from Montreal had to make their way through the bottleneck of the Victoria Bridge. In 1928 neither the Jacques Cartier Bridge nor the Champlain Bridge existed. Two hundred and sixty Montreal policemen had been mobilized. The crush on the Victoria Bridge had to be avoided. They were marched on foot to the wharf of the Longueuil ferry. After crossing the St. Lawrence by steamboat, they boarded a fleet of autobuses and were driven to the airfield. There they controlled the gathering crowd.

Notables were assembling at St. Hubert to celebrate the new era of air mail. Quebec's lieutenant-governor, Narcisse Pérodeau, was there, as was the premier, L.A. Taschereau. The U.S. was represented by its ambassador to Canada, William Phillips. Montreal's mayor, Camillien Houde, arrived, then still new in office but ready with a witty speech.

The airplane, all metal and with three motors, was surprising to the aviation correspondent with its smooth flight. "You will be surprised to know," he wrote, "that it is as easy to stand poised on one foot in the cabin as on the floor of one's bedroom." Exhilaration almost overcame him: "Gradually one experiences a sensation that is certainly one of the most extraordinary man has ever felt. We are

transcending human nature. We feel immeasurably superior to those crawly things we see 2,000 ft. below us."

St. Hubert was drawing near. The "trusty pilot" was now pushing the nose of the great liner toward the earth. In a few minutes the plane was gently bumping its way along St. Hubert airfield. It had arrived at 11:20 a.m., only five minutes late.

Mail and express vans scurried across the field to pick up the airmail bags. The Department of National Revenue had set up a customs house near the entrance to the aerodrome three days before. Parcels were promptly cleared. One parcel was full of merchandise for Henry Morgan & Co. Ltd. (now the Bay). So quickly was it handled that it was in the store in little more than an hour from its arrival. The new airmail service was not only between Albany and Montreal: Toronto was included. Only five minutes after the plane put down at St. Hubert another plane rose into the air and flew off to Toronto. Mail had been transferred from one to the other under the supervision of Victor Gaudet, postmaster-general of Montreal.

At St. Hubert the inauguration of international airmail on the American continent was hailed with speeches. Most of them were formal and predictable. It remained for Mayor Houde to inject the lighter mood. "Time was, and that not so long ago," he said, "when it was considered the characteristic vice of politicians that they were always up in the air. It is, therefore, a particular pleasure for me to be able today to take part in inaugurating another forward step in the new era in which any man can get up in the air as often as he likes . . . and still remain a perfectly competent politician."

The day's program had only begun with the arrival of the airmail from the U.S. and the making of speeches. The event was celebrated with a display of air manoeuvres, "the like of which" (it was claimed) had "never before been seen in Canada." Forty-two airplanes performed over the field. In the clear autumn air four Siskin fighters of the RCAF, flying in formation, looped, zoomed, rolled. They even pelted a corner of the airfield with smoke bombs. The program included races. A derby was flown over a 30-mile course in two heats and a final. Best of 12

JOHN COLLINS SKETCHBOOK

FIRST AIRMAIL
BETWEEN CANADA
AND THE U.S.A.

Albany to St. Hubert

competitors was Capt. F.G.M. Sparks, chief instructor of the Montreal Light Aeroplane Club. He had averaged 110.8 miles an hour.

When the demonstrations and contests were over, a number of planes took passengers on brief flights — just enough to give them their first sensation of being airborne. Huntly R. Drummond, president of the Canada Sugar Refining Co. (and later president of the Bank of Montreal), had arranged an aviation party for about 30 of his friends. He had chartered a plane. This Canadian Colonial Airways passenger plane made a series of short flights. Drummond, as host, remained aboard, entertaining his guests in relays, as they were flown over the airport and the surrounding countryside.

By this time a mail-carrying plane from St. Hubert had taken off for Albany with letters and parcels for Americans. It bore one piece of living air mail. This was a 3-month-old bear cub travelling in a tin carton reinforced with wooden strips. The cub was a gift to mark the inauguration of airmail between Canada and the U.S. — a gift from Montreal's Houde to Mayor Jimmy Walker of New York.

With the early-October sunset, the great day came to a close.

It had been a day of marvels.

Two wandering editors find a resting place

Two editors of *The Gazette* had gone to Lachine for the May 24 holiday in 1871. In a hired skiff they planned to row across the river to Caughnawaga (Kahnawake). Snared by the current, they felt themselves drawn downstream toward the rapids — the wildest rapids on the St. Lawrence River. A farmer named Somerville, on the Lower Lachine Road, saw them "rowing for their lives." He knew nothing could save them.

The two men were George S. Spaight and Charles E.F. Lodge. Spaight was assistant editor of *The Gazette*, Lodge its night editor. Both were Irishmen; both had attended Trinity College, Dublin; both were young — Spaight 32, Lodge not yet 30. They naturally thought the best way to spend their May 24 holiday was to go to Lachine, for both were known to be "passionately fond of the water, and boating was their usual recreation." For some reason, however, Spaight had been reluctant to go that day. Lodge had persuaded him.

At that time Lachine was Montrealers' most accessible resort for "aquatic sports." The waterfront of the city had been taken over by the port and its installations. The river west of the city was broken by the Lachine Rapids. Only when Lachine itself was reached was there the broad smooth lake. In 1868 the Montreal Witness was saying: "Lachine in summer is a favorite residence for Montreal families, on account of the facilities it presents for boating and fishing, and its easy access by rail from the city."

In addition to summer residences for Montreal families, Lachine had summer hotels and boarding houses. The trains of the Grand Trunk Railway easily covered the few miles from Bonaventure Station. At Lachine canoes, skiffs and Verchères boats could be rented by the hour.

Spaight and Lodge were seen by Judge Saxton of Montreal's Recorder's Court. They had rented a skiff and were setting out for Caughnawaga. It was a risky objective. The very name "Caughnawaga" meant "on the rapids." The crossing could be made safely by those familiar with the currents and how to avoid their downstream pull.

Suddenly Spaight and Lodge became aware the current had gripped their skiff. At this point, Somerville, from his farm, saw them being swept into the rapids. He witnessed their death struggle as they were "pulling as never before had men been seen to pull." They could not win and they must have known it. In an interval of frantic strength they were holding the skiff steady. Then it was tossed into the air by the onrush of water. One of the men was hurled out. He dropped into the water and out of sight. The skiff overturned. The other man turned over with it and was gone. Only days later were the bodies recovered.

Spaight was the type of journalist who liked to move from place to place. Versatile and resourceful, he maintained himself by working briefly for newspapers here and there, often as foreign correspondent. He was also a freelancer, contributing articles to magazines. Spaight was said to have "visited every quarter of the world. Paris was as familiar to him as London, London as Dublin, and Sydney, Melbourne and more, all just as familiar."

Lodge, before turning to journalism, had adopted another means of seeing the world: he had joined the British army. He was stationed on different continents. Before settling in Canada, he had been here with the garrison. He was then sent to Gibraltar, where he was in an accident. Both ankles were broken. He was invalided out of the army. Apart from his army experience, Lodge travelled widely. He had gone beyond Europe into the Orient, becoming "a talented linguist and a proficient Oriental scholar." He wrote poetry as well as prose. Some of his poems were published in Montreal.

The characters of the two men were defined by a Montreal journalist who knew them both: "Was there a characteristic belonging to a gentleman? Then Spaight had it. Was there an easy-going, sprightly feature you would look for in an accomplished man-of-the-world? Then be sure you could find it in Lodge."

Spaight and Lodge were buried in Mount Royal Cemetery. After lives of wandering over the world, they had few ties to any part of it. Their brief time in Canada had not attached them closely to the

SKETCHBOOK
John Collins

The CAIRN, CROSS and PLAQUE
IN MEMORY OF TWO GAZETTE
EDITORS DROWNED IN THE
LACHINE RAPIDS

community. Their only circle of friends was within the newspaper fraternity. After their deaths, a meeting of those friends took place. It was agreed that the graves of Spaight and Lodge should not be left unmarked. A committee was formed under Thomas White, editor and joint owner of *The Gazette* with his brother, Richard. Circulars were distributed among the members of the press who had known Spaight and Lodge.

The collected subscriptions were sufficient to erect an impressive monument, designed and made by the Montreal sculptor Mariotti. It was a rustic cross entwined by ivy leaves, symbols of the resurrection. After their varied lives in many lands, both men had come to rest in this valley on a mountaintop. Mount Royal Cemetery was then scarcely 20 years old, but already guidebooks were describing it as "one of the most romantic and secluded burying grounds in the world." Here the monument to these two *Gazette* editors was set up, with the inscription:

GEORGE SPAIGHT
CHARLES E.F. LODGE
DROWNED IN
LACHINE RAPIDS
MAY 24th 1871
A TRIBUTE OF RESPECT
FROM THE
CANADIAN PRESS

A woman's reminiscences of old Montreal

"*There were oyster boats anchored in the river, to which one went out, and paid 25 cents to eat all the oysters one wanted, and throw the shells over the side into the river.*"

Lucy Jewett (Lucy Potter before her marriage) could remember those days in Montreal in the 1880s and 1890s. She also recalled the old root-beer woman down near the wharf, at the west end of Bonsecours Market. That woman "had a barrel of homemade root beer, very good, too, which she sold at a penny a glass and two gingerbread 'hands' for a penny. My father loved to take visitors down for the three-cent treat."

Lucy Jewett was gifted with the capacity for total recall. She left Montreal in 1901, the year of Queen Victoria's death, to live in California. She rarely visited the city again, but her memories of it were clear till she died.

There were childhood memories of picnics on the campus of McGill University, at a time when evidences of James McGill's old farm still lingered. A stream flowed through the grounds and blue violets grew in the grass: "I was born at 70 Cathcart St. at the foot of McGill College Ave. . . . and I, with three other little girls, used to play with our dolls on Saturday mornings up in the 'College Grounds' where the little stream came through the grass (near where the engineering building was built later). . . . Sir William Dawson (the principal) and Lady Dawson lived up above the hollow, and they used to stop by and visit with us little girls and inquired after the dolls' health." The girls came with cookies and one bottle of Gurd's ginger ale, "with the big cork held down by wire."

Her childhood was in the days when Montreal's streets were lighted by gas and many houses had coal-oil lamps: "I can remember the trips to Cole's Lamp Store on St. Catherine St., near Bleury, to bring home a gallon can of coal oil. I was too small to walk that far, but I rode over and back on a friend's sled and was allowed to hold the coal-oil can in front of me, between my feet. Three of us would make the trip . . . to Cole's and back late in the afternoon, just before dark. The lamplighter came around to light up the gas lamps in front of our houses, about that time. It was fun to watch him twist the gas burner with one part of his wand and light the gas with the white taper on the other part."

The 1880s were the years of the great floods. When the ice broke up in the river and began drifting downstream, it might jam near the head of Ile Ste. Hélène. It piled up into a dam. The oncoming water, mounting behind it, overflowed the shore and sometimes spread as far into the city as Victoria Square.

Lucy Jewett remembered the flood of 1886: "One winter we lived in the Albion 'Otel, as their bus driver called it. That was the time of the flood. . . . I rode around in a boat in the 'Otel dining room and out the great front door onto McGill St. and over to Craig and Notre Dame . . . and watched men passing out loaves of bread to people in the second-storey windows. Even Queen Victoria's statue had a lot of water at its base. Never was there a boat ride like that one."

Not many of the landmarks mentioned in Mrs. Jewett's letters are still standing. One of the few is St. George's Church, built in 1870. In her day the rector was Rev. James Carmichael, later dean and eventually the Anglican archbishop of Montreal. Of him she wrote: "The dean . . . was the most marvellous man, with a lovely Irish brogue when he wished to use it. 'Children, th'oye of the Almighty is upon ye,' he would say — and 'the loins and the toigers they girt him round about.' The dean used to demand my services, when I was growing up, to play 'th'hymns for th'infant class . . . and we came out strongly on Work for the Night Is Coming and Onward, Christian Soldiers. Once a year there was a festival, when the orphans had a special treat of buns and sweetened weak tea in mugs, and an orange apiece to take back to their home. It made us all grateful not to be an orphan."

Lucy Jewett went to one of the most prominent girls' schools of the day, Misses Symmers and Smith's School. She had physical training at Miss Barnjum's gymnasium in the back part of the Fraser Institute at the corner of Dorchester and University. Miss Barnjum was "very careful of her young pupils." She would say, "Will someone tell that dear sweet child to pull up her darling little stocking?"

Shops and shopping are described in these letters.

John Collins SKETCHBOOK St. George's Church

At Murray's Flower Shop there was Celia Murray, who "used to have trays of rosebud boutonnieres ready for the men who came over from the St. James's Club on their way home." St. James and Notre Dame were the principal shopping streets at that time. Their rows of shops made a grand display of merchandise — dry goods, jewelry, pianos, Walker's candy (40 cents a pound). And there were the big department stores — Morgan's, Murphy's and Carsley's. She said of Carsley's: "Carsley's was perfectly set up — but cheap for cash. . . . One went round to see Carsley's to see what they had to offer after doing the regular charge-account plugs . . . and maybe (just maybe) climbed into a cab at the corner of Victoria Square and drove home for 25 cents!"

Morgan's moved to St. Catherine St. in 1891. The next year Lucy Jewett boarded, in front of the store, the new electric streetcar. It was on the first day these cars were running on St. Catherine St.: "It was very elegant and warm and large, a far cry from the old horse-cars and sleighs with their straw on the floor and little stove up near the driver."

Lucy Jewett, since she had not lived in Montreal since 1901, was well aware that what she was remembering must nearly all have passed away. "You can't go home again," she would say. In a letter dated Nov. 10, 1958, she wrote: "J'ai vu Madame Albani singing Swanee River in the Drill Hall, Sir John A. Macdonald in the Windsor Hotel on his 70th birthday . . . also in the Windsor Mrs. Langtry in her private suite, wearing the dark red satin dress which became famous on the thread calendar, the toboggan slide which came down Peel St. . . . Louis Rubenstein, the champion figure-skater of the world, practising in a corner of the Victoria Rink (he taught me to do 'the grapevine' and to waltz on skates), the Shamrocks and the Winnipegs playing hockey at the Victoria Rink."

"It is a goodly heritage!" she would say — a heritage of memories of the days that were gone.

Old customs for a new year

In the 1890s, probably the grandest of the New Year's balls were given by Mr. and Mrs. Montagu Allan (later Sir Montagu and Lady Allan). Their mansion, Ravenscrag, perched high on Mount Royal, had been built in the 1860s by Allan's father — Sir Hugh Allan, the shipping magnate. The old building is still there. In the 1940s Sir Montagu gave it to the Royal Victoria Hospital, to become the Allan Memorial Institute of Psychiatry.

Typical of Ravenscrag's dances was the New Year's ball on the last evening of 1894. "Joy and jollity reigned supreme at Ravenscrag on New Year's Eve," says an account of the time. "It was a perfect night; and as the long line of sleighs ascended the slope of the mountain, not the least beautiful sight to their occupants was that of Ravenscrag itself, outlined in points of light against the dark background of Mount Royal."

Two Montreal policemen were on hand to open the doors. Guests were greeted with "A Happy New Year" spelled out in a display of pink and red carnations. The Allans received their guests in a dining room next to the ballroom. More than 400 invitations had been issued. It was said that "the recipients who did not 'accept with pleasure' were only debarred from doing so by unavoidable causes," for the New Year's Ball at Ravenscrag was "one of the most delightful social events of the winter."

Twenty dances were on the program. All were old-fashioned dances, included for that sentimental evening — the waltz, lancers, polka, jubilee, galop, and, as a finale, a Sir Roger de Coverley. Tunes also had a sentimental flavor: Charming, Ecstasy, Child of Fortune, Isle of Champagne, Le Courrier d'Amour. Guests were dancing a double set of lancers when the deep-toned clocks of Ravenscrag sounded midnight.

The dance broke up. All formed a ring at the middle of the ballroom floor. Hand in hand they sang Auld Lang Syne. The New Year was "welcomed in with merry laughter and hearty greetings to one and all." The year 1895 was several hours old when the last sleighload of guests drove away "from what was acknowledged to have been one of the most successful balls ever given in Montreal."

But not all the pleasures of the New Year's Eve had been on the ballroom floor. Many guests withdrew from time to time to Ravenscrag's conservatory. It was "a dream of fragrance and beauty." Rose-colored lights — the wonderful new incandescent electric lights — shone on masses of foliage and rare blooms. Guests "availed themselves of the comfortable seats provided for them, and enjoyed the cool repose of sequestered nooks under the palms."

Gentlemen at the Ravenscrag ball, though they didn't get home till nearly dawn, had to be up again on New Year's Day to make their visits. In 1895 the New Year's visit was still a rigorous social obligation. The ladies, carefully and elegantly dressed, remained at home to receive the visitors. Gentlemen that day were required to call on all relations, all friends, and many of those associated with them in their business or profession. Many also paid their respects to the bishop, the Gentlemen of the Seminary, or the principal of McGill University. On that day such public personages did not themselves make calls; they remained at home to receive their New Year's visitors.

At every house hospitality was extended by serving wine from a decanter. For many years custom required that such refreshment offered by a lady had to be accepted. As the calls were many, the effect was cumulative. Later in the Victorian era a new practice was introduced. Refreshments were placed on a table in an anteroom near the entrance. They were offered by a servant. Gentlemen who would have felt obliged to accept hospitality from a lady felt quite free to decline it when offered by a servant.

One New Year's Day custom required that no caller be turned away. This presented an opportunity for timely reconciliations among those who had quarrelled during the year, or even many years before. If any estranged person wished to call, whether on impulse or by design, he invariably would be received. No awkward invitation need be extended. No call need be made with anxious uncertainty as to what sort of reception might be encountered.

Paying New Year's calls was a custom of French and Scottish origin. But others unacquainted with

SKETCHBOOK
John Collins   Entrance to Ravenscrag

it, who settled in Montreal, soon realized its charm and value. One of these was an Englishman from Kent, Rt. Rev. Ashton Oxenden, Montreal's Anglican bishop from 1869 to '78. On his first New Year's Day in Montreal he received nearly 300 visitors. He might have been a little concerned over the possibility of encouraging excess by offering wine, but he came to consider the custom of New Year's calls courteous and beneficial. "It is a genial and time-honored custom," he said, "and one that I should be very sorry to see discontinued. It draws out much kind feeling; and I have known cases where it has been the signal of reconcilation between persons who have been long estranged from each other."

New Year's calls were brief. Social obligation was met by putting in an appearance of only a few minutes. In most homes new callers were always arriving, making it easy for those already there to leave. The city, of course, was then smaller and far more compact. Distances between calls were often slight. Nevertheless, it was a long, hard day.

How exhausting it could be appears in a description of New Year's Day in the 1870s by Hector Fabre. He was a lawyer and journalist, the brother of Archbishop Fabre of Montreal and from 1882 till his death in 1910 the representative of the Canadian government in Paris. "When a gentleman came home after making his 65 to 85 New Year's calls," said Hector Fabre, "he longed for nothing so much as rest. But that rest was unlikely. His wife and daughters were waiting to be told about everything."

When St. Catherine was a country road

"*S*t. *Catherine St., from Phillips Square to Mountain St., was a country road, with a long open ditch in the fields to the south. On the other side, up to Sherbrooke St., were fields of potatoes and cabbages. The fields from Guy St. to what is now Greene Ave. . . . were covered with crops of grain.*"

This was the picture of St. Catherine St. about the year 1840, as recalled in the 1890s by the Montreal bookseller and stationer F.E. Grafton. The street was then, and remained for some time afterward, little more than a country road, cutting across the farms.

One of the first buildings to appear on St. Catherine was the Protestant Orphans' Asylum. It was built in 1846 on land at the corner of Stanley. The fresh air and rural setting had been considered appropriate for a healthy upbringing for the children. But the orphans' asylum was very lonely. There was almost nothing near it but fields.

Before the end of the 1840s John Birks built a house facing St. Catherine St., where the Birks building was later erected. His son (the founder of Henry Birks & Sons) was to recall that in 1849 there was still nothing west of Phillips Square except two buildings — the house of "a Mr. Ross" and the Protestant Orphans' Asylum. Phillips Square was then the bed for a pond.

The authorities of McGill University, pressed for funds, decided to keep only the portion of James McGill's farm above Sherbrooke St. The rest of it, to the south, would be sold off as building lots. One of the developers who bought land from the university was George Browne, builder and architect. In 1854 he built a residential row on the south side of St. Catherine, covering the block between McGill College Ave. and Mansfield. This terrace, built from his own designs, was named the Wellington Arcade, in tribute to the great Duke of Wellington. On the roof, at either end, a wooden statue of Wellington was placed. Browne took one of the houses in the Wellington Arcade as his own home.

St. Catherine St. was beginning to become a residential street, but it was only a beginning. The north side of the street was still farms. The grandson of George Browne, Gault McCombe, later recalled his mother's description of the open fields: "There

were no buildings on the north side of St. Catherine St. from Mansfield St. to the Anglican cathedral, and my mother used to ride over these fields. My mother used to tell me that when they first moved to St. Catherine St. from the lower part of the city about 1855, the baker only came up about twice a week."

On July 1, 1867, when Montreal had special celebrations to mark the first Dominion Day, a grand display of fireworks took place in the evening on Mount Royal near the reservoir at the head of McTavish St. The civic authorities recommended that the display was likely to be seen to best advantage in the open fields near Stanley St. or McGill College Ave.

The burst of growth in mid-century Montreal soon made St. Catherine, and its cross-streets, a favorite area for houses. By 1864 St. Catherine was sufficiently settled to justify the Montreal City Passenger Railway Co. in adding a St. Catherine St. route to its horsecar lines. Though the central portion of St. Catherine was becoming residential by the 1860s and 1870s, the western end, between Mountain and Guy and beyond, remained more or less countrified. A one-plank sidewalk lay west of Mountain. When E. Phillips Hannaford, chief engineer of the Grand Trunk Railway, built his house in 1868 at the northwest corner of St. Catherine and Mackay Sts., he not only had large grounds about the house itself, but kept a vegetable garden on Mackay, where the Murray Apartments were later built, and pastured his cow just above it. When the Church of St. James the Apostle was built in 1864 one block to the east, it was a pioneering effort on the outskirts of the city.

Bishop and Crescent Sts., between St. Catherine and Sherbrooke, were not opened through the fields. This large area was made up of playing fields for Montreal's various sports. Before the end of the 1860s the tracks for horsecars had been extended along St. Catherine from Mountain to Guy. The street, west of Guy, remained so far out in the country that the extension of the rails to Greene Ave. in 1872 was undertaken only when Robert Mitchell and other owners of the land were ready to subsidize the construction.

When St. Catherine had been established as a

JOHN SKETCHBOOK
Collins St. James the Apostle

choice residential street, those who lived there resented the intrusion of commercialism. The shops had remained downtown, mostly along St. James and Notre Dame. The first big store to make the move up the hill to St. Catherine was Henry Morgan & Co. Ltd., now the Bay.

The decision to go uptown was made by the Morgans at the end of the 1880s. They bought and demolished a row of limestone houses along St. Catherine, just east of Union Ave. In these houses had lived some prominent citizens, including Sir William Hingston and John Lovell. The land cost $100,000. The store was opened on April 21, 1891. Colin Morgan liked to describe the pity displayed toward him, and other members of the family, when the move uptown was made. It was declared to be "veritable madness."

James Ogilvy faced similar warnings when he decided, a few years later, to move his business from St. Antoine to the corner of St. Catherine and Mountain. One old Montrealer remembered, many years later, "how gloomy forecasts were made . . . at the boldness of the firm in building so far west on St. Catherine St. Westmount was then practically only at its beginnings and on St. Catherine St. a businessman west of Peel seemed to be out of active competition for the uptown trade."

Near the end of the horsecar line at Greene were several livery stables. They did a thriving business. People living west of Greene would leave their horses and buggies there and take the horsecars to Montreal.

They would pick up their horses and buggies at Greene on their way home.

Nurses' training in the 1890s

"*A mistaken impression prevails that a nurse's life is all hard, disagreeable work, that she has little, if any, recreation, and has to stand 12 hours a day. Of course, there are times when the wards are crowded, and the nurse is very busy, but it is seldom that she cannot find some time during each day in which to sit down and make dressings for the ward; then there is her hour off duty in which she can rest or go out.*"

So a nurse wrote in 1892. She was a member of the first graduating class of the Montreal General Hospital. The hospital had organized a training school for nurses under the direction of Nora Livingston, a Canadian who had graduated from the New York Hospital. After two years under her intensive training, the first class of young women had completed the course and were ready to receive their diplomas.

The rules for nurses who trained under Nora Livingston were strict and clear. Rising time was 6 a.m. Hours on duty were from 7 to 7, with one hour off. Every week a nurse also had an afternoon off and part of Sunday. Two weeks' vacation was allowed during the year. Though nurses were at liberty to go out when off duty, they had to be in before 10 p.m., unless special permission had been obtained from the lady superintendent. It was rigorous training, but Nora Livingston, as lady superintendent, was convinced that unless high standards were set from the start, a certificate of graduation would have little meaning or status.

One of the problems confronting the nurses in training was the thermometer. Patients were not accustomed to it; many had never seen one before, much less admitted one into their mouths. Many patients broke the thermometers. If the nurse warned them of one danger, they immediately incurred another. "Now, will you please put this little thing under your tongue," the nurse instructed, "but do not hold it with your teeth or you may break it." The uncertain patient did not hold it at all, but merely let it fall to the floor, and then remarked, "It fell, nurse." The nurse tried again: "Put this under your tongue, hold it tightly or it will fall to the floor and break." This time the patent would hold on with such determination that the tip of the thermometer was bitten off.

Some patients dreaded a thermometer. They wondered what effect it might have on them, and whether the hospital authorities really knew what they were doing. Other patients looked on the thermometer as a form of therapy. The results disappointed them. "I kept it in a long time, nurse," a patient might say, "but do not feel much better yet."

Another problem for these early nurses was to get some patients to have a bath. These patients said they had never had one in their lives and never intended to have one. One patient with serious eye trouble got up and walked out. She preferred the risk of losing her eyesight to being given a bath, which in her case was very necessary.

In ambulance cases, the real emergencies, the nurses in training had to clean up patients before the doctors attended them. Nurses were alerted when an ambulance case might be expected. The nurse made a bed ready. The injured person was in for a thorough scrubbing. Over a bed the nurse spread a wetproof mackintosh, then stood waiting with pails of water, brushes, sponges and soap. No matter how thick or hard the dirt on the patient might be, it had to come off. If water, brushes, sponges and soap all proved insufficient, the nurse resorted to turpentine. The turpentine generally worked as a dirt remover. If it didn't, the nurse then tried ether.

Livingston had planned a comprehensive two-year course for these first nurses in training. They attended lectures, at which the principal doctors of the hospital gave instruction in their specialties. Every third or fourth month the student nurses were moved to another ward, medical or surgical, male or female. They were rarely told before the day they were moved where they were going next.

Most attractive of all wards was the children's. It was large and bright, with polished floor, pretty carpets, screens and little red chairs. Nurses thought themselves fortunate to be in the children's ward at Christmas. The whole ward was decorated and a tree was laden with toys. One of the doctors made himself into a Santa Claus. He pretended that he had parked his sleigh and reindeer on the roof. Coming down by the fire escape, he climbed in

The FIRST NURSES' GRADUATION CLASS

The MONTREAL GENERAL HOSPITAL

John Collins SKETCHBOOK

through a window and distributed the toys.

The nurses were all given experience in the outpatient department, where they learned first aid. More formidable was the training in the operating room, but it was found that none of these student nurses fainted at their first sight of an operation. They disproved the expectation that every new nurse would pass out.

These probationers of the 1890s had an authorized uniform: a pink cotton dress, white apron, collar and cuffs and a white muslin cap. Their outdoor uniform was a long cloak of navy blue serge and a small white bonnet with navy blue and white strings. This presumably was the outdoor uniform Livingston modelled one day when she appeared at a meeting of the committee of management. She wanted the hospital to buy it for the probationers to wear. It would have "protective value" when they walked the rowdy streets around the hospital on Dorchester, east of St. Lawrence. The cost per uniform would be $6.30.

The committee members, it turned out, had no objection to the outdoor uniform, but objected to paying for it. The nurses bought their outdoor uniforms themselves.

These first graduates had no word of complaint or criticism. They felt the excitement and fascination of the experience. The work was hard but the career opening before them was a privilege. Though they had little time for recreation, they enjoyed what they had. Their quarters, on the top floor of the hospital, provided them with a parlor or common room. It was "a pleasant room" with a fine piano, easy chairs, writing desks and books. Up there the nurses of that first class had enjoyed many teas and suppers together. Altogether they regarded themselves as fortunate.

As a member of the graduating class of 1892 wrote, "While there may be hardships in the life of a nurse, still, I think . . . that there are many privileges which she enjoys, and that the woman who is a trained nurse is much to be envied."

Brother André's microphone

When Brother André grew old, he began to wonder how he could carry on his work at St. Joseph's Oratory. That work was extremely demanding.

Every day hundreds of pilgrims lined up to tell him their troubles. They came to hear from him words of encouragement and hope — even the hope of a miracle. But when he had entered his 80s, Brother André, more and more, was feeling his strength unequal to the demands.

When pilgrims were hard of hearing, he had to raise his voice to make them understand what he was saying. His exhaustion at every day's end was becoming a serious problem. Yet he could not forsake his central role at St. Joseph's Oratory.

People needed him. They needed him so much that many came miles to see and hear him, even from other countries. Something had to be done to make him able to go on with what he was doing.

By 1909 Brother André had a room, called an office, where he received pilgrims. Though the office was moved to other buildings as the work expanded, the routine established in 1909 scarcely changed through all the following years. In the office was a small counter or table. Pilgrims were formed into a line. They approached the counter, one at a time. Brother André stood or sat at the other side. Those too sick to walk were carried to the counter on a stretcher.

Brother André could not spend much time with any of the pilgrims: he might be receiving as many as 40 an hour. He listened to what each said. Then he repeated to each the words: "Rub yourself with the oil and with a medal of St. Joseph. Make a novena to St. Joseph, and persevere in praying to him."

An observer in 1927, Arthur Saint-Pierre, wrote: "The founder of the Oratory is standing behind a little table, on which occasionally, when completely tired out, he rests his elbows. He is thin and looks frail in his somewhat faded habit. And the tide of suppliants flows by him for hours at a time, some imploring help for themselves, others for relatives or friends."

Long days of such incessant appeals lengthened into long years. When old age lowered Brother André's already limited strengths, he was becoming

simply unable to carry on. One of his close friends, Patrick Lynch, wondered whether the answer might lie in some sort of microphone.

Lynch called Stuart Richardson, then a salesman in the research products division of Northern Electric. A conference was arranged at St. Joseph's Oratory. When he went to the Oratory, Richardson brought Herbert Chadwick with him.

Chadwick was not an engineer by profession but was resourceful, with a vast knowledge of radio, vacuum tubes, microphones, loudspeakers. He was an amateur radio operator with his own station, had served with the CN on trains when they were equipped with radio receivers and headsets, and also had experience with broadcast transmitters.

Lynch was known to the people at the Oratory. They had no difficulty getting into the room to meet Brother André. They found him a small, elf-like figure, with a perpetual smile. He was very warm in his greeting, spoke good English and said how important a solution of his problems would be. He was becoming hard of hearing and his old voice, failing with fatigue, was difficult for others to hear.

He had a third problem. He had to lean very close to the pilgrims to hear and to be heard. Sometimes pilgrims, carried away by hope or gratitude, would fling their arms about him. Such scenes Brother André believed were unseemly.

By this time they were all seated at a table. Chadwick produced a piece of paper and outlined his solution to the problem. There would be a room with doors open at opposite ends — one for the use of Brother André and one for the use of visitors. Across the middle of the room there would be a barrier about three feet high. On Brother André's side would be a chair and a desk with a microphone on it. Behind him, on a table, would be a small amplifier. To the right of the desk, and about four feet away, would be a box containing the loudspeaker.

This arrangement apparently solved all problems. Brother André, seated at the desk, would be out of reach of his visitors. He would just have to whisper into the microphone to be heard clearly by the one at the loudspeaker.

Lynch took Richardson aside and asked what the

ALFRED BESSETTE

THE PORTER OF THE CONGREGATION OF HOLY CROSS

STATUE OF BROTHER ANDRE STANDS NEAR THE ORIGINAL CHAPEL

FRERE ANDRE

JOHN SKETCHBOOK
Collins The Miracle Man of Montreal

cost would be. Richardson made some calculations and told him. It was about $550, with everything installed. Lynch said: "That's great, just send me the bill."

When the equipment had been in use for about a week, Lynch told Richardson and Chadwick that Brother André wanted to see them. At the Oratory they were greeted warmly. Brother André said how very satisfied he was with the arrangement.

Everything had worked out as they had said it would and it was making his day much easier. He wanted to give each of them a religious medal.

So there should be no misunderstanding, Richardson told him that they were Protestants. Brother André's smile broadened as he gave each a St. Joseph medal.

"What is the difference?" he said. "We are all going the same way."

The glory of the vacant lot

The vacant lot had a glory all its own: the glory of childhood, in a simpler era. The vacant lot became a children's playground. And it was a playground the children organized for themselves. The vacant lot was land they claimed.

Nobody objected. Many of these lots remained vacant so long they seemed to have been abandoned forever. Nobody knew who really owned them. Some had signs stuck amid the tall grass, saying the lot was for sale and where one might apply. But the years passed; there were no interested viewers. The signs began to lean like wooden grave-markers in old cemeteries. If the signs were tin, the tin rusted. The paint flaked and drifted away. Then the signs collapsed, or were pushed over. They disappeared into the long grass. And the lots were left without even these futile gestures of being on market.

About 1910 Notre Dame de Grâce, and other suburbs on the outskirts of Montreal, had begun to be opened up. Though much construction was taking place, the land available still far exceeded the demand. The demand itself was erratic. Frenzied booms were often followed by periods of recession when little or nothing happened. So it went from the end of World War I in 1918 until the beginning of World War II in 1939. It was the long, great era of the no-man's-land — an era when the children took over. To them the vacant lots were worlds to explore where nobody would bother them with rules. They fell heir to these forgotten lots, the inheritors of the Earth.

In the social structure of the vacant lot a place was found for everybody. The little ones might play elementary games of their own, such as hide-and-seek. Gradually they were worked into the evolving structure. In baseball games they were at first stationed "in the cow" — on the outskirts of the field — to find a ball that had gone far and astray. As they grew older and more competent, they would move up within the game. Every promotion brought its thrill; it was part of the experience of growing up. The poor little creature "in the cow" might one day be the centre of attention.

Baseball was a game common to most vacant lots. But often the rules had to be accommodated to limited realities. Rarely were there players enough for two competing teams. Baseball declined into "scrub." All players, as it were, belonged to the one team. And each player had a chance of moving up to a higher place.

Another ball game was called Stando. It could be played if a vacant lot happened to be beside the wall of a house. Someone was "it" when the game began. He would toss the ball against the wall and shout out somebody's name. The person named had to catch the ball on the rebound. If he caught the ball, he shouted "Stando!" All players had to freeze, exactly where they were. He then threw the ball to hit the player who happened to be nearest him. If he missed, he had a mark against him — called a "baby." When a player had 10 "babies" against him, he had to stand against the wall. Every other player would take the ball in turn and throw it to hit him. It wasn't as bad as it sounds: the ball was generally soft rubber. But the position of the battered player against the wall was certainly one of humiliation. Stando was not a game to lose.

On many vacant lots clubs were formed. They had presidents and other office-holders. Some clubs even had a librarian — the custodian of a few old battered books and discarded magazines. Clubs had rules and regulations. They emphasized secrecy and mystery. Clubhouses appeared on vacant lots. They were odd little shacks, put together with pieces of wood from fruit boxes, or filched from abandoned construction dumps. Pieces of tin were also useful. The inspiration of many of these clubs and clubhouses was the cartoons of Fontaine Fox — the famed "Toonerville Trolley" sketcher. In his cartoons the Scorpions' Club and their shack with the tottering tin chimney provided a model for vacant-lot organizations.

In the years after the Great War, the dugout was often the model. Boys in vacant lots shovelled out considerable excavations. Boards were placed over the top. On some lots, earth sods were even placed over the boards to provide camouflage.

For children, the chief ritual was some sort of feast in clubhouse or dugout. Peanut-butter sandwiches from the home kitchens seemed tame and effete. Clubs preferred to find their own food. An orchard might still be nearby. It was raided for apples. A

concession to the home larder might be the mother's donation of a few potatoes, or a few potatoes might be taken without her knowing. The excitement and satisfaction came from cooking these potatoes in a vacant-lot fire, often in red hot ashes. An exclusive, conspiratorial air heightened appetite. Even a potato burned on the outside and hard inside became epicurean fare in the aroma of smoky fires.

To the unspoiled children of those generations, every "found object" was a treasure. Bits and pieces discovered lying in the fields were brought to the lot as grand discoveries. The influence of Stevenson's _Treasure Island,_ still a great book for boys, led to the hoarding of fragments of blue Milk of Magnesia bottles. Despite their inappropriate color, they substituted very well for "pieces of eight."

By the 1940s the old unsophisticated way of life was fading, even for children. Vacant lots in summer no longer had their former appeal. But for many who were young before the changes came, those long outdoor summers, near to home and yet away in another world, have in memory a vividness lacking in later experience. Such are the memories of the tall rank grass, the bare diagonal shortcut paths, the wild chicory, daisies and buttercups, the clover and the thistles, even the burdocks.

Life on the vacant lot was not all clubs and games. Lazy, dreamy hours were spent in the midday heat, sitting with the back against the rough bark of some neglected tree and watching the fleecy clouds through the branches.

The glory of the vacant lot belonged to a time of life, and to an era of history, when the wonder of simple things had not been lost.

Burial on the campus

On the campus of McGill University is a small piece of consecrated land. It is consecrated not only in the figurative sense, as land endowed with historic associations. It was literally consecrated — and by a bishop.

The formal "sentence of consecration" has been preserved. This document states: *"We, Ashton, by Divine permission, Bishop of Montreal and Metropolitan of Canada, do hereby declare that the spot of Ground in front of McGill College . . . has been this day consecrated . . . and shall henceforth be set apart from all profane and common uses."* The consecration had been carried out on June 23, 1875, by Most Rev. Ashton Oxenden, the Anglican bishop of Montreal. The "spot of Ground" is the small area just in front of the steps of the Arts Building (known in the 1870s as McGill College). In that spot of ground James McGill, founder of the university, lies buried.

It might seem strange that land was being consecrated in 1875, when James McGill had died 62 years earlier, in 1813. The answer lies in the fact that James McGill had two graves. The first of them was in the old Protestant cemetery south of Dorchester, at the corner of Cheneville, in what is now Complexe Guy Favreau.

When this cemetery was opened in 1797, the "subscribers," for a lump-sum payment, could choose their own burial places. James McGill paid 10 pounds. He selected Lot No. 16. It measured 10 by 7½.

McGill knew his wife would never be buried with him. In 1776, he had married a French-Canadian widow, Charlotte Guillemin Desrivières. Though they had been married by the Anglican rector of Montreal, she had by no means changed her faith but remained a practicing Roman Catholic. When she died, she would be interred in ground consecrated for Roman Catholic burials. She survived her husband and was buried in the crypt of Notre Dame Church.

McGill died in 1813, only a few days before Christmas. Military honors were accorded him, as he had been colonel commandant of the 1st Battalion, Montreal Militia. Among the militiamen who marched to the cemetery on that December day was his neighbor, Robert Cleghorn. "Frost, keen, bitter," he wrote in his diary.

The cemetery on Dorchester St. (now René Lévesque Blvd.) came to represent the old order of things, as the city moved in around it and pressed against it. It belonged more and more to the past, to faded griefs and dusty memories. The old stones were heaved askew by the frosts. Some of them fell apart. The ornamental urn on top of James McGill's monument dropped off and lay in the tall grass. No burials had been made in the Dorchester St. cemetery after the middle of the 19th century. Soon it was overgrown, soon vandalized. Its forlorn condition was described by a visitor in 1872. He wrote an article: "On a Ramble Among the Tombs."

This visitor found the place choked with weeds and tall grass. Earth over graves had sunk, leaving unsightly pits and hollows. Monuments were crumbling, or had been defaced with lewd graffiti. Only a row of fine Lombardy poplars, marking the line of an obscured avenue, recalled more orderly days. A bizarre touch was added by a boys' school. It had been opened in, of all places, the former mortuary chapel in the burial ground.

This dilapidated burying ground could not be left, now that it was near the centre of the city. In 1874 the city of Montreal acquired it. The city surveyor, on Jan. 7, 1875, announced that anyone having claims to remove any of the bones for reburial elsewhere could do so. The cemetery was to be made into Dufferin Park. Most of the dead had been so long in their graves in the old burying-ground that not many among the living were concerned with what happened to their bones. James McGill might have had no one to remove his bones if he had not founded a university.

When the Corporation of McGill University heard the announcement that the old Protestant cemetery on Dorchester St. was to be closed, it held a meeting in April 1875. It appointed a committee to consider "the mode that might seem the best adapted to carry out the project of the removal of the Tomb and Remains of the late Honble. James McGill."

The exhumation was carried out by Richard Spriggins, the first superintendent of Mount Royal Cemetery. He reported "that, owing to the lapse of

John Collins Sketchbook — Arts Building — McGill

time, only the skull and a few of the greter bones and the bottom of the coffin remained." Spriggins had to choose between two skeletons in the McGill lot. James McGill had, in his time, rescued the remains of his friend of long standing, John Porteous, when an even earlier cemetery north of St. James St. had been closed. He had removed Porteous's bones in 1811 and reburied them in his own lot.

The question had been raised. Could a mistake have been made in choosing between the two sets of bones? Could John Porteous's remains be lying today in the consecrated land in front of the Arts Building?

Any such error would be improbable. Spriggins was a highly experienced and responsible cemetery superintendent. A man of his experience would not have much difficulty in distinguishing between the two sets of remains in the McGill lot. The bones of McGill had been in the earth for 62 years, those of Porteous for 93. There would probably have been a difference also in the position of the bones. Those of McGill had never been disturbed since they were

placed in the grave in 1813. Those of Porteous had been in one grave from 1782 till 1811, then taken to the other. They would not be in the same undisturbed position. The condition of the two skulls would probably have been very different. Porteous had been thrown from his horse while riding from Lachine to Montreal. He was hurled to the ground "with great violence." His skull was fractured "in a most terrible manner, of which he died." After 93 years of earth burial his terribly fractured skull would probably have fallen apart.

The dilapidated monument on McGill's grave was also moved to the university. There the pieces were reassembled. McGill's bones, in a box, were placed inside the restored monument. But disintegration set in again.

In 1971 the old monument was replaced by a granite copy. It stands at the same spot in front of the Arts Building in the consecrated ground Bishop Oxenden "set apart from all profane and common uses" on June 23, 1875.

The priest who 'ran' the railroad

A Roman Catholic priest was once the president of the Canadian Pacific Railway. His term in office didn't last very long — only an hour. But during that hour, by courtesy and the vote of the executive, he was the head of Canada's greatest corporation.

It happened on an August day in 1883. The CPR's lines had been laid as far as Calgary. It was an occasion for celebration. A special train set out from Montreal. On board was the CPR's president, George Stephen (later Lord Mount Stephen). Among the CPR directors on that special train were Donald Smith (later Lord Strathcona, one of the promoters of the CPR); William Van Horne, the CPR's general manager (later Sir William and the company's president), and R.B. Angus, another organizer of the company.

When the car reached Calgary, a luncheon was held. An invitation had been sent to Rev. Albert Lacombe, who had left Montreal in 1849 to become an Oblate missionary among the Indians. Stephen had telegraphed Lacombe, inviting him to lunch.

Lacombe was the guest of honor, seated at the president's right hand. Then Stephen stood up, convened a directors' meeting and resigned as president. R.B. Angus moved that Father Lacombe be appointed to replace him. The motion was greeted with applause. It was carried unanimously. For an hour Lacombe ruled the CPR from a railway car at Calgary. It was all in fun, yet serious in a way. The company was paying tribute to the missionary priest who was its guest of honor. The CPR owed much to Lacombe.

He was the most influential of all the Roman Catholic missionaries in the West. He lived with the Indians, travelled about with them, shared their hardships. It was a dangerous life. When the railway builders began entering the territory of the Blackfeet tribe, they sometimes found the track they had laid by day was torn up during the night. The young Indians were said to be ready to attack the track-layers. Even Crowfoot, their chief, a man of moderation, felt he and his people had been wronged and insulted.

As soon as Lacombe learned of these threats, he mounted his horse, galloped to Crowfoot's camp and persuaded the chief to hold a council. The priest acted as though he were the government's agent. He told the Indians they would receive new lands for those the railway was claiming, and he distributed gifts of tea and tobacco he had obtained from the nearest trading post.

The Blackfeet agreed in council, after much ceremonial smoking, not to attack the railway-builders. Lacombe realized that progress could not be blocked. But he wanted to do all he could to see that his bewildered, anxious Indians were given consideration and aid. Because he could see the point of view of both sides, he was the ideal reconciler.

Lacombe, on his visits to Montreal, was entertained at the mansions of the great CPR men. In his diary he wrote of the amazing courtesies extended to him, the poor missionary from the West, in his dusty cassock. But he was good company, with stories of his adventures on the prairies. From his point of view, there was more than pleasurable entertainment in these invitations. He wanted to keep in touch with the railway leaders, to get donations from them for his missions, his schools, his homes for the poor, his translations of books into the Indian languages.

After a Saturday evening dinner at Van Horne's mansion at Sherbrooke and Stanley Sts., Sir William amused Lacombe with card tricks, for Sir William fancied himself something of a magician. Lacombe, fascinated, lost all sense of time. Suddenly he realized it was already Sunday. Hours ago he ought to have been back in the religious house where he was staying. He left in a rush.

On his next visit to Montral he was again invited to Van Horne's house for dinner. This time he was accompanied by a "stern-looking ecclesiastic." Evidently this personage had been sent by his superior to see that Lacombe did not again overstay his time.

Visitors might be invited to Lord Strathcona's mansion (at Dorchester and Fort Sts.) to meet the famous missionary from the West. Lady Aberdeen was one of them. She wrote of "the kindly, noble face." And she added: "His talk with us will always be a happy remembrance; his fatherly solicitude over

SKETCHBOOK

VAN
HORNE
HOUSE

his flock, and the way in which he identifies himself with them is most touching." He said: "You must never drive the Indians, or frighten them; you must draw them by ever telling them of the love of the Father." That evening in Strathcona's house, Lacombe told Lady Aberdeen that when he was quite worn out with active work, he would go to Scotland and build a hermitage in the grounds of Haddo House, the home of the Aberdeens. There he would retire to write books for and about his Indians.

But Lacombe never retired. He died near Calgary on Dec. 11, 1916, aged 89 and still at work. The CPR, which had given him a lifetime pass, provided a funeral train.

With the locomotive draped in mourning, it carried Lacombe's body north from Calgary to his Indian mission at St. Albert.

Three important men and their lookalikes

Montreal has three monuments to historic men who bear striking resemblances to three other historic men living in their time. The monument to King Edward VII in Phillips Square resembles Sir William Van Horne, president of the CPR. In Lafontaine Park the monument to Sir Louis-Hippolyte Lafontaine, the French-Canadian political leader, resembles the Emperor Napoleon. The monument to Sir John A. Macdonald in Place du Canada (the southern part of the old Dominion Square) resembles Benjamin Disraeli, Earl of Beaconsfield, the British prime minister.

While the three men depicted in these monuments were alive, their resemblance to their living counterparts was widely observed and caused much astonished comment. One day Van Horne was travelling in an English train. With him was his daughter Adaline. The conductor ("guard") collecting the tickets eyed Sir William. He turned to Adaline. "If this gentleman," he remarked, "were less stout and not so tall, I should take him for King Edward."

The resemblance was sufficient to deceive even those who had occasion to know the king's appearance well. Among them was the headwaiter at Henri's, a celebrated London restaurant of the Edwardian era. The king often went there, informally and incognito. On these dining-out evenings he was accompanied by Lord Elphinstone. Van Horne, on one of his visits to London, went with his son to Henri's — and Lord Elphinstone accompanied them. The headwaiter hurried forward, with an air of obsequious recognition suitable for royalty. Assiduous and bustling, he led the party to a table. Evidently he was convinced that His Majesty had arrived on one of his customary visits, accompanied by Lord Elphinstone as usual. Van Horne, not easily embarrassed, felt the awkwardness of his unreal situation. Without intention he had beome an imposter.

Van Horne's likeness to Edward VII was equalled by the resemblance of Sir Louis-Hippolyte Lafontaine to Napoleon. Like the emperor, Lafontaine was short with a massive figure, aloof, immobile face, regular features and large head —

and assured dignity of bearing.

Lafontaine played a commanding role in Canadian history during the years while Ontario and Quebec, then known as Canada West and Canada East, were constitutionally combined as the Province of Canada. The custom was to have the government headed by a political leader from Canada West and one from Canada East who, together, would share the administration. In 1842, and again in 1843, Lafontaine shared this leadership. Lafontaine's resemblance to Napoleon startled Lady Bagot, who came to Canada in 1842 as the wife of the governor-general, Sir Charles Bagot. In her youth she had lived in Paris where she had seen Napoleon. When she saw Lafontaine for the first time, the resemblance made her cry out in surprise. Napoleon had been dead since 1821, yet he seemed to be standing in front of her. "If I was not sure he was dead," she said, "I would say that it was he."

When Lafontaine visited Paris, old soldiers of Napoleon's army were just as surprised. He went to the Hôtel des Invalides, the old soldiers' home. They crowded about him. Old memories, old loyalties were reawakened. "Bon Dieu!" they exclaimed, "Monsieur, how you resemble our emperor!" Lafontaine was aware of the resemblance. He did not dislike it. He tried to make it all the more complete by allowing a lock of hair to fall over his large forehead, in Napoleonic style.

Most striking of all the resemblances was between Sir John A. Macdonald and Disraeli. It may be seen in the monument facing René Lévesque Blvd. in Place du Canada, though in real life it seems to have been far more amazing. Macdonald's likeness to Disraeli is supported by the testimony of many. The correspondent of the London World wrote in 1879: "The Canadian Prime Minister supplies a likeness to Lord Beaconsfield which is almost bewildering in its exactitude."

When Sir John A. was awarded the honorary degree of DCL by Oxford University, the students, seeing the resemblance to Disrael, shouted, "Dizzy! Dizzy!" The resemblance was seen not only in facial features but in mannerisms as well. The correspondent of the Edinburgh Daily News wrote: "The resemblance is further carried out when Sir

SIR
JOHN A.
DISRAELI'S
DOUBLE

BOHN
Collins SKETCHBOOK

John talks. He has the same shrug of the shoulder, the same outspreading of the hands, and, in brief, all the little mannerisms so familiar in our Benjamin."

After Disraeli's death those who saw Macdonald might feel sure that they were looking at Disraeli's ghost. The vision shook them. In 1881 Sir Charles Dilke, shortly after visiting the dying Lord Beaconsfield, was taking a train at London's Euston Station. The clock had just struck midnight. Looking at the door of the railway carriage, he thought he saw Disraeli standing before him. He later became aware of his mistake, but never forgot his shock. A similar shock proved too much for "one noble lady." She had gone to a reception some time after Disraeli's death. Macdonald, visiting London, attended the reception also. The lady fainted when Macdonald approached. She was convinced Disraeli was out of

his grave.

Both Macdonald and Disraeli were aware of their resemblance. When Sir John A. was on a visit to Fredericton, a friend of his asked "a certain gentleman" to meet him when the steamboat arrived, saying: "You will know him by his likeness to Disraeli." Sir John A. was told how the man had recognized him. "Yes," he remarked, "they do say we look alike."

Benjamin Disraeli, two years before he died, had an opportunity to form his own opinion. Sir John A. came to visit him at his country estate in the early autumn of 1879. The day after the visit Disraeli wrote to his friend Lady Bradford: "By the bye, the Canadian chief is said to be very like your humble servant, tho' a much younger man. I think there is a resemblance."

The battle against the demon rum

One day in the 1850s Montrealers crowded a lecture hall to hear a speaker on temperance — the most improbable temperance lecturer that could be imagined. He was P.T. Barnum, the American showman, the exhibitor of freaks and fakes in his New York museum.

Barnum — tall and robust, with a round head, square face, short nose, an intelligent but severe expression, hair not lanky, but cut even all round the head — came to the front of the platform in a genteel suit of black. While he spoke he held his hands together, fingers touching.

As the incomparable showman, Barnum knew how to hold the attention of an audience. "I drank a great deal myself," Barnum admitted, "but now I see it is a universal evil."

"I have never seen a drunken man succeed in business," he said. "If he did, I, being fond of curiosities, would exhibit him in the New York Museum."

Barnum knew that his audience expected him to be peculiar, and he didn't wish to lose his audience. To make his points, he told quaint little stories. One of them illustrated the evils of companionable conviviality. An Irishman often used to come home drunk. Once he was watering his horse. His wife remarked that the horse was more sensible than he was: the horse knew how to leave off when he had had enough. The Irishman retorted: "Oh, it's very well to discourse like that, Biddy, but if there was another horse at the other side of the trough to say 'Here's to your health, my ould boy!' would he stop till he drunk the whole trough, think ye?"

Barnum spoke again as the keeper of the museum of curiosities and wild beasts when he concluded: "If a tiger got out of my menagerie and killed a man, would it not be justifiable to take a rifle and shoot it? So liquor, which rages like a tiger . . . must be put down, and you will all sing hosannas if it is so here."

Barnum was only one of a long series of temperance lecturers who came to Montreal. Drink was felt to be a public scourge. From the beginning of the 19th century, drinking was hard and heavy. Thomas Storrow Brown, a temperance advocate, described conditions as he had found them after he came to Montreal in 1818: "With men, drinking was too much the great pastime. Those young men who could stand the most liquor were often the most thought of by their employers. At some dinner parties all were expected to get drunk, and lest any should be delinquents, the door would be locked to keep them from escaping. . . . At an early lunch given on the launch of a vessel . . . and with our leading men present, all got furiously drunk before noon, and two of our most sedate respected citizens pulled off their coats for a fight."

One host had a distinctive procedure. After he had locked the door, he would toss the key into the grate. No one could hope to get it out until the fire had sunk into cold ashes.

The forces for temperance in Montreal were varied. For the evangelical Protestants, abstinence from alcohol was only part of a general puritanism. Many were also opposed to the theatre, tobacco and the dance. Among Roman Catholics a number of temperance leaders arose. Conspicuous among them was Rev. Patrick Dowd. He encouraged a strong temperance league in St. Patrick's Church. Montreal had its temperance press in John Dougall's paper, the Montreal Daily Witness. It had its temperance hotels where no liquor was served. The Women's Christian Temperance Union, founded at Owen Sound in 1874, was soon represented in Montreal. In Victoria Square the Montreal Temperance Society erected a drinking fountain inscribed with the words Fountain of Health.

The first of Montreal's temperance picnics took place about 1839. A famous English temperance lecturer, J.S. Buckingham, spoke on the deck of a steamboat which took 300 Montrealers on an excursion down the river.

Christmas and New Year's were, naturally, the busiest seasons for the temperance workers. On Christmas Day in 1877 a temperance organization, the Independent Order of Good Templars, put on "the Great Temperance Drama — *The Drunkard's Home."* They had hired one of Montreal's principal theatres, the Academy of Music on Victoria St. (on ground now occupied by Eaton's).

New Year's was an even bigger day than Christmas. Paying New Year's calls was Montreal's

SKETCHBOOK
East Wing of the
Arts Building

John Collins

social custom. As many as 30 or 40 calls might be made in the one day. Custom required that alcohol in some form should be offered to every visitor. The principal of McGill University, Sir William Dawson, decided to take a stand against the custom. On his first New Year's Day in Montreal a long stream of visitors called at his residence in the East Wing of the Arts Building. "In 1855, the old French and Scottish custom of New Year visits was in full force . . . and our visitors were naturally numerous," said Dawson. "To their surprise, instead of wine, invariably offered on these occasions, they were provided only with tea and coffee. It often happened, too, that at the various dinners and entertainments to which we were invited, we were the only guests present who did not take wine."

Even those seriously ill sometimes refused to take any alcohol, even though their physicians had prescribed it as a needed stimulant. One such instance was described by P.L. Kinmond, manager

of the first railway on the island of Montreal, the Montreal and Lachine. In the 1840s many of the railway's workmen took down with cholera. Kinmond wrote of a man who, though dying, would not break his pledge: "We had to look after the sick men, the doctors were so busy; and one distressing case I remember well. I held the man's head on my arm as he lay, and I had in my other hand a cup full of medicine, the principal parts of which were hot tea and fine brandy. The man asked what was in the medicine and I told him there was brandy and tea, etc. 'I have taken a pledge not to taste strong liquor,' said he, 'and I shall keep it if I die for it.'

"I told him not to push his pledge so far as that as the brandy was only part of the medicine and it might save his life. He could not get better without some medicine. 'I shall not break my pledge; I'll die first,' said he. Well, I held him until he died, poor fellow. He was true to his pledge unto death. He could not have carried it further."

The Montrealer who wrote O Canada

Every week in the winter and spring of 1926 (the year of his death) a bearded, dignified man went as a volunteer to the School for Crippled Children, to help the handicapped children develop a love of music and to instruct them in choral singing. He was Robert Stanley Weir, a "judge in admiralty" of the Exchequer Court of Canada for the district of Montreal. Twenty years earlier he had been the writer of an English version of O Canada.

It was only one English version among about 20, but something about its spirit and fervor raised it above the others. The Association of Canadian Clubs and other national organizations had chosen it as their national patriotic song, and it was taught in the schools in preparation for the visit of the Prince of Wales in 1919. From 1921 on, it was printed in the public-school readers of a number of provinces.

Gradually Weir's lines were to win official acceptance. In 1927 they were published in an official form when the diamond jubilee of confederation was celebrated. They were officially approved again in 1939 when King George VI and Queen Elizabeth visited Canada. Weir's version still remained only "a national song." But in 1975, at the July 1 ceremonies on Parliament Hill, a modified version was officially proclaimed Canada's national anthem, together with the French version by Sir Adolphe Routhier and the music of Calixa Lavallée.

Obviously, Robert Stanley Weir was a Canadian patriot. His patriotism was not an aggressive nationalist boasting, but something far more subtle: an inner response to the deep and varied loveliness of the land. He was a man of much tenderness, as his voluntary visits to the crippled children reveal. And he was tender in his feeling for his country.

This poetry-writing judge of the Exchequer Court was also a lifelong musician. He was the organist, at different times, of Zion Congregational Church, Erskine Presbyterian Church and the Unitarian Church of the Messiah. He loved the fitness of things, especially in church worship, and composed responses in the Gregorian style for certain services. He taught singing and the piano and was a skilled accompanist. "His charming courtesy," said a friend, "and kindness, and fair though liberal criticism,

made him beloved by all who knew him."

In the last months of his life he was making musical arrangements for staging the *Antigone* of Sophocles with Mendelssohn's music. This, he thought, would be fittingly performed at the opening of the classical new Moyse Hall in the reconstructed Arts Building at McGill University. Music to Stanley Weir was something more than the achievement of technical proficiency. It was part of the inner harmony of nature. In one of his poems he wrote:

O that the dull sense keener were to hear
Earth's softer music ever breathing near! —
Chimes of the chaliced lily as it grows,
Or the melodious murmur of the rose.

As a sportsman, Weir favored golf. In competitions he won nine cups. One year he held a senior championship. But here, again, golf to him was something more than skill on the course, or competitive superiority. It brought the player closer to nature — to "the God of the Out-of-Doors." At a club he wrote a poem on The Hills:

When I look out upon the hills
My heart, with heart's brief rapture, thrills.
Does God feel rapture, too, when He
Looks out upon the hills with me?
And was my rapture His
All down the centuries
(Mine of so short a span)
Or, is all rapture one in God and Man?

All such musical and poetic feeling, the mystical feeling for the land, was combined with impressive legal erudition. This writer of O Canada was also the writer of learned works. The Code of Civil Procedure, An Insolvency Manual, The Education Act, The Municipal Code. In 1899 he had revised the charter of Montreal.

Stanley Weir believed there was a place for tenderness even in the law. From 1899 till 1915 he was a judge in the Recorder's Court in Montreal. There, morning by morning, the drunks and waifs were paraded before him for judgment. He sought to do justice to them and to society alike. His studies were extended beyond the law into sociology — into an examination of the failures of society that had resulted in such pitiful delinquents.

The essential tenderness of his character was the

MUSICIAN

GOLFER

ROBERT
STANLEY
WEIR

JUDGE
and
POET

_John
Collins_ SKETCHBOOK.
The man who wrote O Canada

theme of the tribute paid to him by the Royal Society of Canada at his death (he had been a member of the society since 1923): "Of him it can be truly said he was 'just in the exercise of power, generous in the protection of weakness,' and beloved for his rare charm of kind courtesy to the timid souls of all classes." His other interests were characteristic. He was president of the Montreal Parks and Playgrounds Association and president of the Grace Dart Home.

When such a man wrote the English version of O Canada, his patriotism was not a vain boast; it was a profound sentiment, a thing of memory and affection. As he believed all deep sentiments become

religious, he felt the religious reality in the love of one's own country. The spirit of religious dedication in his poem was obscured and largely lost when the official adaptation of what he had written deleted the final verse, which reveals the religious context of the original version of O Canada:

Ruler Supreme, Who hearest humble prayer,
Hold our Dominion in Thy loving care.
Help us to find, O God, in Thee,
A lasting, rich reward,
As waiting for the Better Day
We ever stand on guard.
O Canada, glorious and free!
We stand on guard for Thee!

The crime of Dr. Crippen

Late in July 1910 *The Gazette's* editor had to choose his most graphic, his most vivid writer to cover a major assignment — someone who could rise to a rare opportunity and turn in a story everyone would have to read. He chose John Bassett, a 24-year-old Irishman from Tyrone, only recently on the staff. Bassett had Irish eloquence, whether in the spoken or written word. He also could meet people well and get stories out of them.

Bassett was sent to Father Point on the lower St. Lawrence near Rimouski, where incoming ocean liners paused to take on the river pilots. The liner Montrose was on its way. Wireless messages claimed Dr. Hawley Harvey Crippen was aboard.

The Crippen case was already big in the news, all the bigger because it was a mystery. Crippen was an English dentist whose wife had disappeared. Crippen told contradictory stories: first he said she had died of peumonia in California, then he said she wasn't dead but had just gone off and left him.

Friends of Mrs. Crippen were not satisfied by these explanations, and even less satisfied when they found him living with a young woman, Ethel LeNeve. Crippen was questioned by Inspector Walter Dew of Scotland Yard. Then he and Ethel LeNeve both disappeared. Inspector Dew examined Crippen's London house. Beyond a revolver and cartridges, nothing suspicious was found, until the inspector came upon an unpleasant odor in the cellar. He tore up the brick floor — and uncovered the remains of Mrs. Crippen, largely destroyed by quicklime.

The search spread across the world, but no trail was found. In July the liner Montrose put out from Antwerp on its voyage across the Atlantic to Quebec. The captain, Henry Kendall, spotted a passenger aboard who seemed to resemble descriptions of Dr. Crippen: a small man, about 5 foot 3, with brownish sandy hair, wearing gold-rimmed glasses. Unlike Crippen, he was clean-shaven. But removing a mustache would be one of the first things any criminal would do to escape detection.

Crippen was known to have false teeth. Kendall made a point of talking to the passenger who had aroused his curiosity, and told him a funny story. The man laughed. The captain saw that his teeth

were false. In the ship's register the man was listed as "John Philo Robinson," travelling with his young son, "John George Robinson, student." The captain scrutinized them, as father and son paced the deck together. Something about the boy did not seem right. His walk was certainly unboyish. He also had "well-developed bust and hips which were not usually found in lads."

The captain also noticed the odd insistence of "Robinson" that he and his son should have the end seats at the dining table. Robinson always placed his son in the very last seat, next to the wall, so that no one but he would be sitting beside him. The captain realized Robinson was guarding his son from having conversation with anybody. Kendall's suspicions were confirmed by the bedroom steward. The steward went to the captain to report that the boy in Cabin 5 seemed to be a girl. Apart from appearances, he noted that Robinson and his supposed son were invariably up and dressed before he entered their cabin. And he thought it odd that, between them, they had no baggage except a valise — a fact that suggested they had made a hasty departure.

The Montrose was equipped with the newly developed ship's wireless. Kendall wired his suspicions to Scotland Yard, and Inspector Dew was rushed to Canada on the liner Laurentic. The Montrose was a slow sailer. By taking passage on the swifter Laurentic, Dew would get to Canada in time to meet the Montrose in the St. Lawrence.

Day after day went by. Robinson and his son, keeping to themselves, were seen walking up and down the deck. Robinson seemed at ease. He was passing much of his time in reading.

Meanwhile John Bassett was waiting at Father Point — and he wasn't alone. Reporters were arriving from many papers and from all the news services. It was a boring wait, but Bassett made something even of nothing in a preliminary despatch: "The clang of the city's cars are not heard here, but the deep bass voice of the tide vies with the fog horn to lend enchantment to the air."

In the early morning of July 31 word came that the Montrose was steaming up the river. At 7:30 a tender put out from shore. Aboard were a pilot and Inspector Dew with the Quebec police. Crippen was

DOCTOR
H.H. CRIPPEN
and the moustache
he shaved off

GUARDING
CRIPPEN
IN HIS CABIN
IN THE
MONTROSE

John Collins SKETCHBOOK... *From Photos of the time*

pacing the deck on the port side. As the pilot boat came near, he grew visibly nervous. "It's a cold morning, Mr. Robinson," said Dr. Stewart, the ship's physician. "Yes," replied Crippen. Then he added: "There seem to be a lot of men in that boat."

The men reached shipside and climbed the rope ladder. Dew came on deck. As he approached, he said quietly: "Crippen, I want you." Crippen recoiled involuntarily when he recognized Dew. Blood left his face; his breath came in short gasps; he "gurgled incoherently." Dew and the police led him away. Crippen recovered, saying: "Thank God. The suspense is over, and I am glad."

Then reporters reached the Montrose in the boat Eureka. They clambered up the ladder in heavy rain. They found where Crippen was being detained, and crowded in front of him. "He sat in the small lounge with his head buried in his manacled hands, huddled back in a corner. . . a small puny creature, without anything about him to suggest the criminal, save the eyes, which occasionally blazed forth dangerously and then took on a vacant look. In his room he kept

twitching his hands nervously and during the time the detectives were searching him he looked sheepish, like nothing so much as a small boy caught stealing jam."

Bassett then went to see Ethel LeNeve: "She is slightly taller than Crippen, with grey eyes, unusually large, and although she was crying in a frightened sort of way when being questioned, it was evident, in spite of her tear-stained face, that she was a decidedly pretty girl."

Crippen was hanged.

Young Ethel LeNeve, who was judged more sinned against than sinning, was released and faded out of the news.

Kendall became commander of the Empress of Ireland and four years after the Crippen affair, in the same part of the St. Lawrence, near Father Point, his ship was rammed by the Norwegian collier Storstad, with a loss of more than 1,000 lives.

John Bassett, the talented 24-year old Irish reporter, was to become president and later chairman of *The Gazette*.

Reflections of a World War I air ace

"*You have to hit the enemy in the right place, and that right place is the pilot, and when you hit him, you must kill him.*"

Major William Avery Bishop, VC, DSO, MC ("Billy Bishop"), the great Canadian air ace of World War I, was speaking to the Canadian Club of Montreal. It was Jan. 11, 1918, and the war had nearly a year to run.

Bishop told his audience that a day's work in the flying squadron was to hit and kill as many as possible: "The work of a pilot consists of going out and looking for a fight, and we have no other orders."

As a pilot Billy Bishop was all alone in his plane. In a single-seater the pilot had to double as the gunner. In his machine the two machine guns fired only straight ahead, through the revolving blades of the propeller.

If he wished to fire, he headed his machine directly at his enemy, using his telescopic sight. When directly in line, he pressed a button.

Machine guns were fired by the same control that managed the plane. Once the pilot had pressed that button, the guns rattled away by themselves. He did not aim his guns; he aimed his plane.

In his speech to the Canadian Club, Billy Bishop gave the secret of his success: "The great difficulty in fighting in the air," he said, "seems to be to get people to close in." In most successful fights in the air he had closed in at 100 yards before opening fire. Sometimes he had been only 15 or 20 yards away before firing the first shot.

"At this range," Bishop remarked, "with bullets passing out at the rate of 1,200 a minute, there is only one side to the fight and it is over very quickly at that."

It was a precision operation. Hesitant pilots, unready to close with the enemy, could never hope to be winners. They were more likely to be casualties.

Being a fighter pilot in a one-seater was not all a matter of dogfights in the sky. Instructions for a fighter pilot about to set out were to shoot up anything he might find. Bishop spoke of pilots swooping down on a transport or a convoy on a road, or on a car carrying officers, or a moving railway train, or on soldiers in a rest camp behind enemy lines.

Bishop surprised his audience by describing how low he flew his plane coming back from a flight over enemy territory: "The trip home is not dangerous, but it is the most exciting part of the whole game and the most thrilling to hear about. We fly pretty close to the ground, sometimes within five or ten feet of the ground, and you go along from one field to another zigzag, altering your course often, making a complete turn whenever you see anything ahead of you."

Low flying was safer than flying high. A high-flying plane was a better target for anti-aircraft artillery. Its flight could be plotted; there was time for aim to be tested and improved, till a shell hit. But a plane flying only a few feet above ground was a poorer target. It was safe from anti-aircraft artillery.

Its greatest risk was from machine-guns. Machine-gunners had trouble seeing a low-flying plane till it was nearly upon them. Flying only a few feet from the ground, its approach might be hidden by a hill, by a clump of trees, even by farmhouses and barns. When it came into view, speed was on the side of the pilot. The machine-gunners might be 200 yards away. But the plane might be coming on at 120 miles an hour. It might pass over them before they could aim and fire.

Billy Bishop didn't seem to mind this kind of dashing and dodging. What he did not like was being detailed to shoot down enemy balloons miles behind the enemy's lines — balloons sent up but anchored to the ground to give observation of what was going on along the Allies' lines and beyond them. Shooting down a balloon was no dogfight. It meant flying into a trap that had been carefully prepared.

Whenever the enemy sent up a balloon, he knew it would be attacked. Anti-aircraft guns, a whole battery, were placed on the ground around it, supported by a battery of machine guns. The enemy also set up guns to fire "flaming onions" — balls of fire that came up very slowly. Special enemy planes were detailed to patrol over the balloons.

Airmen were encouraged, while on the ground, to forget about flights. "Otherwise," said Bishop, "every pilot coming down would be discussing his

SKETCHBOOK
Billy Bishop — Ace of World War I

work, and a man's mind would never be off flying in the air, and hearing what a tight corner the other fellow had been in would make him more nervous than he would otherwise be inclined to be."

Life on the ground had some luxuries. Airmen's huts had been papered and carpeted. The mess was very good. They had a piano, a phonograph, two big open fireplaces, lots of reading material. After an American bar was added to the mess they had more visitors than ever. Such means of recreation were needed: "The result was that when airmen were told off to do a patrol, up to the last minute they were laughing and talking; cases of nerves or anything of that sort were very rare. They would go up in the air with the same spirit in which they played on the ground."

Before the war was over, Billy Bishop was to be given command of the 85th Squadron, promoted to lieutenant-colonel and awarded the DFC. In civilian life in the years after the war, Bishop lived in Montreal. He was vice-president of McColl-Frontenac Oil Co.

The gorgeous opulence of Molsons Bank

The tellers in Molsons Bank at the southeast corner of St. James and St. Peter Sts. (St. Jacques and St. Pierre) were armed with revolvers. These revolvers were kept near at hand, ready for use. Andrew D. McCrindle, an office boy at the plumbing firm of J. McGuire, recalled in his old age seeing an armed teller when he went to Molsons Bank with the manager of McGuire's, R.J. Macaulay, to draw out the cash for the company's payroll. "When we got to the bank," McCrindle said, "Mr. Macaulay handed in the cheque for the cash and I could see on the counter a loaded revolver, but, alas, I never saw the teller use it."

At Molsons Bank employees were required to take their turn in guarding the premises at night. A junior clerk named A. Lebrun recalled his guardian duties: "It was the custom in those days to have one of the employees of the bank sleep there at night while the caretakers were doing their chores. I was told that the insurance companies insisted on this. When your turn came around, you had to be in the bank by 10 or 11 p.m. and get up at 7 a.m. The caretaker would set up a nice, very good and clean bed in the office of the assistant manager on the right-hand side of the entrance, and would put the office back in proper shape the next morning. An extra pay of 50 cents per night was added to your regular salary; that was very much appreciated."

On the facade of the building, at the top, are the arms of the Molson family. This building was once the headquarters of Molsons Bank, an institution that did banking in Canada from the 1850s till the 1920s. The entry of the Molson family into banking in the middle years of the 19th century was nothing new. The family had been engaged in banking, in a private and informal way, at least as early as 1815. This was even before Canada's first chartered bank, the Bank of Montreal, commenced business in 1817.

Such private, informal banking did not prevent the Molsons from having a role in chartered banking as well, through a connection with the Bank of Montreal. John Molson Jr. became a director of the Bank of Montreal in 1824. Two years later, in a time of serious financial troubles, a prestigious and reassuring public figure was needed as president. The

Bank of Montreal turned to John Molson Sr. He was elected president, his son resigning to make a place for him on the board. When old John Molson resigned in 1830, his son was re-elected to the board. His brother William joined him as a director in 1843. They continued as directors till the 1850s.

The situation changed in 1853. A "Free Banking Act" was passed. Hitherto the government had prevented private bankers from having a charter on the ground that a chartered bank should be an institution in its own right, not merely an offshoot or sideline of those engaged in other types of business. Now the way was open, under the new Free Banking Act, for the Molsons to set up a bank of their own among the chartered banks. On Oct. 1, 1855, the new Molsons Bank received its charter by an act of Parliament.

The status of a chartered bank depended, to an extraordinary degree, on the impressiveness of its head office. At first Molsons Bank was housed in two undistinguished buildings on St. James St. Plans were being made for headquarters that would hold its own among the other head offices of the city. Instead of going to one architect and asking him for his designs, the Molsons believed they could achieve superior results by opening a competition. All architects were invited to submit plans. The best of the submissions would be selected.

One set of plans was approved unanimously by the jury — submitted by George Browne and his son, John James. The name of George Browne, in fact, is carved into a stone on the St. Pierre St. side of the building. In working with his son on the plans for Molsons Bank, George Browne aimed for a tremendously impressive presence. The new bank should have dignity. But the age of classical austerity (as seen in the facade of the Bank of Montreal farther east on St. Jacques) was not his model.

The mid-Victorian mood called not for imposing austerity but gorgeous opulence. The interest of the Brownes' design today is how successfully they achieved what they set out to do. They abandoned the "good gray limestone" of Montreal's own quarries. They chose, instead, the warmer, richer reddish tones of Ohio limestone and Scottish granite. All materials were rich, such as the lavish use of

MOLSONS BANK
A WINTER SKETCH SHOWING HOW SNOW
BRINGS OUT DETAILS IN MONTREAL'S OLD BUILDINGS

Spanish mahogany for the woodwork. Ornament was profuse but graceful. Into the stone of the walls, here and there, are carved wreaths of flowers and fruits. Even the chimney pots were carefully designed, with their ornamental rubbed sandstone.

Molsons Bank, as its name implied, was primarily a family business. A certain proportion of the shares, however, were publicly held. There was a board of directors, including — besides members of the family — a number of the city's businessmen. At the beginning, the business of the bank was entirely local. The first branch was established in London, Ont. At the end Molsons Bank had 125 branches.

Its greatest era of expansion was from 1898 till World War I. A comparatively small bank, however, was becoming less and less viable under modern conditions. A crisis came in 1924. The country was undergoing economic strains. Loans could not be called in but had to be extended. Firms that had borrowed money were having trouble even paying the interest. An easy-money policy by the government, after a period of inflation, made it hard

for the bank to earn needed revenue.

The Molsons decided there was only one course: they merged their business with the Bank of Montreal early in 1925. As early as 1916, nine years before the merger, a member of the Molson family, Colonel Herbert Molson, was elected to the Bank of Montreal's board. And, as a part of the merger, the president of Molsons Bank, Frederick William Molson, also became a director of the Bank of Montreal, the number of directors being enlarged to make his entry possible. On a December day in 1924, just a few days before Christmas, the last special general meeting of shareholders took place in the ornate Molsons Bank.

The building became the St. Pierre St. branch of the Bank of Montreal, till this branch was closed in 1981. But the building is still there. A contemporary critic said of Molsons Bank that it had a "bold and imposing character."

The adjectives were well chosen. The boldness of its design, the confidence of its ornateness, still make it impressive.

Montreal's own stone

Montreal was long known as "the old gray city" — from the limestone used for much of its construction.

Limestone has undoubted dignity. The long gray streets were sombre, perhaps, but in wonderful harmony. The graystone looked good in all seasons. It was a good background for green trees, or for snow. It was best of all in autumn when it merged with a certain poetry into the gray twilights, an effect caught in many of the paintings by Robert Pilot.

Across Canada in the 19th century, many cities had their own chief building material taken from the quarries of their rock formation. These various building stones gave different cities a distinctive architecture, something of their own. This is the character now being lost. Montreal was fortunate in its geology. Much of the island consists of Trenton limestone. Where there were notable outcroppings, quarries were developed. So many buildings in Montreal were built with limestone that whole streets and districts took on an impressive stateliness.

The great age of limestone construction in Montreal began a little before the Victorian period, about the 1820s. Previously, Montreal's chief building stone had been mere rubble — stones of all shapes and sizes gathered from the fields and fitted together with a lavish use of mortar. When limestone blocks came into use, the appearance of Montreal was transformed. Limestone, chiselled and smoothed, gave buildings a new elegance.

The impression first made on Montrealers by this finished material was remembered in old age by Thomas Storrow Brown. In 1870 he recalled the new buildings as he saw them after his arrival in Montreal in 1818: "Hammer-dressed stone had come into use and some coarse-cut, but the only specimen I remember of fine chiselled, such as now used, was Mr. Torrance's block, corner of St. Paul and St. Nicholas Sts.; its beauty was a wonder in our eyes."

Limestone from the quarries back of the mountain could meet the most exacting requirements, the biggest orders. It was the stone used in the construction of Notre Dame Church in Place d'Armes in the 1820s. This order might have been the biggest ever given for a single building in North America, for Notre Dame Church, at the time it was constructed, was North America's biggest building, ecclesiastical or secular.

In *The Gazette* in 1824 advertisements called for tenders for "the Cartage to Town from the Quarries in the rear of it." This cartage had to be kept up for the length of the contract "in such manner that the works may not be delayed." Long processions of mule teams hauled the limestone blocks from the quarries to Place d'Armes. When Place d'Armes became overcrowded with building stone, other blocks were stored in Place Viger, about a quarter of a mile away.

Among the good qualities of Montreal's limestone was its endurance. It withstood even the exceptional rigors of Montreal's climate, resisting erosion. Experiments by Victorian contractors with imported graystones only redounded to the better reputation of Montreal's own limestone. When Christ Church Cathedral was being built in the 1850s, Montreal limestone was used for most of it, but the architect, Frank Wills of Salisbury, England, appears to have wanted a superior stone (as he believed) for the openings and trimmings.

Wills had already been the architect for the Anglican Cathedral at Fredericton and had imported stone from the quarries in Caen, France. Caen stone was imported again for trimmings at the cathedral in Montreal. It proved a bad choice. Wills was ignorant of what the Canadian climate would do to imported stone. Not half a century had passed before the stone from Caen began to decay and fall away. Early in the 1920s much of it was removed, and similar repairs and replacements followed. The old Montreal limestone has weathered well, while much of the "superior stone" from Caen ended up as chippings for the paths around the cathedral.

From the 1880s onward, however, newer types of building materials were becoming evident. Sandstone, in its various reddish and brownish tones, became limestone's first chief competitor. It was bringing a new sense of color to the old gray city. It was also introducing greater ornamentation, as sandstone lent itself to carving more easily than limestone.

Unlike limestone (so conveniently quarried back of

the mountain) the variety of sandstones were brought into the city from outside. Some were of Canadian origin, such as the brown sandstone from quarries in the Thousand Islands. Other types of sandstone came from other countries. Some were from the U.S., such as the sandstone used for Molsons Bank. Much sandstone was imported from the famous quarries of Scotland.

As the 19th century moved toward its close, not only sandstone but other building materials were gradually displacing limestone's architectural ascendancy in Montreal — such materials as glazed bricks and terra-cotta tiles. By about 1910 the great era of old gray limestone was practically over.

Montreal lost most of its downtown limestone heritage in the years after World War II. The reconstruction of Montreal's centre, especially the surge of office construction, swept away whole streets of limestone houses. The time is rapidly approaching when limestone houses, once so conspicuous a presence, will be only random and rare. Yet an impressive limestone heritage has survived in larger buildings. There are still such old limestone Roman Catholic churches as Notre Dame, St. Patrick's, the GESU, the Cathedral of Mary Queen of the World and such Anglican churches as Christ Church Cathedral, St. George's, St. James the Apostle and St. John the Evangelist. And there is St. James United (the old St. James Methodist). The limestone tradition is also impressive in such landmarks as Bonsecours Market, the old courthouse, Windsor Station and some of the older buildings on the McGill campus.

Every time Montrealers cross the St. Lawrence River on the Victoria Bridge, they are passing over the massive limestone piers of the 1850s. Most of these piers were constructed with limestone from the quarries at Pointe Claire. Though most of Montreal's limestone past is gone, what remains is a reminder of the days when it gave Montreal "an air of solidity and grandeur surpassed by no other city on this continent."

Art saved by the sword

The roof was about to collapse when the officer of the 39th Regiment made his way into the cathedral. The flames, in a roar, were leaping up into the cold December night. The lead from the roof was beginning to melt and pour down into the street; particles of the burning roof were dropping to the cathedral's floor.

Above the altar hung a huge oil painting, a copy of Leonardo da Vinci's Last Supper. The painting in its wide frame was too heavy for one man to carry; perhaps it had been affixed too firmly to the wall to be dislodged easily. There was only one way of saving it. The officer drew his sword. With the blade he sliced the canvas out of its frame and carried it out to safety.

In that furious night fire of Dec. 10, 1856, the old Christ Church Cathedral was utterly destroyed. It had stood on the north side of Notre Dame St., a little east of Place d'Armes — a fine, large, classical building. When the new cathedral was built, a site was chosen up the hill in the block on St. Catherine St. between University St. and Union Ave. The painting, reframed, was placed in the new cathedral. It was hung inside, over the main entrance. Its great size, its elevation high on the wall over the doors and its soft, clear lighting give it a memorable majesty. In 1980, when Christ Church Cathedral was renovated, the painting was moved to its new position in the chancel.

At a meeting at Christ Church Cathedral on Feb. 17, 1825, the vestry had considered whether the painting should be bought. It had been offered for 170 pounds, "including the frame." Some objection was apparently raised to spending the parish funds on something that was not essential but only a decoration. Other members of the vestry, impressed by the beauty of the painting, did not believe the opportunity to purchase it should be lost. If Christ Church didn't buy it, some other church (probably Roman Catholic) might do so. A compromise was reached: the picture would be acquired, provided that the 170 pounds could be raised by subscription, without diminishing the parish funds. The subscription was successful.

Who painted this copy of the Last Supper? The record of the vestry meeting in Christ Church on Feb. 17, 1825, says that the picture was offered to the vestry by "Mr. Drake." The reference here is undoubtedly to the English artist John Poad Drake. He had come first to Halifax, then to Montreal. In Montreal his copy of the Last Supper was exhibited. The advertisement reads:

"THE LAST SUPPER"
"An Historical Picture of THE LAST SUPPER, painted by J.P. DRAKE of this City, is now open for Exhibition at the Exchange Coffee House, St. Paul St., from 9 a.m. till dusk. Admittance is 3d. General Admission Ticket 3 shillings."

The exhibition opened at the end of January 1825, the month before Drake offered the painting to the vestry of Christ Church. It was John Poad Drake's practice to paint a large, impressive picture, then to place it on public view and charge admission. The most famous of the pictures he painted and exhibited in this way was one of the emperor Napoleon.

Drake had the opportunity of actually seeing Napoleon. His father, Thomas Drake, was an official in the navy yard at Plymouth. Napoleon was brought to Plymouth Sound in July 1815. After the collapse of his fortunes following his defeat at Waterloo he had surrendered himself to the commander of the British warship HMS Bellerophon. He had done so partly for protection; he was fearful that he might be killed if he fell into the hands of some of his other enemies. The ship sailed to Plymouth Sound. Thousands seized the chance of getting a glimpse of Napoleon.

Napoleon obliged the crowd by appearing on deck from time to time. During those summer days at Plymouth, John Poad Drake made the most of his opportunities for seeing Napoleon. He later painted a colossal picture of the emperor standing on the deck of the Bellerophon.

Drake was gifted as a portrait painter. When he came to Halifax in 1815, a subscription was raised for a portrait of Chief Justice S.S. Blowers. Drake was given the commission. His portrait of the chief justice in official scarlet robe and wig hangs today in the Halifax courthouse. When Drake came to Montreal, his work was praised. Competent artists were rare in Montreal in the 1820s. Drake shone

JOHN COLLINS SKETCHBOOK

The LAST SUPPER
CHRIST CHURCH
CATHEDRAL

with brilliance in this limited environment.

Drake, however, did not receive the patronage he had hoped for in Montreal. In 1827 he returned to England. He largely turned away from painting to become an inventor. His upbringing in the navy yard at Plymouth had given him a taste for pondering new ship designs and new weapons of war. He patented a number of his inventions. Again and again he tried to persuade the government to adopt them. His ingenuity was praised, but little was done to make use of his designs.

Colonel Munro, commander of the regiment, later admitted that his men might have saved a number of the handsome memorial tablets in the cathedral. But he felt he had no authority to carry out such wrenching; it might have damaged the walls and possibly the tablets. Fortunately, no such untimely inhibitions delayed the resolution of the officer of the 39th Regiment who saved the painting. He probably had to stand on the altar to slice the canvas from its frame. He then leaped to the floor. With the roof burning over his head, he ran for the door.

Redpath's progress

One of the oldest factories in Montreal closed in January 1980 when Redpath Sugars Ltd. ceased making sugar on the bank of the Lachine Canal, and its parent company, Redpath Industries Ltd., concentrated its manufacturing in Toronto. The canal-bank factory was the first to manufacture sugar in Canada: construction started in 1854, manufacturing the next year.

This factory is historic in another way: it was one of the first in Montreal to be run on waterpower. Under the conditions of the day, the Redpath factory was an enterprise of startling proportions. It required an outlay of 40,000 pounds on land, machinery and buildings. An equivalent amount was needed for working capital. These huge sums of money were provided by John Redpath.

This Scot from Berwickshire had come to Montreal in 1816 at the age of 20 with no capital other than his training as a stonemason. He went on from working with his hands to become a contractor. One of his first opportunities came when he built a Montreal dairy. Soon he had moved on to building some of the major projects in the country. In 1821 work began on one of the first important St. Lawrence projects — the construction of the Lachine Canal, a foreshadowing of the St. Lawrence Seaway.

Redpath was one of the two contractors. It was a big project — about 8½ miles long, needing four years to complete. How rapidly John Redpath had progressed is seen in the fact that he was awarded this contract only five years after coming to Canada and when he was still only 25 years of age.

Redpath's success with the Lachine Canal gave him high status among contractors. In the late 1820s, when the Rideau Canal was under construction, he was awarded the contract to build the lock at Jones Falls. That lock was the most difficult of all on the Rideau, even the most difficult ever built anywhere in North America. The British government had sent one of its engineers, John Mactaggart, to report on the falls and the problems it would raise. Mactaggart described the river as "rolling down a narrow ravine, scarcely a mile in length, and having a 60-ft. fall. The banks of this narrow and crooked ravine are lofty, averaging 90 ft. in height; and on their west side there are deep bogs, surrounded by high land." Redpath, however, undertook the awesome project. He was working in a wilderness, hauling stone by oxen from a quarry in a forest, and in a region infested with swamp fever. Yet the project was brought to completion.

Meanwhile Redpath was active as a builder in Montreal. He had a part in erecting many of the city's most conspicuous landmarks. He was a contractor for the Montreal General Hospital on Dorchester St. He provided stone for the building of Notre Dame Church in Place d'Armes in the 1820s. And he was contractor for the first construction on the McGill campus: two sections of what is now the Arts Building, the central portion and the east wing. Though the Arts Building over the years has undergone much internal remodelling, the walls built by Redpath in 1839-40 still stand.

Redpath's success as a builder enabled him to accumulate capital, which he invested in a wide spectrum of enterprises. He bought heavily in Bank of Montreal stock, becoming one of the bank's directors and a vice-president. He was also involved in shipping, mining, real estate, telegraphs, fuel and insurance.

His greatest opportunity came in the 1850s. Hydro-electric power was becoming available to Montreal for the first time. In those days the idea of transmitting water power by high-tension wires from such remote waterfalls as Shawinigan would have seemed incredible. Water power then was to be had only at the very site where the water flowed.

At the beginning of the 1850s water power was being provided along the Lachine Canal, which had been enlarged since its first construction in the 1820s. The tumbling water at the locks, instead of being wasted, could be put to industrial use. The Canadian government offered leases — virtually in perpetuity — to industrialists who wanted to establish factories right on the canal banks. Redpath began to buy land on the canal from the Sulpicians. He obtained a lease from the government at the St. Gabriel Lock. His plan was to do something never done in Canada before: he would manufacture sugar. To give his industry a chance to grow, the government imposed a tariff on imported sugar.

SKETCHBOOK
John Collins — The "Sugar House" on the Canal

Redpath lit his factory with gas obtained as a by-product from the animal charcoal used in the sugar-making. He had his own ships for bringing in the raw sugar from abroad — ships he named after his daughters. Alongside his factory, in a basin off the canal, these ships unloaded at his own wharf.

Redpath manufactured sugar in the manner of his day: he turned it out in solid form known as the "sugar loaf." Liquid sugar was poured into molds shaped like cones, where it hardened. Cones weighing 14 pounds stood in rows on grocers' shelves. In an era of rough handling, the sugar loaf was easy to transport. There were no bags to break open. The sugar loaf was so hard it would ring like iron if struck. The consumer would grind a loaf to get "pulverized sugar." Or he could ask his grocer to grind it for him. Redpath made some pulverized sugar as well. Leftovers at the factory were made into syrup or molasses.

Redpath was active in charities and in educational institutions, not only with financial support but in administration. He was an active Presbyterian, a founder of the Presbyterian Foreign Missions and the Montreal Presbyterian College, as well as the Côté St. Presbyterian Church. He was a member of Montreal city council from 1840 to 1843.

Redpath died in 1869, in his early '70s. He had invested in many farms on the slope of Mount Royal, convinced these farms would one day be among the most valuable areas of the city. One of these properties bears his name — Redpath St. In the 1850s the trustees of Mount Royal Cemetery wanted to expand the cemetery's boundaries. Redpath owned land adjoining it. They asked him to sell a portion to them, and he agreed, on condition that he could pick a sixth of an acre for a family burial plot. There he lies buried on what was once his own farm.

All aboard for the West

xcept for the fur trade (a wilderness trade), Montreal had had little contact with the West. Apart from small settlements on the shores of the Red River, and on the Pacific coast beyond the Rockies, the West had few communities with which significant commercial relations could be established. The way west from Montreal was long, circuitous, danger-filled.

One of the Montrealers (other than fur-traders) who had penetrated into the Canadian prairies in the years before the CPR was an artist, Henri Julien, on the staff of a Montreal weekly, the Canadian Illustrated News. In 1874 the News arranged for Julien to accompany the new North-West Mounted Police to make a pictorial record of their first trek from Manitoba to the Rockies.

When Julien returned to Montreal, he was haunted by the wild loneliness of the western wilderness. "This had truly been called the Great Lone Land," he said. "Its silence and its solitude weigh on you like a mechanical power. . . . It is a real desert, a land of desolation."

Once the CPR had been granted its charter in February 1881, the Great Lone Land of the Canadian West suddenly assumed a new meaning. The railway would bring development to the land of desolation. The West would become a land of opportunity. In Montreal, where the business interests of Canada were concentrated, a railway to the West would create new horizons for enterprise. Prominent among Montrealers exploring the economic prospects of the West in 1882 was Senator Alexander Watson Ogilvie, founder of the firm of millers and grain merchants. In 1882 he was active in the Qu'Appelle Land Co., interested in developing land 400 miles west of Winnipeg. Already the company was seeking emigrants in England, Scotland and Ireland, offering them inducements to become settlers. Ogilvie was also prominent in the Montreal and Western Land Co., formed to develop a tract of land on the north side of the Qu'Appelle River.

S.O. Shorey, president of H. Shorey & Co., a Montreal clothing manufacturer, reported on the rising land values in Winnipeg. His firm had paid $9,500 for a Winnipeg lot. Three days later it was offered $15,000 for it. Another Montrealer had

bought a lot about eight miles outside Portage la Prairie for $3 an acre. He offered it for sale. Word soon reached him in Montreal that it had been sold at $20 an acre. Such soaring prices did not seem to Ogilvie to be unreasonable, or merely inflationary. He said he "had great faith in the new country, and did not think that the price of land could go beyond its value."

Everyone in Montreal seemed confident that the CPR would make the West the land of the future. In 1882 the Montreal firm Vipond, McBride and Co., wholesale fruit and provision merchants, was planning a wheat farm in the West. François-Xavier Bissette of Montreal was opening a Winnipeg soap factory. A.M. Duperrouzel, former proprietor of Montreal's Grand Hotel, was leaving to cultivate a flower and market garden in St. Boniface. Montrealers of all trades, occupations and professions were heading west. A.M. Béliveau, master carpenter, was leaving. So was William James Akin, a young accountant, formerly with the Montreal firm Court and McIntosh. Two young Montreal advocates, S.W. Jackson and Fred Carter, had gone to Winnipeg, intending to pass examinations for the Manitoba bar.

Prospects of cattle-ranching attracted other Montrealers. Among them was Duncan McEachren, Montreal's leading veterinary surgeon, later dean of the faculty of comparative medicine and veterinary science at McGill University. McEachren and his business partners made their exploratory expedition west in the summer of 1882. As the CPR had not yet reached Winnipeg, they had to follow a route through the U.S., then sail up the Missouri River on the steamboat Red Cloud to Fort Benton in Montana. From Fort Benton they set out in prairie wagons for the Canadian west. At Fort McLeod they saw the mounted police in their "smart and soldier-like scarlet uniform," and Indians "resplendent in earrings, necklaces, brass wire twisted in the hair and their faces painted hideously a yellowish red."

The hard western journey proved worthwhile. At High River, Alta., McEachren and his associates found the sort of land they were seeking: "one of the best cattle ranges in the whole Northwest — pasture

SKETCHBOOK *John Collins*

ON THE BUILDING THAT USED TO BE ON NOTRE DAME EAST OF BERRI THERE WAS A MARKER INDICATING THAT BELOW NOTRE DAME WAS THE SITE OF THE CPR'S DALHOUSIE STATION

First Train to Winnipeg 1885

abundant, water good and plenty of shelter on the well-wooded river banks." The West, in anticipation of the coming of the CPR, was already developing at such a rate that some wondered whether it was destined to rival eastern Canada. Shorey, who claimed he was the first Montreal commercial traveller to visit the Red River, had seen the western growth getting under way, and he said: "The tail will wag the dog some day."

The railway was advancing westward. At 2 p.m. Nov. 2, 1885, the first through-passenger train left the CPR's Dalhousie Station (Windsor Station didn't exist) on its way to Winnipeg. Many Montreal merchants gathered at the station "to give a congratulatory cheer" as the train set out, its locomotive "gaily decorated." West of Winnipeg the tracks were being thrust out into the Great Lone Land, being laid down at a rate of three to four miles a day. The former general manager of the Grand Trunk Railway, C.J. Brydges, visited the construction scene and declared: "The extent of average daily tracklaying done has never yet been

equalled on any railway in the world." Several trains a day were sent west from Winnipeg to the end of track, each carrying everything needed to lay a mile of track — "a mile of rails, a mile of joint fastenings, a mile of bolts and nuts, a mile of spikes and a mile of ties."

By the late autumn of 1885 the railway had been completed. Lord Strathcona left his Montreal house to travel by rail to Craigellachie, a wayside station in the Rockies near the Columbia River. On Nov. 7 he drove in the last spike, four years and 11 months from the day the CPR had received its charter. By the next summer the CPR was ready to begin its service to the Pacific.

On June 28, 1886, its first through-passenger train left Montreal for the Pacific. The next month Montreal's new contact with the Pacific was celebrated with a cargo of tea, brought by ship from Japan and sent by train from Vancouver. It was consigned to the Montreal firm James Magor. Montreal's commercial route across the West, in all-Canadian territory, was now a reality.

The old kirk on the waterfront

One of the oldest churches on the island of Montreal is St. Andrew's United on the waterfront at Lachine. St. Andrew's was built by Presbyterians, mostly Scots, and at first it was known as "the Scotch Church." It is typically Scottish in architecture — the "auld kirk" of gray stone, plain and solemn, strong and firm. When opened in the 1830s, it had square box pews, a choir loft and a raised central pulpit, but for 32 years it had no organ.

The organ was regarded as an interruption and a distraction, more a form of entertainment than an aid to worship. Choir and congregation sang unaccompanied, with noble simplicity, out of the heart. Such singing, however sincere, tended to become somewhat confused. In 1861 a precentor was engaged, James Law. He would stand up before the congregation, a tuning fork in his hand. He struck the fork on wood, got the right pitch, then led the singing. For this Sabbath duty he received a stipend of 10 pounds a year.

Lachine was still countrified and rather primitive back in the 1830s. An English traveller, Mrs. E.C. Porteous, stayed there for a few days in 1830, while waiting to leave with the Hudson's Bay Co.'s canoes for the Northwest to enter service in the household of Mrs. McTavish, wife of the chief factor of the company. She was accommodated during her stay at Hudson's Bay House, the headquarters of the Hudson's Bay Co. in Lachine. It stood alongside the land where St. Andrew's Church was to be built. At Lachine she attended a prayer meeting, possibly a meeting of the Presbyterian congregation. This congregation had been formed as far back as 1818, but in 1830 it had no church and held services in any makeshift accommodation it could find. "I shall never forget," she wrote, "going one evening to a prayer meeting to which our party was invited before commencing our hazardous journey up country. The arrangements were on the most primitive scale, and we were compelled to climb up to a vacant garret. . . . The only accommodation provided in the way of seats was a rough piece of lumber supported by blocks, and access to the rude apartment was obtained by mounting an old and rickety ladder. But the heartiness of the little service certainly compensated for all these disadvantages. The minister gave an edifying discourse; we all joined heartily in the singing; and we left with a very good impression of the earnestness and deep religious fervor which characterized the whole proceedings."

St. Andrew's Church, when built, faced the river. It looks upstream — the way all Lachine was looking at the time, for it was the point of departure for all travellers setting out from the island of Montreal for the vast unsettled territories of the west. Montreal was then a port that received thousands of arriving immigrants, but it was not the port of their departure. The Lachine Rapids blocked the way upstream. Before the building of the Lachine Canal, and even for many travellers long after, the route was overland from Montreal to Lachine, by carriage, wagon or on foot. At Lachine they took the boats that carried them up the St. Lawrence on the way to their scattered destinations.

St. Andrew's Church owes its origin to a Scot, John Grant, who was in the business of upstream transportation for passengers and freight. He had a fleet of bateaux and Durham boats — big strong boats that could be propelled against the current by oars, sails or poles, or dragged through rough water by ropes pulled by oxen along the shore. Such transportation was big business at the time, Lachine's chief industry. Grant transported the pioneers who founded or expanded the settlements of Upper Canada. He carried their supplies up and brought their first produce down. Grant also had an inn at Lachine, where travellers often stayed a night or two, waiting for the boats to leave, or for their luggage to arrive from Montreal. When he died in 1817, his body was taken to Montreal and Grant's neighbors, "as a last token of their respect," carried the body on a palanquin — a covered stretcher, borne by poles on the shoulders of men who carried his body not only for these nine miles, "but even to the grave, not allowing the hearse in attendance to be used."

Grant, a Scot from Glenmoriston, near Inverness, had been making plans to found a Presbyterian church in Lachine. He died before he could carry out the plans, but his heirs respected his intentions and fulfilled them. His sons, Robert and J.C. Grant, gave

John Collins SKETCHBOOK
St. Andrew's Church—Lachine

the congregation the land where church, parish hall and manse were to be built, and for the churchyard that received the dead till the last burial in 1915. The church today probably stands on or near the site of John Grant's old house, as is suggested by the wording of the memorial tablet on the east wall. The tablet is above the Grant family pew.

The old registers of St. Andrew's, which have been preserved, give a picture of the role the church played in a very active community. As the only Presbyterian church for Lachine, and for a wide area around, it served Presbyterian people from communities as far away as Châteauguay. The records of baptisms, marriages and burials give the varied occupations of the time: farmers, bakers, tailors, blacksmiths, schoolmasters, soldiers, a miller,

a weaver, a surveyor, a tollgate keeper and a laborer who signed with an X.

Old St. Andrew's Church is now 1500 St. Joseph Blvd., as the lakeshore road at Lachine is known. Historic in itself, it stands on one of the most historic spots in Canada. The shoreline in front of it, and nearby, saw the canoes manned by the voyageurs putting out for the fur posts of the wilderness, and the clumsy bateaux carrying the immigrants, their baggage piled as high as a haystack, or the troops for western forts such as the 1,000 redcoats seen by James Somerville, a farmer on the Lower Lachine Rd., as they marched past the rapids on their way to take the bateaux at Lachine to join the army on the Niagara frontier in the War of 1812.

The deserters

In the summer of 1803 Washington Irving, the American author who created Rip Van Winkle, was on his way through the wilderness from New York to Montreal. Other travellers were encountered rarely, but one day he came upon a traveller with "a remarkably striking appearance."

He was standing under a twisted tree that grew in the middle of the road, wearing "a red jacket with something like military decorations," and with a round black hat stuck on the side of his head. His hair hung about his ears in wild disorder. Over his left shoulder a bundle was slung, on the end of a cutlass. Irving says that "his countenance was rugged and almost savage," and "found out he was a deserter from the English garrison at Montreal . . . making his way to the Black River."

That deserter was only one of thousands from the garrisons in Montreal and other posts who crossed the border, breaking loose from the discipline of army life to snatch at sudden freedom. Dealing with deserters was one of the most constant and most baffling problems that the garrison commanders faced. The British garrisons in Canada were stationed close to the American border. It was a temptation to a soldier to make a dash to cross over it. The U.S. was then wide open to immigrants: no questions were asked. The temptation to desert was all the greater since at that time British emigrants were setting out for the U.S. by tens of thousands. Many of the deserters from the garrison in Montreal must already have had friends and relations below the border.

Even when the long era of the British garrisons in Canada was drawing to its close, desertion was still a problem. One wintry day in 1862 the war correspondent of the London Times, Sir William Howard Russell, was travelling by train from Point Lévis to Montreal. He had been sent to North America to report the American Civil War, but as the war seemed in a lull that winter, he had come north to see Canada. Russell wrote: "There were several companies of H.M.'s 63rd Regiment in the train also going up to Montreal. It did not escape me that at the station pickets were looking sharply out for intending deserters who might have cut away in the darkness." Russell learned how ingenious some of the methods of desertion might be when soldiers had been "seduced by high pay," and were "seized with an irresistible desire to quit the service abruptly."

Sometimes the act of desertion was collective. A whole guard would march off, non-commissioned officers and all. In one instance, a soldier put on a sergeant's coat, or sewed chevrons on the sleeve of his own, and marched off with a whole party. Sometimes one of the party would submit to being handcuffed. He would be marched out of the post by his comrades like a deserter when he was only concealing the act of desertion by playing the deserter's role.

Penalties for desertion were often severe. Some soldiers were sentenced to imprisonment with hard labor in the penitentiary at Kingston. There were heavier penalties: deserters might be transported as felons to penal colonies in Australia or elsewhere. Sentences for transportation might be for 10 to 20 years, or even for the prisoner's "natural life."

Despite such severe penalties, desertion was only imperfectly discouraged. The criminal records of the Montreal Jail show that early in May 1839, 24 soldiers (belonging to the 85th and 34th Regiments) were committed for desertion and transported. At the end of the month two soldiers (of the 73rd Regiment) were transported. Early in July five more deserters (of the 85th and 32nd) were transported, and there were two more before July had ended.

Still another penalty was branding a deserter with the letter D. This might be done together with a sentence of imprisonment in the penitentiary or a sentence of transportation. If the deserter had been notorious for bad conduct in other ways, the letters BC might be added. In the records of the old Montreal Jail is one concerning a private of the 43rd Regiment who was sentenced "to be transported as a felon for the term of 14 years and further to be marked with the letter 'D' in the manner prescribed in the Mutiny Act." The practice was to burn the D into the breast or shoulder with a red-hot iron. According to an old tradition, the deserter would be told that the moment the iron touched his flesh he was to repeat the words "God Save the Queen" three times. As soon as the last words were spoken the iron

Champ-de-Mars

would be withdrawn. Even in this short time the iron would have hissed into his flesh and left a scar that nothing could ever efface.

On a Monday afternoon in July 1862, "an immense concourse of people" had gathered on the Champ de Mars. An English visitor wanted to see what was about to take place, but the crowd was so great that he might have been able to see nothing had not Judge Coursol admitted him to his chambers in the courthouse overlooking the parade ground. From this window the visitor saw the troops of the garrison drawn up in columns; they formed three sides of a hollow square. In the space at the centre stood Maj.-Gen. Lord Frederick Paulet and his staff. Two soldiers were then led into the centre. They were handcuffed and guarded by a corporal and four men with fixed bayonets. The adjutant read the charges in a voice was so firm and clear it could be heard from the courthouse window. Courts martial had decided "that Privates McKay and Bryan, having been found guilty of desertion and mutinous conduct, should be branded with the letter 'D,' according to the articles of war, and that the remainder of their natural lives should be spent in servitude."

The English visitor, watching the prisoners intently, saw that they were two young men who "stood uncovered during the reading of their sentences and seemed to feel acutely the humiliating position to which their bad conduct had reduced them." In the silence that fell when the adjutant had finished reading the two young men were led off under a strong escort.

Then followed something the visitor thought typical, yet dramatic, for the life of the army must go on, though punishment had been pronounced and the guilty sentenced. The troops "marched past" Lord Paulet and his staff, and left the parade ground, "the bands of the several regiments playing gaily meanwhile."

To the visitor, this spectacle on the Champ de Mars "was both a sad and imposing one."

Montreal's Russian guns

Two Russian guns stand pointed at René Lévesque Blvd. — captured from the Russians at the Black Sea fortifications of Sebastopol in 1855. Queen Victoria presented them to Montreal following the Crimean War. They are the two cannon in Place du Canada (formerly the southern half of Dominion Square).

When the guns arrived in Montreal in the 1850s, they were first set up on either side of Nelson's monument in Place Jacques Cartier. When Montreal's Roman Catholic cemetery was closed and the area converted to Dominion Square in the 1870s, the guns were brought uptown. At first they stood on wooden platforms. When these rotted, excavations were made for foundations of cement. Spades turned up bones from the old cemetery.

Britain, France and Turkey found themselves at war with Russia in 1854. Fighting was concentrated in the Crimea, the Russian peninsula on the northern coast of the Black Sea. There the heart of the struggle was Sebastopol, the Russian stronghold.

Though Montreal was far from the Crimea, the effects of the war were felt. The British garrison in Montreal (maintained there, as in other Canadian cities, to warn the Americans against aggression) soon dwindled. Troops were moved to Crimean battlegrounds. Names of many of the officers Montrealers had come to know were appearing in the Crimean casualty lists.

Capt. Maximilian Montagu Hammond is an example of the British officers, stationed for a time in the Montreal garrison, who were to die before the walls of Sebastopol. Known as "Maxy," he made himself conspicuous for his courageous piety — a characteristic not common among garrison officers. (In 1869 Hammond's uncle, Ashton Oxenden, was to be appointed the Anglican bishop of Montreal.) Hammond came to the Montreal garrison in 1846 with his regiment, the Rifle Brigade. He thought of himself as a Christian soldier, fighting alike in the army of the queen and in the hosts of the Lord.

"Satan has been very busy amongst us," he said. He tried to set a better example. Courage was needed to withstand ridicule. To a younger brother at Eton, he wrote: "If we would serve the Lord, we must most cheerfully and gladly put up with sneers and scoffs. . . . We must never be ashamed."

He went into the wards of the Montreal military hospital, kneeling and praying at the bedsides of sick soldiers. He regularly visited a solder dying of tuberculosis and tried to turn his thoughts to faith. He raised funds to help soldiers' families and for Irish immigrants arriving in Montreal in poverty and sick with typhus. When the rector of Trinity Anglican Church, Rev. Mark Willoughby, contracted typhus while ministering to the immigrants, Hammond risked his own life by nursing him till he died. A private in the Rifle Brigade wrote: "The French people when they meet Capt. Hammond in the streets, hearing of his kindness to the poor, would uncover their heads and invoke blessings upon him."

This man, known in Montreal as "the praying captain," was one of the officers called away to the Crimea. At the very end of the war, the day before Sebastopol surrendered, he took part in the assault on the parapet. He was struggling to break through and was "seen to cut down several of the enemy with his sword." The color sergeant of another regiment said the next day: "I saw an officer of the Rifles whose name I do not know — a fine tall man — behaving heroically." A bayonet punctured his heart. He fell over backward into the ditch. The next day his servant told another officer that on the morning of the battle Hammond had called him in for prayer in his tent before going out.

The Crimean War was a dreary struggle, with fumbles, frustrations, heavy losses. Discouraging prospects made victory all the sweeter when it came at last. Even good news travelled slowly in those days. On Sept. 28, 1855, *The Gazette* ran the headline:

BY TELEGRAPH
VIA MONTREAL LINE
GLORIOUS NEWS!
SEBASTOPOL TAKEN
SEPTEMBER 9.

There was to be a day set aside for public rejoicing. It was postponed because of rain: "Skies seemed to be weeping for the slain." On the morning of Oct. 4 the mayor ordered the churchbells rung, a signal the celebration would take place that evening.

SKETCHBOOK John Collins

The CRIMEAN GUNS
—Place du Canada

It rained again in the afternoon, but cleared. Crowds swarmed out, heedless of deep mud in the streets. The illuminations dazzled. Every window of public buildings and private houses (even the dwellings of the poor) had candles or lamps. St. Andrew's Church (of the Church of Scotland) on Beaver Hall Hill (where the Bell Canada building stands today) was floodlit, "its outlines showed distinctly through the darkness."

The grandest feature of the night was the Bank of Montreal at Place d'Armes. Its portico and facade (the same today as then) fluttered with lights. Gas pipes circled the bank's tall Corinthian columns. With the jets in these pipes all aflame, the columns became "climbing wreathes of light." Around the dome were colored lamps. Above the dome, gas jets had been arranged to make a crown. From the bank's roof, rockets were fired into the night sky.

Other celebrations came later. Regiments were coming back from the Crimea to resume garrison duties in Canada. On the morning of Saturday, June 28, 1856, the 39th Regiment arrived in Montreal from its Crimean service. Montreal went wild with welcome.

The war in the Crimea was believed to have ended Russia's ambitions for conquest in the area round the Black Sea. In an editorial headed Victory, *The Gazette* declared: "The Russian power in the Crimea is broken, and Russian power over the Black Sea forever at an end." But about 16 years later Russia repudiated the treaty that had ended the war. It began to reconstruct the shattered fortifications of Sebastopol and planned the building of a Black Sea fleet. The Russian guns in Place du Canada, marked with the Tsar's eagles, are the trophies of a very uncertain victory.

The collector: David Ross McCord

The McCord house was named "Temple Grove," and it looked like a Greek temple: a large, many-columned mansion in the Greek Revival style of the early 19th century. Few of the temples of ancient Greece could have had a more advantageous setting. Temple Grove stood on the rising slope above Sherbrooke St. on the east side of the old Côte des Neiges Rd. (Cedar Ave. was one day to be opened through the grounds, north of the house).

Not only was Temple Grove lifted up above the distant city; it was really grove-like in its surroundings. When it was built in 1837, Sherbrooke St. had been only a country road through pastures, and Côte des Neiges was only the road leading to the village of Côte des Neiges.

In this temple-like mansion, David Ross McCord gathered Canadian historical relics. All his life he was impressed by the words of the hymn that time, like "an ever-rolling stream," is bearing everything away. He was determined to snatch as many things as he could from the stream, to assemble and preserve them and make a gift of them to the future.

This is not to say that he was without other interests. He was a McGill graduate of the 1860s (BA, MA and BCL) who successfully practiced law and was made a QC in 1895. He was a Montreal alderman. For many years he was secretary of the Conservative Association. But none of these other activities ever deterred or eclipsed his historical collecting.

McCord turned away from nothing that seemed to have historical meaning. Into Temple Grove he brought Indian relics of every kind: letters and manuscripts; guns, swords and other weapons; military uniforms; old pottery, porcelain and silver; period furniture; ecclesiastical relics, from crucifixes to pieces of church furnishings; prints and drawings; portraits and paintings of historical scenes and buildings.

A visitor in 1914 described the house: "A year or two ago when I first visited the place, the drawing room and reception room, as well as other rooms, had been utilized to store the collection. Quite recently when I was there, the dining room and every other room on the ground floor had been invaded, and the family had been driven for house room to the upstairs apartments. Even these are being invaded by relics, and the family, retreating before them, will apparently soon find itself on the roof, so rapidly is the collection growing."

David Ross McCord was a small spare man with a beard. Some called him "quaint," others "eccentric." Sometimes he wore the gown of a Japanese nobleman, though he had no connection with Japan. His manners were brisk and whimsical. When saying goodbye to a visitor on a wintry night, he would step outdoors in his Japanese nobleman's gown. With the lights of Montreal twinkling below in the frosty air, he would go on talking rapidly about his historical interests. Then he would abruptly say "Good night!" His feet would crunch in the snow. The "odd little figure" would withdraw between the tall columns of the Greek portico and disappear beyond the closing door.

McCord was determined that his historical collections not be dispersed after his death. He was not collecting for the auction rooms, but with patriotic purpose: saving the heritage of the nation. Already he was calling his collection "the David Ross McCord National Museum." But there was a problem. Who would provide a suitable museum building where the collections might be open free to the public?

McCord favored McGill University. But McGill, preoccupied with other needs, had no money to build and maintain such a museum. Offers came from Toronto and Winnipeg. It was reported that "certain gentlemen — or perhaps certain institutions — in either city would provide the money for a suitable building at once." The Public Archives at Ottawa was also known to be interested. But McCord's roots were deep in Montreal, and, as a McGill graduate, he still hoped that the university might be able to make some arrangement.

In 1919 his collections were given to McGill. The university, however, had difficulty in finding space for a historical museum and for financing its maintenance.

In 1957 Mr. and Mrs. Walter M. Stewart began providing funds for a conservation program. Then the possibility of using a vacant building arose. The

The
Mc CORD
MUSEUM

JOHN COLLINS $KETCHBOOK

McGill Union, at 690 Sherbrooke St. W. on the southeast corner of Victoria St., became redundant; a new Students' Centre had been built on McTavish.

The Union was not only a very large building but it had architectural and historic interest of its own. Sir William Macdonald had given it to McGill in 1907 as a place where students might "meet together freely, not as members of different faculties, but of the university as a whole." Designed by Percy Nobbs, in association with Hutcheson and Wood, it was one of the most notable buildings of this architect's career.

Mr. and Mrs. Stewart provided funds to reconstruct the McGill Students' Union as the McCord Museum. In 1970 the university, in financial difficulties, withdrew its support. However, Mrs. Stewart and her daughter, Mrs. T.H.P. Molson,

together with the McConnell Foundation, enabled the museum to keep its doors open.

A new era lay ahead. On April 9, 1990, the federal and Quebec governments joined in making a grant of $5,836,000 to the McCord Museum. This sum, added to a previous special grant from the J.W. McConnell Family Foundation, made a total of $30,546,000.

These financial resources provided the museum with the means to improve its equipment and more than double its building's size, greatly expanding its services.

With all these developments, and with the increase of its collections by gifts and purchases, the historical items gathered by David Ross McCord in Temple Grove will always remain the museum's extensive nucleus and many of its principal treasures.

The Franciscans in Montreal

One of the last of the wayside crosses standing in Montreal (in the traditional form of the crucifix or "calvaire") is on the south side of René Lévesque Blvd. about halfway between Fort and Closse Sts., on the grounds of the Franciscan monastery. Behind it is the graystone church of St. Joseph. Just to the east are the monastic buildings of red brick, starkly plain.

This is not a remote, secluded site, but very definitely a city monastery. Motor traffic rolls in front of it, railway trains behind. Commuters on the CPR have a glimpse of the gardens to the rear — narrow and steep, only a few feet from the tracks.

The Franciscans have been on Dorchester (which became René Lévesque Blvd.) since 1890. But the association of this religious order with the island of Montreal goes back to the dawn of the region's history — even farther back than the history of the city itself.

On June 24, 1615, Franciscan priests celebrated the first mass on the island. The Franciscans in New France were from a branch of the order known as the Récollets. Samuel de Champlain had brought three Récollet priests and a Récollet brother with him. On that day in 1615 two of the Récollet priests, Joseph LeCaron and Denis Jamet, were with Champlain and his men on the shore of the Rivière des Prairies, the river flowing by the northern shore of the island of Montreal. Both priests took part in celebrating the mass. Indians looked on, as Champlain noted, "in admiration at the ceremonies and at the vestments which seemed to them so beautiful as being something they had never seen before."

In 1692 the Récollets began the construction of a monastery in Montreal. They brought the work to conclusion in 1706 when the chapel was ready for worship. This chapel faced Notre Dame St., a little east of what today is McGill St. The monastic grounds extended southward as far as Lemoine St. and westward to St. Pierre St.

With the coming of British rule to Montreal in 1760, the Récollets faced gradual extinction. The new government did not look with favor on such religious orders, regarding them as links with France. The Récollets were granted the use of their property in Montreal, but only so long as the priests in the

order lived. They would recruit new brothers but no new priests. When the last of the Récollet fathers died, their monastic property would become the property of the Crown.

An air of mortality brooded over the monastery of the Récollets. They could look forward only with melancholy. One by one the priests died, carried in turn by the survivors to the burial place in the chapel's crypt. The last Récollet priest in Montreal was Louis Demers. In contemplation of his own death he disposed of what remained of the order's belongings. He died in 1813.

Four years later an American traveller, Joseph Sansom, visited the deserted chapel on Notre Dame St. "Nothing presents itself to the street," he wrote, "but the dingy facade of the chapel, and the outer walls of the cloisters, which are still overshadowed by coeval elms." He stepped into the chapel. It was empty, "dark with age, and dreary with neglect and desertion." Lamps hung before the altar, but no lights glimmered. The chapel was lofty in proportion to its other dimensions. Windows were 20 feet from the floor. Between them still hung pictures of the mystical "ecstasies of St. Francis." Sansom felt chilled by the deathly desolation. He hurried out of town into the neighboring fields, "more sensible than ever of the cheerfulness of open air and daylight."

The monastic grounds and buildings had become the property of the Crown. For a time the old cloister of the monks was used as a garrison barracks. But the British authorities had their eye on Ile Ste. Hélène. They needed to fortify that island to defend Montreal from the threat of an American invasion. A deal was worked out with Charles William Grant, husband of the last baroness of Longueuil: Ile Ste. Hélène was part of the ancient holdings of the Longueuil family. An exchange of properties was arranged in 1817: the Crown would take over Ile Ste. Hélène, and Grant would receive the Récollet property and some other Crown land in Montreal.

Grant may have had plans for developing the old Récollet property. In 1818 he opened a street through the grounds, a street below Notre Dame and parallel to it. That little street is still known by

John SKETCHBOOK
Collins Cross of the Franciscans —

the name he gave it, Rue des Récollets. He didn't hold the property long: the Sulpicians bought it from him later in 1818. They repaired the dilapidated chapel, which became the first church of the Irish Roman Catholics in Montreal. They worshipped there till they moved to St. Patrick's in 1847. The old Récollet chapel then became the church of a francophone congregation. It was demolished in 1866.

The Franciscans, however, were to return to Montreal. In the meantime the old name "Récollets" had become obsolete. The order had been reorganized by Pope Leo XIII. They came back to Montreal in 1890, at first with a very small chapel on Richmond St. Help soon came from two pious and beneficent women, Mrs. Tiffin and Mrs. MacConkey, whose aid enabled the Franciscans to establish their monastery on Dorchester. The

Franciscans occupied their residence on Dorchester in 1892 — 200 years after the Récollets had established their monastery on Notre Dame. In 1893 a wing was added. The wayside cross was set up in 1896. St. Joseph's Church was completed in 1901.

These Franciscans on Dorchester wanted some reminder of their Récollet predecessors. When the old church on Notre Dame St. had been demolished, the bones of the Récollets had been removed from their graves in the crypt. They were reinterred in the church of Notre Dame des Anges at the corner of la Gauchetière and Cheneville. When the Franciscans returned to Montreal, they obtained fragments of these bones and buried them under the choir in the crypt of their new St. Joseph's Church on Dorchester. These bones became a link between the Franciscans who came back and those who had been in Montreal long before.

The smartness and snap of the 'Vics'

Montreal's Victoria Rifles claimed to be the first militia regiment in Canada to have its own armory. There were older Canadian armories. But they were huge barn-like drill sheds built by the government for the militia units in the area. In these drill sheds each unit was assigned its quarters.

Montreal had such an armory — the drill shed on Craig St., facing the Champ de Mars. Officers of the Victoria Rifles, however, wanted an armory they could call their own. No financial aid could be expected from the government for such a project. Funds were raised by private subscription, supplemented by such money-raising events as a bazaar.

In 1887 the "Vics" armory was opened on the north side of Cathcart St., a little west of University. Elegant for the times, it was the envy of every other militia unit. It had rooms for the officers' mess, the sergeants' mess, the band and every company of the regiment. There were also a shooting gallery, bowling alleys and a billiard room. Drilling took place in a big hall equipped with a platform for concerts.

The Vics liked to do things in style. On one of the nine occasions when the regiment was called out to uphold the law against rioters, the quarters assigned to the men were considered miserable. The officers believed the Vics deserved better and, at their own expense, rented a hotel and moved the men into it. Other regiments promptly nicknamed the Victoria Rifles "the Featherbeds." The name stuck.

The regiment showed its style again in 1901. It had been called to Quebec to take part in the grand military review put on for the visiting Duke of York (later King George V). The Vics chartered a steamboat from the Richelieu and Ontario Navigation Co., forerunner of Canada Steamship Lines. In this boat the Vics journeyed to Quebec in comfort. At Quebec it served as their floating armory.

The Victoria Rifles never lacked recruits in those days, but it was not an easy regiment to join. Privates were carefully screened for character and quality. An unwritten law in the regiment for half a century required all officers to serve in the ranks first.

The Vics were known for their "smartness and snap." They worked hard for precision in drill. In 1898 the Militia Department, in its report of annual inspections, gave the Victoria Rifles the highest marks among all the country's infantry regiments. The regiment liked to have extra features. It claimed to be the first militia regiment in Canada to have a machine-gun, known in those days as the Maxim gun. The Canadian government wasn't providing the militia units with such modern equipment. The officers of the Vics bought one in 1892 and presented it to the regiment. It made its appearance, drawn by a horse, whenever the Vics were on parade.

The Vics had been formed back in 1861, mostly by members of the Beaver Snow Shoe Club. It was during the American Civil War, and there were fears that Great Britain, friendly to the Confederacy, might become involved in war with the northern states. Canada might be invaded. It would need defenders. Conflict was avoided at that time, so it was not until 1870 that the Victoria Rifles won their first battle honor. The Fenians, an Irish organization in the U.S., were hoping to advance the cause of Ireland's liberation from British rule by making raids on the British colony of Canada, "twisting the lion's tail." When an attack from Vermont seemed imminent, the Victoria Rifles were stationed at Stanbridge in the township of Missisquoi, ready to move to any point on the frontier. On the afternoon of May 25 orders came for the Victoria Rifles to march at once for Eccles Hill, a rocky mound close to the border. On the hill there were already a small number of local volunteers, including the Red Sashes of Missisquoi, who had armed themselves with Ballard sporting rifles. They had fired when the Fenians ventured over the border and driven them back. When the Vics arrived at Eccles Hill, reports came that the Fenians were being reinforced by more men from New York. Another attack, and a stronger one, seemed likely. By 6 p.m., when no attack came, the defenders of Eccles Hill moved down the slope to drive away any Fenians who might be lingering on Canadian soil.

The Victoria Rifles were stationed as a reserve on the spur of the hill, ready to charge down wherever any serious resistance might be encountered. But the

ARMORY
ON
CATHCART

John Collins SKETCHBOOK

few lingering Fenians, faced with this advance, withdrew. The battle was over.

Eccles Hill was only the beginning of the Vics' long war record. They sent 89 officers and men to serve in the South African War. Six died. In World War I the Victoria Rifles contributed many officers and men toward forming the Royal Montreal Regiment for overseas service. The Vics then raised other battalions for overseas. Altogether the Vics sent 4,827 men and won 307 decorations (including the Victoria Cross won by Lt.-Col. W.H. Kennedy while serving as officer commanding the 24th Battalion at the battle of Arras).

In World War II the 1st Battalion of the Vics provided 15 officers and 460 other ranks as reinforcements of the Canadian forces overseas. When the 1st was brought back to strength, it was again broken up to provide further reinforcements urgently needed by other overseas regiments. The 2nd Battalion of the Vics was formed. In the first 20 months of its existence alone, 28 officers and 313 other ranks went for overseas service.

In the years between the two wars the old armory of the Victoria Rifles on Cathcart St., thought splendid in the 1880s, had become outdated and outworn. It was demolished. The regiment donated the site, by then a valuable property, to the Canadian government. In return the government built a handsome new armory for the Vics. It was opened in 1933.

In the mid-1960s the government revised Canada's reserve forces, reducing the number of regiments. The Victoria Rifles was one of those chosen to go out of existence. In the spring of 1965 the armory on Cathcart St. was vacated. It is now the armory of the Régiment de Maisonneuve.

1929: panic in the stock exchange

St. François Xavier St. in front of the old Montreal Stock Exchange (now the Centaur Theatre) is narrow. And in the late autumn of 1929 it was crowded for blocks — with people from sidewalk to sidewalk, from wall to wall. Prices on the exchange had collapsed, and stocks in shoals were being shoved upon the market, to fetch whatever they could get.

Hardly anyone in Canada had thought good times would ever cease. The year 1928 had been the most prosperous in the country's history, and the prosperity of 1928 was followed by the prosperity of 1929. Confidence in perpetual growth was reflected in the Canadian stock markets. The market was no longer the preserve of professional traders, but had become everybody's market, almost everybody's plaything.

In 1928 the Montreal Stock Exchange had doubled its previous peak in the number of transactions, from about 9 million shares to about 18 million. This was almost three times the total for 1926. Faith ran highest in two stocks: Brazilian Traction and International Nickel. Some days they accounted, between them, for as much as two-thirds of all the Montreal market transactions.

In 1929 little clouded the investor's self-assurance. A nasty jolt or two earlier in the year were followed by swift recoveries and still higher peaks. Right through 1929 to the beginning of September, the market lost none of its gleam or glamor.

If the stock market had been only reflecting the general economic prosperity of the country, it might have been closer to realities. But it had parted company with realities; it had made a world of its own and was trying to live in it. Prices of stocks had been bid up to 20, 30 and even 40 times their annual earnings. Investors were borrowing money at 8 to 10 per cent to purchase stocks yielding 2 to 3 per cent. No longer did transactions of this kind represent responsibile investment in sound companies. It was overpricing stocks for the sake of their presumed and automatic rise. The speculative was being regarded as though it were the inevitable.

Investing was made still more unsound because so high a proportion of the stocks were being bought on margin. Brokers were going heavily into debt to raise marketing funds. The Canadian banks had seen the danger in such loans. In 1929 they had started to restrain their lending: in that year, Canadian call loans increased by only 5 per cent. In New York there was no such restraint. Speculation had been given free rein on Wall St. The true reckoning came at last on Thursday, Oct. 24, 1929. Wall St. gave way. It was compared to the sickening fall of an elevator in a New York skyscraper, all its braking mechanisms failed.

In Montreal's classic exchange on St. François Xavier St., financial terror soon broke loose. A total of 382,521 shares were sold — a record for all time. Desperation spread. Stocks were dropping five or 10 points between sales. Some fell as much as 40 points. The bigger the decline in prices, the faster the pace of sales. Better, it seemed, to sell without a moment's delay than to hold back and lose still more. As one Montreal trader remarked: "It's better to lick a ghastly wound than to suffer a fatal one."

Next day, Friday, Oct. 25, seemed to bring back some self-control. The nightmare had passed. The Montreal Exchange (like Wall St.) made a considerable recovery. Twenty leading securities on the Montreal market moved up an average of 2.45 points. Brazilian Traction and International Nickel led the moderate improvement. But 2.45 points was only a small fraction of Thursday's losses. Everyone was still nervous, dejected. The big bubble had burst.

Another crash came on Monday. It was even worse than the catastrophe of the Thursday before. The wreckage left from Thursday was tossed on Monday's market: it was the sharpest drop ever experienced in a single day. The margin accounts that had survived, badly battered, were beaten again and folded up. New York's debacle became Montreal's. The strongest stocks suffered along with the weakest. The "Big Two," Brazilian and International Nickel, plummeted — Brazilian more than 11 points, International Nickel more than seven.

On Tuesday the market fell again. New York described it not only as panic but as "blind panic." Montreal was just as bad. A commentator remarked: "Stock values on the Montreal Stock Exchange crashed with a reverberating roar . . . and when the

STOCK ◉ EXCHANGE

The OLD STOCK EXCHANGE

John Collins SKETCHBOOK

din of trading had ceased in the afternoon, new records for all times had been established in the matter of volume and extent of decline. The total turnover of 540,151 shares on the local exchange has never been even closely approached."

Hope, however, still fluttered. Some suggested the frenzy was nothing but hysteria. The chairman of the Montreal Stock Exchange, Edgar M. Smith, said that "the drastic decline in prices here with the wholesale dumping of stocks for what they would bring has reflected nothing but a certain hysteria which has been altogether the result of the panicky conditions prevailing in New York."

In the weeks that followed the markets in New York and Montreal had their ups and downs, without any pronounced trend one way or the other. Recovery and decline were on a seesaw. Enough uncertainty prevailed to give some leeway to hope. Then, in the middle of November, came another crash. Stock prices proved that they could sink even

lower. By this time hope practically expired. The Montreal market was likened to a prizefighter, once a renowned champion, who had fought gamely, round after round. He had been knocked down again and again and was almost out, but had scrambled back to his feet and made a brave show of recovery. But with that last mid-November blow he had to concede defeat. The market had fought — and lost.

One hope remained, outside the stock markets. The economy of the country seemed to be sound. Economic experts believed the disaster could be confined to the markets. Among them was Professor W.T. Jackman of the department of political economy at the University of Toronto. He contended that no serious reaction upon industry would result from the stock-market crashes. Even this hope soon died away. The long cold winter of 1929-30 ushered in a season that was to become even longer and even colder — the Great Depression, the winter of deepest discontent.

The historic gates to McGill

Perhaps the most completely graceful feature of Sherbrooke St. is the Roddick Gates, the entrance gates to the campus of McGill University.

Officially opened by Lady Roddick on May 28, 1925, the gates have acquired their own history. Through them thousands of students walked out of McGill in procession, during the years when spring convocations were held in one of the big theatres on St. Catherine St. Also through these gates the longest and most impressive military funeral in Montreal's history made its way on a misty morning in early December 1933. The procession formed on the campus, proceeded down the avenue and turned east on Sherbrooke on its way to Mount Royal Cemetery. Sir Arthur Currie, McGill's principal and the commander of the Canadian Corps in World War I, was taken to his grave with all the military honors the nation could bestow.

When the Roddick Gates were constructed in the early 1920s, the architect and builders ran into troubles with the foundations. The soil at this spot is treacherous. Concrete piles were sunk to boulder clay, 30 feet down. On top of the piles concrete was poured for the foundation.

This method served well enough for the inward curves of the gates, but it could not be adopted for the two square columns, where the gates come to an end on Sherbrooke St. Piles couldn't be driven there because the city's gas and water conduits lay underneath. The solution was ingenious. A huge reinforced girder was laid. It ran from the last column on either side, straight under the McGill driveway.

This was a massive, difficult, strong foundation for a structure so much lighter than a building, and not much higher than a building's first story. But the same poor soil was to raise problems a little way to the southeast when the old stone spire of Christ Church Cathedral began to tip in the 1920s. The foundations of the Roddick Gates had to have unusual thoroughness. Indiana limestone was selected for the gates. It was chosen by the architect, Grattan D. Thompson, because he needed very large pieces without flaws and uniform in color. Each of the columns is cut from a single piece.

The architraves — the two long curving stones that rest on the column heads on either side of the entrance — are also solid pieces, neither with steel supports. The iron railings between each of the columns is handwrought throughout. The square column on Sherbrooke St., on the west side of the gates, was also designed to serve as a clock tower. It is entered by a bronze door in the rear. A narrow passage leads to the clock chamber. Here on a stone table lie the clockworks and the four bells for sounding the Westminster chimes.

There is a story about this clock in the gates. Sir Thomas Roddick, dean of the McGill medical faculty, always wanted McGill to have a clock, prominently displayed. He had a keen sense of time, of the need to be punctual and to make use of every minute. He wanted a clock on the campus to be a reminder to students and others that time is passing and it is later than anyone likes to think.

Roddick's regard for time is described by a medical historian, Dr. H.E. MacDermot, in his biography of Roddick in 1938. It was Roddick's custom when going to his surgical lectures at McGill, or for university meetings, to drive up in a carriage in summer, or in a light sleigh in winter. He was always insistent on arriving exactly on time. Roddick's old coachman was deaf and not particularly conscious of time. On approaching the college avenue Roddick would lean forward and poke the coachman in the back, to warn him to hurry up if he was late, or to go slower, if he was ahead of time.

Lady Roddick usually accompanied Sir Thomas to the college; there she would leave him and be driven elsewhere. On these drives he would always remark to her that a clock tower on the campus would be a good idea. The idea grew on him. When the Roddicks were travelling abroad, they made a point of looking at clock towers as examples of what might be done. Though the plan to give the campus a clock was not carried out in Roddick's lifetime, Lady Roddick remembered his wishes. She had the clock tower incorporated in the gates.

Roddick is one of the pre-eminent figures in the history of McGill and of the history of medicine in Canada. A McGill graduate, he belonged to the Osler

John Collins SKETCHBOOK

RODDICK
GATES
McGILL UNIVERSITY

era. He introduced into Canada Lister's practice of using aseptic methods in performing surgical operations. Roddick also played an important part in the history of the Royal Victoria Hospital: he was the chief professional adviser in surgery to the cousins Lord Mount Stephen and Lord Strathcona, when they were planning to give the hospital to Montreal to commemorate the jubilee of Queen Victoria. He was the Royal Vic's first surgeon-in-chief and the dean of McGill's medical faculty from 1901 to 1908.

Roddick was also determined to reform the laws governing medical practice in Canada. He sponsored a law that would establish a medical council for all Canada and give every Canadian doctor the right to practice throughout the country. He went so far as to get himself elected to Parliament to see the bill through.

The gates built to honor Roddick were not McGill's first gates. The previous ones, standing in about the same position at the foot of the campus avenue, had been made of wood. Inside them, on the west side, was a picturesque little lodge. There the keeper of the grounds lived.

These old wooden gates had their place in the history of sport. Here the St. George Snow Shoe Club used to assemble under the moon on wintry nights, ready for the tramp over Mount Royal. There is a Notman photograph of such a gathering at McGill's wooden gates, with the little lodge in the background, icicles sparkling from its eaves. But snowshoeing was fading into skiing by the time the new stone Roddick Gates were built in the 1920s. The picturesque little groundkeeper's lodge had been rudely shaken when the Mount Royal Tunnel was built more or less under it. The lodge had to be taken down.

The country-like wooden gates then gave way to stone, and the entrance to the campus attained the classical touch that it has today.

A preacher for the Scots

The Montreal doctor Norman Bethune, renowned in the world for his heroic and inventive battlefield roles in Spain and China, was the great-grandson of Montreal's first Presbyterian minister, Rev. John Bethune. The coming of this Scottish minister had roused the Scots of Montreal like the sound of the bagpipes. At last they could look forward to having a congregation of their own, a Presbyterian congregation.

Till that month of March 1786, Montreal's Scots had been attending the only church they could — the Anglican church that today is Christ Church Cathedral. Anglicanism, in the eyes and hearts of Scottish Presbyterians, was no substitute for their own kirk. In Montreal the substitute was all the less satisfactory because they could not really understand what the preacher was trying to say.

The clergyman in charge of the Anglican congregation was Rev. Charles Chabrand Delisle, a native of France. He had been chosen by the government as the minister for Montreal's Protestants. This odd choice had an explanation: the government hoped he might be influential in converting the French Canadians to Protestantism. The trouble was that Chabrand Delisle was not really bilingual. When he preached in English, as he often insisted on doing, he was incomprehensible. Nor could he easily understand English when he heard it.

When a true Highland preacher arrived in town, bilingual in English and Gaelic, the Scots rallied to him. They rapidly left the Anglican congregation to form a Presbyterian one. Support for John Bethune was certainly liberal. Much of it came from the Scots who were partners in the North West Co., the fur-trading company with headquarters in Montreal that had established a trading empire from Lake Superior to the Pacific and from the sources of the Mississippi to the Arctic Ocean. On the subscription list a donation of 10 guineas (a substantial amount 200 years ago) stands opposite the name of each of the "Gentlemen of the North West Co."

John Bethune was everything Montreal's Presbyterians could wish for in a minister. He was a true Highland Scot, born on the remote, historic Isle of Skye. He was Gaelic-speaking, well schooled at the University of Aberdeen. Hardships in the Highlands had driven him, as they had driven so many other Scots, to emigrate to North America. After settling, with 2,000 Scots from Skye, in North Carolina, he made his choice when the American Revolution broke out. Loyal to the Crown, he became the chaplain to a regiment of Loyalists.

Defeated in battle, he was among the prisoners of war. When released, he went to loyal Nova Scotia. There he helped to raise another regiment, the Royal Highland Emigrants, and was appointed chaplain to the first battalion. He served with his regiment in Quebec when an American army of invasion commanded by General Richard Montgomery was repulsed in its attempt to take the city on the last night of 1775.

His record certainly commended itself to the Scots of Montreal. So did his character. He was described as "a man of noble countenance," with the self-possession that characterized Presbyterian ministers, a sense of "the dignity of the cloth."

When he died, 29 years later, *The Gazette* said: "Mr. Bethune was a man remarkable for the mildness and agreeableness of his manners, but at no time deficient in that spirit which is requisite for the support of a Christian and gentleman. He understood what was due to 'the powers that be,' without losing sight of that respect that was due to himself."

From March 12, 1786, till May 6, 1787, Bethune preached in a room on Notre Dame St. He then left for Upper Canada. Whatever considerations might have influenced his decision, one was probably greater than all others. He had a large and growing family. It amounted in the end to nine children — six sons and three daughters. He had few resources, having lost everything through his loyalty in the American Revolution. In only one way could he hope to provide for every member of his family.

Bethune, like all veterans, was entitled to land grants from the Crown for his military service. Since he had been an army chaplain, his award would be equal to that of a captain: 3,000 acres. What was more, all his children (whether already born or born later) would be eligible for grants.

The land granted him was at Williamstown in the Glengarry region of Upper Canada. At the time it

SKETCHBOOK

John Collins

REV. JOHN BETHUNE

MONUMENT TO
DOCTOR NORMAN BETHUNE
— Guy and de Maisonneuve

was rough bushland, but bushland with a potential, certain to rise in value as settlement spread.

Bethune's move from Montreal to Glengarry in 1787 by no means meant that he was giving up the ministry for the sake of free land. On the contrary, he entered upon a new ministry under far harsher conditions. In fact, the range of his ministry had widened immensely. In addition to Williamstown itself, he ministered in Martintown, Cornwall and Lancaster. He even went into the borderlands of Lower Canada, into Coteau and Dundee. He was a Presbyterian version of the saddlebag preacher, riding rough country roads or wilderness trails.

The extent of his ministry is seen in the records. After moving to Glengarry he performed 2,379 baptisms. He was exacting on himself and expected action from his people. "No excuse can . . . be sustained from want of means," he said. "The only real want there can be is want of will."

In the War of 1812, when the frontier was menaced by American invasion, he reverted to his old role as an army chaplain. He accompanied the force that crossed over the frozen St. Lawrence to destroy the fort at Ogdensburg in New York state.

Bethune died at Williamstown on Sept. 23, 1815, "in the 66th year of his age and the 44th of his ministry." Though his ministry in Montreal was brief, the results were lasting. This first experience of the Scots in Montreal of meeting together as a congregation led to the establishment in the early 1790s of the St. Gabriel St. Presbyterian Church, the mother church of Presbyterians in Montreal.

The battle of the Victoria Bridge

"*I 'll be blamed if anyone is going to tell me that a canal has got priority over a railway!*"

Donald Gordon, president of the Canadian National Railways, uttered those words in the 1950s, when the future of the old Victoria Bridge was in question. The St. Lawrence Seaway would bring about a revolution in Canada's inland waterways. The bridge, with a history going back to the 1850s, might be an obstacle to the Seaway's construction.

It was a low bridge, not far above the water. The ships in one of the Seaway's proposed locks would have to pass beneath it. The low level of the bridge would not provide clearance enough to let the ships get through.

The Victoria Bridge belonged to the CNR. It had been built in the middle of the 19th century by the Grand Trunk Railway. In 1923 the Grand Trunk was one of the distressed railways combined as the CNR. Along with the Grand Trunk's liabilities, the CNR had inherited its assets, one of which was the Victoria Bridge.

By the 1950s, however, many were questioning whether the old bridge was still an asset, or an obsolete liability. Various proposals were made. One was that the bridge be scrapped, another that a lift span be inserted. Such a span could be raised to allow ships to go by, then lowered to allow traffic to move over the bridge as before.

The Victoria Bridge, though with a history going back about a century, was not entirely the same structure as at the time of its completion. Originally it was in the form of a grotesque iron tube, a sort of tunnel built above the river. This tube enclosed a railway track but nothing else. No provision had been made for wagons or carriages, or for people crossing on foot.

In the 1890s the Grand Trunk overhauled its bridge. The old iron tube was removed. The bridge became, as it is today, an open structure. In alterations completed in 1898, a roadway for vehicles was provided, and a walkway for pedestrians.

Donald Gordon regarded the bridge as his property. He was not going to allow other people to start meddling with it, if it would interfere in any way with his trains. He ordered his engineers to make a thorough, objective appraisal of the bridge's condition. They reported that it was in good, sound, serviceable shape.

Gordon came out fighting for the CNR. The president of the Seaway Authority, Lionel Chevrier, thought he ought to have an informal talk with Gordon to see whether some friendly agreement could be reached.

As Chevrier described the negotiations in his book *The St. Lawrence Seaway,* he went to Gordon's Montreal office, taking with him Charles Gavsie, the Seaway's vice-president. They had no sooner entered the office than they realized this would be no informal talk. Gordon was flanked by his chief engineer and his legal adviser. The atmosphere was stiff, formal — even chilly. After some discussion Chevrier realized that compromise seemed improbable. He resorted to an assertion of his rights.

The needs of navigation, he reminded Gordon, took priority over those of rail traffic. It was at this point that Gordon exploded, and made his declaration that he'd be damned if anybody was going to tell him that a canal had priority over a railway. This exploratory meeting had run into an impasse. Chevrier suggested that their only course was to take the disagreement to the federal transport minister, George Marler. On this suggestion, at least, they agreed.

When Chevrier and Gavsie left the CNR office, they could understand why Gordon had been so unyielding. No president of a railway, in direct competition with the Seaway, would be likely to admit that his competitor had prior and superior rights. It might be an admission with far-reaching consequences. At the same time, they were annoyed. Chevrier did not want to see this whole international project held up indefinitely, just because Gordon would not let anybody touch his bridge. The next meeting took place in Ottawa in the transport minister's office. Soon it ended in the same impasse as the meeting in Gordon's office in Montreal.

Chevrier says he lost his temper: "I told Gordon exactly what I thought of the CNR attitude. . . . After my outburst I realized my mistake and formally apologized. Whether my apology mollified him, I

don't know, but Gordon said, 'Well, one thing is certain: You are not going to take any action on that bridge without paying me damages'."

Chevrier explained that the Seaway Authority would pay for a vertical lift span on the bridge and for the approaches. Gordon again was adamant: "The vertical lift isn't good enough. It will delay my trains." The meeting ended with no solution yet in sight. A solution, however, was found by the engineers of the Seaway, who had been working on the problem for some time. They said they could install a lift span in the Victoria Bridge in such a way that the CNR's trains could keep running, even while the span was up. This apparent impossibility might be accomplished by building an offshoot (an auxiliary bridge) from the Victoria Bridge. This would provide a detour near the southern end of the

bridge leading to the South Shore. The Seaway planned to have a lock near the South Shore, partly under the Victoria Bridge. When a ship coming up the river entered the lock, a lift span in the bridge would be raised to let it pass. But trains wouldn't be held up. The offshoot would be built diagonally from the upper side of the bridge, leading to the South Shore. While the lift was up, trains would make a detour by this alternative route. When the ship had passed under the Victoria Bridge, the lift span would be lowered. Trains would then follow the direct route on the bridge, as before.

The irresistible force had been reconciled with the immovable object. The old Victoria Bridge, originating in the 1850s and remodelled in the 1890s, would still be functioning in the new Seaway Age of the 1950s. It functions still.

Not much of a mountain, but what a view!

"**Y**ou have chosen to take a mountain for your park but, in truth, a mountain barely worthy of the name. You would call it a hill if it stood a few miles further away from the broad, flat river valley."

Frederick Law Olmsted said that about Mount Royal. He was disappointed, almost amused, when he first saw it. Hailed in his day as the greatest landscape architect in North America, he had been persuaded, against his wishes, to come from New York to Montreal to make a park of the mountain that Montreal's city council had purchased. When he arrived in Montreal in 1874, he found that the "mountain" was nothing but a hill. But if Montrealers wanted to call their new park a mountain, he would do his best to make it look like one. After all, it was, he conceded, "relatively mountainous" in its flat surroundings.

This downgrading of Mount Royal continued right into the 20th century. The writer of a guidebook in 1924 remarked: "As a 'mountain' Mount Royal is a failure, for it is . . . less than the height of the Woolworth Building in New York." Since the Woolworth buidling has since been much exceeded in height by more modern office towers, Mount Royal's claims to be a mountain have shrunk still further.

Montrealers have had an answer to all these tendencies to diminish Mount Royal's stature. They have said they are not really interested in comparisons. They like Mount Royal the way it is. W.D. Lighthall, one of Montreal's chief historians, put it this way: "Mount Royal is an ideal crown for a city. Not too lofty to be ascended, nor too low as to be insignificant."

The same point of view had been held by another Montreal historian, S.E. Dawson. He insisted that Montrealers did not want a higher mountain. The higher the mountain, the more useless it would be as a civic park. "They feel," Dawson said in 1884, "that it is a great ornament to their city, and it answers their purpose much better than Mont Blanc or Mount Washington would because, being the height it is, they have been enabled to turn it into a park which is their delight and will be that of their children."

The height of Mount Royal, even if only hill-like, was sufficient to provide tremendous views over its flat surroundings. Even sophisticated travellers, who had seen the world, were surprised by the grandeur that suddenly lay spread before them when they had reached Mount Royal's summit. Though they might say that this mountain was scarcely a mountain when seen from below, it was almost incomparable when the landscape was viewed from its top. Among such travellers was the English railway promoter Sir Edward Watkin. "There can be no view more beautiful, few more extensive," he exclaimed in 1851. "It gives North American scenery in its largest and finest features." From this mountaintop he had looked upon the distant city, the St. Lawrence, "the dark forests of the Ottawa," and even as far as "the 'green mountains' of Vermont."

Watkin's voice was only one in the chorus of perpetual praise. Visitors used such expressions as "one of the greatest panoramic views ever beheld," a vision of "natural beauty," difficult "to surpass," and "grand beyond description." James S. Buckingham, a writer who had travelled and lectured in many lands, said after his visit to Mount Royal about 1840: "The view of the City of Montreal from the brow of the mountain is one of the finest that this or any other country could produce, and is worth a long voyage or journey to enjoy."

Montreal realized early that the view from Mount Royal was one of its greatest assets. A road had been made around the top as far back as the 18th century. Mount Royal was not then public property, but was divided among private proprietors. Though a road for visitors had been made, and a few lookout platforms seem to have been built, the private owners had been careful to discourage anyone from leaving the road to linger or intrude on their properties. In the summer of 1815 these proprietors combined to give public warnings that trespassers would be rigorously prosecuted. In 1850, when the New England author Henry David Thoreau went one evening for a solitary ramble on the mountain, he had to scramble "across lots in spite of numerous signs threatening the severest penalties to trespassers."

When the city decided in the 1870s to proceed

PATHS
ON
MOUNT ROYAL

with plans to make Mount Royal a public park, it set out to purchase or expropriate the holdings of private owners. A few proprietors resisted and delayed the legal process.

Today the view from Mount Royal still has astonishing grandeur. But it was probably seen to best advantage when all the area round about was still flat.

Its geographical environs have not changed, but the rise of high buildings, almost to the foot of Mount Royal, has ended much of the surrounding flatness that enhanced its stature. It is difficult now to conceive how Mount Royal appeared when farmlands or country estates lay all about it, and the city was far off, close to the waterfront. The mountain was then described as "standing like a bulwark against storms." Its southern slopes, sheltered from harsh winds, became a splendid apple district. Here were grown the Pomme de Neige (which seemed to melt like snow in the mouth), the Pomme Gris, the Bourassa, the St. Lawrence, the Fameuse.

Many of the apples from these southern slopes were exported. Standards were high. Those who picked and packed the apples on the mountainside wore gloves to prevent their fingernails from puncturing the skin of the apples and impairing the fruit.

Other kinds of fruit were also being grown in the protection offered by Mount Royal. On his farm (the upper portion is now the McGill campus) James McGill, about 1802, was harvesting peaches, grapes, nectarines, apricots and melons.

He was doing well with apples, too. In one season he filled 285 bags with them.

Nothing then challenged Mount Royal — certainly not the little low-built city straggling far away along the waterfront, or the fields and orchards shielding themselves on its southern slope. No man-built pinnacles, no clusters of soaring highrises, crowded in then to challenge Mount Royal's "relatively mountainous" height.

The wonders of the Victorian house

The Victorian house was not just another house. It had a character and a structure all its own. For one thing, its kitchen and dining room were in the basement. The ground floor was made up not of a living room, dining room and kitchen but of the front and back drawing-rooms, or parlors. These two parlors were sometimes almost one, with little division between them save pillars on either side, or perhaps a curtain of heavy material suspended from a long brass rod.

In other cases (mostly the later Victorian houses) the two drawing-rooms or parlors were equipped with sliding wooden doors, so that the two rooms could be made one, or separated, as might be desired. These doors were of heavy, thick wood, and when they had been brought together, the two rooms were as securely cut off as with a wall.

Getting rid of the kitchen and dining room by putting them into the basement meant that the two parlors could be rooms of stately dimensions, occupying the space from the front to the back of the house. This sense of space was increased by the height of the ceilings. Those who have lived only in newer buildings can have no idea of the sense of graceful elevation given by these high ceilings, 14 feet or more above one's head. This sense of height was still further increased by the tall windows that looked out upon the street from the front parlor, and upon a little garden from the back parlor.

Often there would be three windows at each end. They would begin quite near the floor, with sometimes a very low window seat beneath them, and they would rise to within a few inches of the ceiling. Their great height was emphasized by the long curtains. The inner curtains, nearest the glass, would be of white lace, rather stiffly starched. The over-draperies would be of a heavy and richly colored material of a rather plush-like quality, in red or purple, or of a deep brown. These over-draperies hung from magnificent curtain rods both of whose ends were often shaped like spears.

In the Victorian house, plaster was not merely a covering or concealment for the laths but for the most elaborate ornamental ceilings. At times it might have been overdone. But at its best this plastering added a touch of grace to a room. Sometimes the festooned design on the ceilings would be in an oval which gave the impression of lengthening the rooms still further.

The Victorian house had many a fireplace. This may now be seen where walls with chimneys have been exposed in demolition. The fireplaces can be seen one above the other. The bottom one, of course, would be the fireplace in the dining room in the basement. The second fireplace would be in the parlor, the third in the second-floor bedroom and so on to the top floor. Many of these fireplaces were of white marble, a color and material that contrasted agreeably with the small iron grates. The arched lines of the fireplaces lent themselves easily to the Gothic sentiment of the period and they were often cut in the shape of a Gothic window. At other times the point at the top of the arch would be carved in some ornament — a flower, perhaps, or the face of a child or a serene young girl.

Seeing these white marble fireplaces as they are now being removed, it is often remarkable to find them still very white and unstained by smoke. That's because the marble fireplaces were often ornamental, and their whiteness was carefully preserved. Heat was supplied in a manner more suitable to Quebec winters — by stoves and, in later days, by radiators. These radiators of the late Victorian era were covered by painted iron grills with colored marble slabs across the top. Radiators emerged from such coverings for a considerable period in the 1920s but have since retreated again behind grill coverings of different designs.

Some recent demolitions have revealed the use made by Victorian builders of colored or stained glass. In some houses the front doors had twin panels of colored glass, sometimes purple, sometimes ruby. They were not particularly pleasant when seen from the outside, with little light behind them, but when seen from the inside, from the porch or hall, they cast a deep glow. It was like that colored glow that collectors of Victorian glass now admire so much when they place their vases and jugs and plates on shelves against a sunny window. An adept use of colored glass was sometimes made in the skylight over the main staircase. On a sunny day these skylights might cast a wonderful patch of color over

SKETCHBOOK
John Collins
Victorian Doorway

the stair carpet. Anyone mounting or descending the stairs was transfigured for a moment in passing beneath it.

In 1860 when the Prince of Wales (later Edward VII) was a guest at Sir John Rose's mansion (where Percy Walters Park is today), the skylights were emblazoned with Prince of Wales's plumes, "chiefly in ruby color." Stained glass was artfully used. Such glass was most often inserted in a window on the landing, halfway up the stairs, at the landing. This position on the stair landing served two purposes: it made an attractive piece of color on the stairs itself, and it gave an attractive view from the hall below. The designs in the glass were often of flowers, though some more ambitious pieces showed little landscapes

with winding roads or rivers.

The staircase was itself one of the chief glories of the Victorian house. The very height of the ceilings, especially on the ground floor, gave length enough for grace. The landings halfway up are mostly of later date. The early and mid-Victorian house accomplished a curve in the stairs with wonderful skill, creating a recess or alcove in the wall for a piece of statuary — probably of Parian ware (as white as marble).

It is easy to imagine the dramatic way those stairs could be "descended" in the costume of the Victorian age. People in modern houses no longer descend stairways.

They only come downstairs.

Other rocks than 'rock the cradle'

The highest mountain in all Canada is Mount Logan in the Yukon. And a street in Montreal is named after the same Canadian scientist, Sir William Logan, a Montrealer.

It was Logan, for about 25 years director of the Canadian Geological Survey, who first made Canadians really aware of what lies beneath the surface of their own country. Logan is interesting today not only because of his scientific work, wide and precise as it is, but also his personality.

He was the sort of man ready to take his chances with the unknown, to invite adventures, to suffer hardships. His scientific reports were written each night by the light of his campfire. In the cause of science he was ready to be battered and bruised. On an August night in 1843 in unknown Gaspé, he wrote in his journal:

"It is 12 o'clock at night and I am fagged. I have just put into ink my observations of the day which has required four hours; and before that I had been hard at work measuring, and noting, and cracking stones for specimens from six o'clock in the morning. I have had a blow on the head from a great stone weighing half a hundredweight which fell upon me, fortunately from no great height. It has bruised my temporal muscle on the left side, and I can masticate only with difficulty. . . . I have had a tumble, too, on a slippery stone, striking my elbow; and I put my foot between two stones and pinched my instep so that I am all bruises, and my limbs are as stiff as sticks. I'll go to bed."

Logan was given to his work, heart and soul. He cared for nothing else in life. Marriage never seemed to have entered his thoughts. When a lady with attractive daughters asked him why he didn't marry, he replied: "I really have not the time to spare. Other rocks than 'rock the cradle' claim my whole attention."

His appearance often astonished those who didn't know him. The sort of clothes he wore in the wilderness were sometimes worn in town. One description pictures him as he appeared in the streets of Montreal in 1871: "The slouched hat, much the worse in color for exposure to sun and shower; the ill-fitting suit, innocent of acquaintance with a clothes-brush; the muddy kneeboots, the long hair, shaggy beard and spectacles, altogether, gave him the appearance of a gardener out of employment." Another account likened him to "a shipwrecked sailor."

Logan had bachelor's quarters in the offices and museum of the Canadian Geological Survey, a building on St. Gabriel St. on the site of the present Palais de Justice. His one room on the second floor, a sort of den, was his office, his mapping room, his reception room, his bedroom, his wardrobe. There was one large window looking south. Since it had neither screen nor curtain, the unbroken rays of the sun shone on his unheeding head. Of such superficialities as rugs or carpets there were none.

Sir William enjoyed the freedom of his bachelorhood, not only because he could keep his room the way he wanted it kept, but also because he could spend his day as he wished. No one seemed to know when he started work, but it appeared to be about 5 in the morning. About 7:30 or 8 o'clock he breakfasted at a boarding house around the corner in Little St. James St. He never took lunch but indulged in a hearty dinner at 7, after 12 hours of continuous work. Anyone passing the museum building, even long after midnight, might see the gaslight burning brightly beyond the curtainless window and Sir William working busily over his mapping table.

The austerity of his quarters was exchanged for an austerity still greater when he went on his geological expeditions all summer long. "We are all patching small leaks in our covering," he wrote in one of his camping journals, "in order to sleep as dry as we can. Our provisions being rather short, we go to bed supperless. The poles of our cabin are spruce, and wherever the branches have been cut gum oozes out. As we sit the poles touch our heads, and a multitude of the drops of gum have attached themselves to my hair."

On his journey into the interior of Gaspé they travelled long distances without water. He was kept alive because his Indian guides scraped the innermost bark of birch trees and gave it to him to suck. "Capital it is!" he wrote. "It is cool and has a faint sweetness which makes it very pleasant." He dined on porcupine, roasted on a stick over his campfire.

HOUSES
ON
LOGAN
STREET

John Collins SKETCHBOOK

Yet not even such rigorous hardships distracted his mind from his zeal for geology. One day he failed to return to camp at sundown. His companions feared he had lost his way and might never be found again. They waited for dawn and made preparations to set out to search for him. But "suddenly, a little after day had fairly broken, he was perceived emerging from the bush, hammer in hand, occasionally pounding a rock as he advanced and seeming quite unconcerned, though his trousers were torn to rags and his boots completely minus the soles!"

By this total concentration on his work, Logan mapped out the geological structure of the Gaspé, the area around Quebec City, the Eastern Townships, the Laurentians, the region up the Ottawa and around the Great Lakes. His discoveries altered the geological opinions of the world. He was knighted.

His extreme austerity and sacrifice, his scorning of all comforts and luxuries and indulgences, are all the more remarkable because Logan was a man of considerable and increasing wealth. His grandfather, James Logan, was a Scottish baker who immigrated to Montreal about 1784. He made money by establishing a large Montreal bakery and bought land near the city. One of his properties was a farm, now Lafontaine Park. Sir William inherited that property, known as Logan's Farm, from his brother. There he lived after his retirement from the Canadian Geological Survey.

In fact, private wealth was useful to Logan in his geological work. The Canadian government was reluctant to advance enough funds to the survey. Logan bought his own scientific books and instruments. From time to time he would meet the cost of the survey out of his own pocket, hoping to be reimbursed in due course. Yet, while he was director of the Canadian Geological Survey, he had lived in that bare room on St. Gabriel St. and often looked like an unemployed gardener or a shipwrecked sailor.